RUSHDIE, KUREISHI, SYAL
Essays in Diaspora

Esterino Adami

Prestige

an international publishing house

Published by
PRESTIGE BOOKS
3/28, East Patel Nagar
New Delhi 110 008
Ph. 9818755529
Email: prestigebooks@gmail.com
Website: www.asiabookclub.com
ISBN: 81-7551-184-2

The publication of this book was assisted by a grant from the Department of Oriental Studies, University of Turin (Italy).

Printed at Chaman Offset Press, New Delhi 110 002

Contents

Acknowledgements

This book is based on my Ph.D. dissertation discussed at the University of Turin (Italy) in 2003. Many people have contributed to my research thesis in different ways and times, through discussion and conversations, help with references and other expressions of interest. The guidance of my supervisor, Prof. Alessandro Monti (Head of the Department of Oriental Studies, Faculty of Arts, and DESHI, Centre for the Study of Indian English), has been highly rewarding for me. He was a constant source of inspiration; each meeting with him made me feel confident and I wish to express my full gratitude to him.

In recording my acknowledgements, I should probably cite too many of my family members, friends and colleagues at the University of Turin, who have lent me their support and provided me with wise counsel, but I would like to make special mention of G. who motivated me to give out my best to the work.

Esterino Adami

The English Weather

To end with the English weather is to invoke, at once, the most changeable and immanent signs of national difference. It encourages memories of the 'deep' nation crafted in chalk and limestone; the quilted downs; the moors menaced by the wind; the quiet cathedral towns; that corner of a foreign field that is forever England. The English weather also revives memories of its demonic double: the heat and the dust of India; the dark emptiness of Africa; the tropical chaos that was deemed despotic and ungovernable and therefore worthy of the civilizing mission. These imaginative geographies that spanned countries and empires are changing, those imagined communities that played on the unisonant boundaries of the nation are singing with different voices. If I began with the scattering of the people across countries, I want to end with their gathering of the people in the city. The return of the diasporic; the postcolonial.

Homi Bhabha, *The Location of Culture*

List of Abbreviations

All primary texts refer to the following editions and are indicated parenthetically with page reference in the text:

Salman Rushdie

MC	*Midnight's Children* (1981) (London: Vintage, 1995)
SH	*Shame* (1983) (London: Picador, 1984)
SV	*The Satanic Verses* (1998) (London: Vintage, 1998)
EW	*East, West* (1994) (London: Vintage, 1995)
GF	*The Ground beneath Her Feet* (1999) (London: Jonathan Cape, 1999)
IH	*Imaginary Homelands* (1991) (London: Granta Books)
STL	*Step across This Line* (2002) (London: Jonathan Cape 2002)

Hanif Kureishi

PO	*Plays One* (1992) (London: Faber and Faber, 1992)
BS	*The Buddha of Suburbia* (1990) (London: Faber and Faber, 1990)
BA	*The Black Album* (1995) (London: Faber and Faber, 1995)
LBT	*Love in a Blue Time* (1999) (London: Faber and Faber, 1998)
I	*Intimacy* (1998) (London: Faber and Faber, 1998)
MBL	*My Beautiful Laundrette* and *The Rainbow Sign* (1986) (London: Faber and Faber, 1986)
MAD	*Midnight All Day* (1999) (London. Faber and Faber, 1999)
SWM	*Sleep with Me* (1999) (London: Faber and Faber, 1999)
GG	*Gabriel's Gift* (2001) (London: Faber and Faber, 2001)
DS	*Dreaming and Scheming* (2002) (London: Faber and Faber, 2002)
BSS	*The Body and Seven Stories* (London: Faber and Faber, 2002)

MEHH *My Ear at His Heart* (London, Faber and Faber, 2004)

Meera Syal

AM *Anita and Me* (1996) (London: Flamingo, 1997)

LAH *Life Isn't All Ha Ha Hee Hee* (1999) (London: Anchor, 2000)

Introduction

D like Diaspora

> If religion is the opium of the people, tradition is an even more sinister analgesic, simply because it rarely appears sinister. If religion is a tight band, a throbbing vein and a needle, tradition is a far homelier concoction: poppy seeds ground into tea; a sweet cocoa drink laced with cocaine; the kind of thing your grandmother might have made. To Samad, as to the people of Thailand, tradition was culture, and culture led to roots, and these were good, these were untainted principles.
>
> Zadie Smith, *White Teeth* (p. 193)

The complex experience of the Indian diaspora should be located within a wider social phenomenon of mass migration towards the UK, a process that achieved its peak in the post-war era. Whereas the countries that once made up the British Empire gradually gained independence, Britain started dealing with the ethnic question and the consequent re-elaboration of the concept of nation and nationhood. The idea of the Commonwealth that substituted the imperial grandeur was accompanied by a radical transformation of society that led England into an endured phase of debunking. An iconographic representation of the beginning of such pregnant process lies in the image of the steamship "Windrush" approaching the British coast: the boat crammed with West Indian immigrants dramatically anticipated the consequences of the cultural and social displacement implied in the condition of exile. Nowadays we may even consider the "Windrush" as a forewarning sign, if we look at the derelict fleet of ships that illegally carry migrants to the coasts of Mediterranean countries, miserable victims of a cruel criminal exploitation.

The diasporic memory was celebrated in Britain some years ago by an itinerant exhibition entitled 'Roots of the Future,' which was installed in major cities between 1996 and 1997. Supported by the Commission for Racial Equality, it illustrated the various phases of English multiculturalism, the thorny aspects of racism or the attempts of antiracism policies, and the present ethnic components of the nation. The scope of my research however has not a historical character, but rather it concentrates on the literary scenario that the Indian diaspora, with its juxtaposition of tradition and modernity, has recently produced. Whether we consider the notion of diaspora as a category which helps us to record the metamorphosis of a nation, we implicitly realize that "literature and visual arts—first poetry and fiction, then films and videos, photography and painting—become the migrant's territory where the English language is appropriated and transformed into something rich and strange, a new medium, a new style."[1]

This work is based on my Ph.D. dissertation, whose original title (*'English Writers Born and Bred, Almost': Patterns of Tradition and Modernity in the Indian Diaspora across Britain*) was intended as a pun and clearly indebted to the incipit of Hanif Kureishi's *The Buddha of Suburbia*, a novel which by now has become a groundbreaking text concerning the mongrelisation of cultures in the UK. The provoking act of labelling expatriate writers from Asia as 'English,' heralds of Englishness, suggests at once an ironic gaze that is necessary to assess the definition of contemporary English literature. By asserting his self-proclaimed inclusion in the canon of Englishness, Karim, the character conceived by Kureishi, who defines himself as "English born and bred, almost," strikes monolithic assumptions and reverses constructed clichés: in his position of second generation migrant, he perceives his mixed family milieu as a positive feature which, in a paradoxical manner, enables him to elaborate on the meaning of British identity, a concept now revised and updated in a multicultural society transformed by historical changes. It is the adverb "almost" that signals an unstable balance and hints at the confusion of the individual confronted with the peril of displacement. Diaspora then parallels a sense of double belonging as the characters created by Hanif Kureishi, Salman Rushdie and Meera Syal strive to demonstrate. These anti-heroes represent a textual strategy of subversion whilst the expatriate novelists work as the intercultural interpreters of the maladies of English society, to misquote Jhumpa Lahiri. However the idea itself of belonging, in this case, is born out of a splitting of terms, a dichotomy that is dramatised in Karim, being both Indian and English, both suburban and metropolitan.

At the turn of the century, this peculiar identity crisis, in which the paradigms of nationhood and belonging are weakened or questioned, functions within the UK as well. Indeed the national consciousness of Britain is presently being re-read and re-imagined because of the stimuli propelling from the devolution that is taking place in Scotland, Wales and Northern Ireland. As a consequence, now the contours of the discourse of political and cultural unity appear to be blurred or broken, detached as they are from an imposed frame of hegemony. The contraposition of nation and ethnicity, which is expressed as a paradox of anxious postmodernity, has to be singled out from racist ideology and move on to spotlight the social and cultural composition of society. With reference to Britain, any reflection on nationhood, theorised in various forms of Englishness as a tool for cementing the national unity and cohesion, does not lead to a univocal response but rather, in a problematic way, it highlights the uniqueness of each single component. Not only does it delete the opposition of Englishness versus ethnic identity but it also questions the very meaning of being English and disjoins the different parts of the UK:

> The cultural definition of 'race' is sometimes conveyed in an attempt to define the English as a 'race' separable from the Scots, Welsh, and Irish whose skin colour they share. Britishness, as if it

> is discussed rather than simply extrapolated from Englishness, is seen to emerge as the sum of these cultures. Alien (i.e. black) cultures have been introduced into this country with disastrous effects.[2]

Postcolonial studies, notably through the voices of Homi Bhabha and Edward Said, have charted the rise of diasporic communities and their fictional representations. Such type of literature overflows and breaches the boundaries of modernity by absorbing the language of national belonging and establishing the disruption of identities. It is this atmosphere of fragmentariness that lies behind the category of diaspora, given its manifold status and hybridity of styles and modes. Such awkward lack of unity however should be addressed as a positive feature, one in which the notions of home and origins are encoded in rhizomatic extensions, which compose an intricate web of meanings.

The structure itself of this research tries to evoke the sense of intricate complexity that seems to characterise the Indian diaspora, from both a social and a literary point of view. This tortuous kind of migration, which includes not only Indians, but also Pakistani and Bangladeshi, and alternates writers as diverse as Salman Rushdie, Sunetra Gupta, Ravinder Randhawa and Farrukh Dhondy, constitutes a primary sign of difference, an heterogeneous intermingling of regional and *deshi* (that is, national) cultures that deconstruct and re-build the value of being and living in contemporary Britain. They are added to the essence of Britishness so that a new perspective is moulded. As a whole, my study is devoted to the intercultural matrix that the Indian diaspora has produced in the UK whilst distinctively each chapter focuses on a particular author, or genre, and on their peculiarities, in a monographic manner. My idiosyncratic vision of the Indian diaspora discards the Western dichotomy that discriminates the metropolitan and the migrant viewpoints: indeed the miscellaneous corpus of Indian narratives and histories, a whole universe of cultures, languages and beliefs that should not be indicated by worn stereotypes of Babel-like mess, draws on the prismatic heritage located in the subcontinent and affects modern and postmodern nation-states.

The writers I examine here deftly illustrate the process of giving voice to those subjects and communities previously exploited and marginalised by mainstream white society. Through the registers of fiction and cinema, theatre and music, migrant characters affirm their identities and react to the silencing of subalterns. The "rainbow coalition," to employ a definition coined by Kureishi, articulates an alternative sense of national belonging and elaborates on new forms of resistance. The diasporic context is affected by both the periphery and the centre, and intermixes urban cultures with the migrant's heritage. Often diasporic literature becomes not only a vehicle for communicating a new cultural approach—let us think about the characters of Rushdie like Saleem Sinai and Gibreel Farishta who express the anxiety of liminality, the oscillating position of in-betweenness—but also acknowledges the denunciation of intolerance, discrimination and abuse. Karim, the picaresque hero of Kureishi, endures the claustrophobic climate of ethnic persecutions and he stresses his condition of displaced subject whenever he manages to come back home without being kicked or punched by racist culprits. In Rushdie's case, the accusations against British racism are rendered in the grotesque scenes of *The Satanic Verses*, in which the detention centre looks more like a deportation camp than a municipal social service. The stylistic features of diasporic authors are rather variegated: while Rushdie elaborates on ingenious and proliferating plots and is close to the techniques of magic realism, postmodernism and fantastic literature, Kureishi and Syal prefer to deploy social realism, sometimes in its coldest and aseptic version in the case of Kureishi, whereas irony and wit abundantly add colour to the narrative tissue. Further Syal's astute use of different genres requires a new type of assessment and highlights the notion of hypertext and literary contaminations: Meena's stories may remind one of Karim's quest or be modelled on the author's autobiographical experiences but at the same time they reflect the actual travails of childhood.

Whether the diaspora conveys the perspective of Indianness, a term whose scope covers the cultures and literatures of the whole Indian subcontinent, we have first to consider the code of Englishness, or Britishness in a wider perception, which I discuss particularly in the second chapter. Provokingly we may agree with Vijay Mishra, and Iain Chambers,[3] when they theorise two types of Britishness, which are (paradoxically) quite antithetic. The first kind is strictly Anglocentric and imbued with the praise of an imperial past, a dream of power that sustained the racist feeling of white superiority and the belonging to the British nation; the second type, conversely, is linked to the potentiality of hybridity and the interconnection of various cultures and ethnic communities. Social anthropologist Kate Fox seems to side with such position and in her exploration of Englishness she states that "ethnic minorities are included, *by definition*, in any attempt to define Englishness. [. . .] Although ethnic minorities constitute only about six per cent of the population of this country, their influence on many aspects of English culture has been, and is, considerable. Any snapshot of English behaviour as it is now [. . .] will inevitably be coloured by this influence."[4] To return to Mishra and clarify the argument concerned with diaspora and nation, we should keep in mind how he borrows the term 'differend' from Jean-François Lyotard's vocabulary, which indicates a conflict between two or more factions that are characterised by different systems of legitimacy and thus not completely comparable. Therefore the structural collision that derives from the clash between nation and diaspora reflects a nebulous tension because progressively the discursive staging of identities becomes elusive and divergent. This is particularly evident in *The Satanic Verses*, an ambitious text which chaotically provides a climatic vision of the migrant's experience. It eventually functions as a narrative site in which "the rupture, the drift, the inconclusive begin to designate the diasporic condition itself."[5] The deceptiveness of diasporic authors who probably should be distinguished from postcolonial writers is here again at work.

NOTES

1. Itala Vivan, "The Impact of Postcolonial Hybridisation on the Britishness of British Literature," in S. Bassi, S. Bertacco and R. Bonicelli, eds., *In That Village of Open Doors* (Venice: Cafoscarina, 2002): 29.
2. Paul Gilroy, *There Ain't No Black in the Union Jack* (1987) (London: Routledge, 2002): 66.
3. Vijay Mishra, "Postcolonial Differend: Diasporic Narratives of Salman Rushdie," in *Ariel*, Volume 26, Number 3, July 1995: 7-45.
4. Kate Fox, *Watching the English* (London: Hodder, 2004): 16-17 (Author's emphasis).
5. Vijay Mishra, cited: 43.

A Question of Place

> This is my hidden city. It has no past and no present, but what is not yet reached frames the world we shall inhabit. I can remember the future.
>
> Abdullah Hussein, *Émigré Journeys* (p. 246)

Whether the term diaspora suggests an immediate sense of physical and cultural displacement, in fiction we have to consider the topographical representation, the construction of spaces which may also incorporate a biographic reference. Eastern and Western cities are manipulated in narratives and films so as to express the tension that the encounter of different cultures brings along. Bound for Britain, the migrant feels catapulted into labyrinthine London: the English capital plays a relevant role in the works by Kureishi, Rushdie and in a different measure Syal, and also in films like *Bend it like Beckham*, *London Kills Me and Sammie* and *Rosie Get Laid*. The diasporic artist works out a characteristic *poétique de l'espace* and pictures the complex metropolitan site: Rushdie, for instance, imagines London as a cobweb in which the émigré gets lost in a perpetual wandering, which is a symptom of the burden of exile. The ethnic protagonist scans the place in search for a new home, but such act of surviving has to come to terms with the feeling of alienation that grotesque London releases in its process of cleaving identities. *The Satanic Verses* identifies a monstrous aspect of the city now dominated by surrealism: it appears like a sick *civitas diaboli* that incorporates a dystopic threat and is evocatively renamed Mahagonny, Babylon, Alphaville.

Gibreel Farishta's crisis and plan to turn the city into an exotic location is more than a blast of 'meteorological' folly: rather it is an example of the textual stratagems that Rushdie deploys to deconstruct and assemble the imaginative cartography of diaspora. Consequently boundaries and spaces are dilated and treated by virtue of magic realism, so that through the geography of otherness the novelist gives shape to an alternative scenario. Ironically he overthrows the rational modernity of London, the former centre of power and heart of the Empire, to extend the enchantments and myths of the subcontinent, to introduce elements of popular culture like comics and music, films or songs. The final result is a mongrel instance of urban and suburban location, one in which the ethnic and the metropolitan eerily interplay in a reciprocal symbiosis.

The cartographic foregrounding conceived by the writer concerns also Eastern metropolises. Bombay, Karachi, Islamabad, Calcutta, as pictured in *Midnight's Children* and *Shame*, are grounded upon the ancient legends and built like the invisible cities dreamt by Italo Calvino.[1] Whilst the former colonies retrieve original place names, in India (Mumbai instead of Bombay, Varanasi instead of Benares) but also in Africa and elsewhere, the great expectations brought about by Independence and the injection of modernity into the traditional setting gingerly draw a blurred map. In the teeming urban site, Internet cafes arise next to temples and mosques, the towers of muezzins are now surrounded by industries and the streets are covered with decaying cars, 'three-wheelers' and horse-drawn carriages. The devouring disarray of the subcontinental city however is processed in the migrant's mind that envisages an imaginary homeland: in order to escape the postmodern city of the West, a nightmarish nowhere, the exile turns back to the repository of collective memories to conceive 'Indias' of the mind, which are utopian interstices or strategies for surviving, according to magic realists.

In Kureishi's narrative, a different treatment of urban spaces is displayed: whether the intrusion of fancy is abolished, the style of realism determines the mundane dimension and grey shabbiness of geographical spaces. London, which is the mirror of a dialogic relationship between centre and periphery in physical and metaphorical terms, becomes a real character, endowed with Dickensian brio. In films and novels, the author establishes a figurative mapping of London, in various diachronic phases. The pivotal point is that the values and meanings attributed to the suburbs and the inner city are not univocal and strictly oppositional; apparently, the outskirts are the reign of chaos and racism, with huge tower blocks as symbols of anonymity, whereas central London is the pulsing heart of the nation that unfolds a vibrant social milieu. However we should question such pattern because also the suburbs can suggest a certain positive degree of Englishness, in a vision *à la* Orwell. Similarly the very centre of the city is sketched as a jigsaw of contrasts: in Kensington, old Victorian houses which resemble theatrical sceneries are restored and decorated by Eva and Haroon. It is the bourgeois innovation that substitutes the old metropolitan spaces and brings up the new intercultural site. Kureishi asserts the peculiarity of London as a unique site of negotiations of identities, opposed to the idyllic representation of 'Heritage' England with its corollary of cottages and meadows. On the contrary London, in spite of its alienating power, functions as a hybridising laboratory of cultures which designs new styles. Such aspect is markedly highlighted in *The Buddha of Suburbia*, a novel in which the metamorphosis of characters is allowed through the experiences of theatre, music and fashion: for instance Karim manages to transform his perspective in a chameleon-like manner when he is onstage. This narrative device perhaps echoes a Kiplingian matrix and while interviewed by Bart Moore-Gilbert, Kureishi recognises the cathartic quality of London and the dynamic propensity of the character:

> BMG: I suppose it's a fairly obvious point, but there does seem a strong connection in your films between the idea of London as various and changing and the stress in your work on the malleability of identity. I suppose it's an idea which connects with *Kim* again, the emphasis on disguise and the way a character like Karim is constantly changing his wardrobe as if he's trying on new roles or identities.

HK: Yes, in London there's a sense that you make yourself up. At the beginning of the TV series, and in the novel, Karim sees his father turned upside down, literally, and then he's transformed into this other creature. Or in *The Black Album*, where Shaid could become a Muslim fundamentalist. Then he goes to a rave. And so on. That idea of mutability, it excited me very much, it was happening to me already. I was a Pakistani boy when I was with my Pakistani family, then I'd go to school, and I'd be a mod. And then you saw you could make more of it and enjoy it and it was rather liberating to think that you didn't have to be stuck in one identity. I suppose one of the things I liked about *Sammy and Rosie* was all the stuff on the tube, the trains and the travelling, which is also a metaphor for other kinds of fluidity.[2]

The configuration of the urban surface develops into a virtual text that is akin to the diaspora: narratives and personal histories of the migrants are inscribed in special re-mapping, whereas the ethnic community becomes an indelible constituent of the city and its ramifications. In this light, for the expatriate writer the operation of mapmaking Britain does not simply constitute the flowering of dreams and nostalgia for his/her idealised remote homeland, but on the contrary it fortifies the discourse on multiple identities and intercultural spaces, in which 'newness,' as prophesised by Rushdie and theorised by Bhabha, takes place. From Tollington to London, the migrant subject deterritorialises the literary coordinates and creates a new textual area of confrontation, one in which little Indias can now grow.

The terrorist attacks of September 11th in New York and the brutal London bombings in July 2005 have brought death and destruction into the metropolitan sites, they have dramatically reshaped urban spaces, and sharpened the question of global migrations, cultural confrontations and international relationships by increasing the rise of Islamophobia and racial intolerance. In spite of such rancorous feelings, it is essential to reformulate the debate in an attempt to go beyond all types of strict boundaries, hierarchies, traditions. The category of diaspora, deemed as a series of networks or transnational links of individuals forced to leave their countries, could turn out to be a pacific, life-enriching experience that celebrates the interconnection and compatibility of cultures. Speaking of the 'Windrush' generation and the West Indian migrants, Mike and Trevor Phillips outline the transformational power of migrancy diaspora and the positive role of minority groups vis-à-vis mainstream society:

> The culture we created allowed us to face towards the Caribbean and towards the African diaspora, but it also opened a doorway into some of the deep structures of British life. British 'black culture' from the beginning, therefore, was dynamic and ambiguous, swapping valued between four or five different sources, tapping whatever roots were available and useful. In that sense, what the black British became was little to do with biological characteristics determined by skin colour, or with mystical connections to the African diaspora, and it was not exclusively shaped by resistance to white racism. [. . .] The product which has resulted is unique and unmistakable, but also marked by the ambiguity and many-sided quality of black British life.[3]

I would like to expand such vision in order to incorporate other cultural, social and political perspectives. Let us stop and listen to the voices of diasporic communities then.

NOTES

1. See Stefano Manferlotti, "La città degli immigrati. Memoria e spazio in Salman Rushdie e Hanif Kureishi," in Carlo Pagetti, ed., *La città senza confini* (Rome: Bulzoni, 1995): 301-31.
2. Bart Moore-Gilbert, "London in Hanif Kureishi's Films: Hanif Kureishi in Interview with Bart Moore-Gilbert," in *Kunapipi*, ed. John McLeod, Volume XXI, Number 2, 1999: 13.
3. Mike Phillips and Trevor Phillips, *Windrush. The Irresistible Rise of Multi-Racial Britain* (London: Harper Collins, 1999): 384.

Literary Curries and Postcolonial Recipes: The Strange Case of Salman Rushdie

The Writer of the Writers

> What do I tell her, and how, that I want this, a language, like God has a language and my mother has hers and my father his own, even Jenny with a single tongue-wrinkle of a missed soft d has a separate voice, but not I, I have the verbs and nouns and adjectives and all the grammar but no language, I speak like everybody else and I am not everybody else; and this too (God of peacock, help me stop this clatter in my skull so I can know what I want), a nameless anonymous being to find its way into me, enter me, plunging head-first as a diver from a great height into an ocean, zealous and furious, shining like a great white fish in the bright sun, tracing perfect arcs in the air that stay visible against the sky long after the body has vanished, defining the time of the jinn, one of my very own.
>
> Abdullah Hussein, *Émigré Journeys* (p. 246)

In the fermenting world of postcolonial literatures, Salman Rushdie has become the author *par excellence*, notably after being awarded the 1993 Booker of the Bookers, and is now broadly assimilated by canonical curricula and literary establishment. In spite of the accusations of being partially or completely westernised, the writer who at the moment lives in the United States unfolds a paradigmatic approach to diasporic issues, dealing with the core topics of minority communities and ethnic consciousness. His ground-breaking works have been followed and somehow imitated by a large number of Indian and Pakistani authors. Given the complexity and multi-shaped quality of his writing, my research will touch on the first phase of his production, roughly covering the 1980s, though mention of more recent texts will be made in order to point out a changeable creative itinerary. Rushdie is much debated in universities and critics propose different interpretations of his oeuvre—the number of essays and articles dedicated to him throughout the world is rather abundant and reflects a growing theoretical interest in a versatile artist. My double orientation will try to balance a general introduction to the writer and a more specific analysis on some selected aspects of his narrative.

As well as providing a Babel-like fabric in his fiction, Rushdie also adds his personal biographic background by admitting his plural cultural identity: indeed his multiplied personality and imagery derive not only from his eastern/western collocation but also from his idiosyncratic conception of liminality, one in which shattered examples of intertextuality and the imprint of Indian storytelling can coexist. Born in 1947 (a fundamental year in modern Indian history) to a family of Kashmiri Muslims, he builds up a unique Indian lore by drawing on different pre-colonial sources, like the *Ocean of the Streams of Stories*, a classical collection of Kashmiri tales. In a parallel manner, living in a hybrid metropolis like Bombay, now renamed Mumbai, accentuates the westernising seal as most postcolonial cities nowadays are structured as heterogeneous and mixed urban conglomerations that are representative of the entire world. It is the author himself who emphasises his peculiar controversial position, mixing together geographical boundaries, religious references and literary styles: "It seems to be that I have been in minority groups all my life, a Muslim in India, immigrant in Pakistan and England. Now, of course, I find myself belonging to a serious deprived culture whose entire way of life is threatened by the uncaring attitude of the majority, that is to say, writers."[1] The quotation, which dates back to the 1980s, incorporates a main *locus* of Rushdie's writing, that is the idea of multiple homelands and different traditions juxtaposed in the same site. His novel-making is soundly grounded on a net of narrative structures, one in which plots can be easily manipulated and combined with postmodern influences. It is not just a question of handling imaginary cartography or re-inventing improbable characters or even worlds; the pivotal starting point is to try to keep memories and look for significance behind the mere historical analysis.

Reality and language are also formed as an accumulation of details, including even mundane facts because eventually "meaning is the shaky edifice we build out of scraps, dogmas, childhood injuries, newspaper articles, chance remarks, old film, small victories, people hated, people loved" (*IH*, 12). The meaning of perception in Rushdie's characters and texts is imbued with the essence of memory, and does not constitute only a repetitive procedure of listing; on the other hand, we are shown a display of fantastic devices and magical creatures (djins, half-goat men, angel-like prophets, telepathic boys). Apparently this seems to be the world of chaos and nonsense, one in which the reader is puzzled and continuously challenged because of the lack of order and logic linearity and ultimately happens to loose himself in the realm of the fable and myth. The complex discourse formulated by Rushdie may be deemed within Mikhail Bakhtin's critical approach to literature through the notion of carnivalization, namely a dynamic process of transformation and/or camouflage of identities. In this light, carnival may be observed as "a pageant in which everyone participates: there is no division between performers and spectators and between high and low,"[2] and thus it activates a revisitation of norms, roles and conventions. As a consequence, Rushdie's characters show a high degree of malleability and discard the status of flat type to the blasphemous pleasure of carnival. Obviously under the glittering façade of the genre of the marvellous and sublime, we can identify a subtle and pungent criticism against social and political systems. Whether it is true that Rushdie's self-imposed task is to detect reality and life at a deeper level, simultaneously the presence of his peculiar encyclopaedic knowledge assimilates the individual and the universal, the personal and the collective.

In a real Pinter-like style, Rushdie is interested in the comic and grotesque aspect of a decaying world, and this approach is pointed out by his intent to 'exile' reality to the margins of his narrative discourse, so that the wor(l)d can be (re)forged and given substance. However, we should note that this is not an easy way to escape actuality: on the contrary, with a parodic attitude it functions as a powerful tool to deconstruct events which seem to be stuck in history. The narrative masquerading that we find in *Midnight's Children* (1984) or *Haroun and the Sea of Stories* (1990) relies on the very 'once-upon-a-time' frame that can encircle the universe of fables and fantasy.[3] The literary bonanza conceived by the writer is then influenced by and grafted onto a rich intertextuality, one that interpolates the epic narratives of the subcontinent with the postmodern inclinations of the West.

On the linguistic level, the task is arduous and requires a new, polysemantic idiom to express a non-autochthonous genre[4] and substantiate it with the orality of the vernacular tradition. The author employs a number of techniques to mould his narrative in order to translate the linguistic extravaganza of India, a country that claims eighteen official languages along with a myriad of local dialects. English therefore acquires a regional characterisation, pulling down geographical barriers and cultural confines, and becomes a linguistic pastiche that permits cross-cultural interactions. Let us look upon the vivacious miscellany of local Indian languages mentioned in *The Ground beneath Her Feet* (1999):

> Not only in English. Because it was only me, she [Vina] could prattle on in Bombay's garbage jargon, *Mumbai ki kachrapati baat-cheet*, in which a sentence could begin in one language, swoop through a second and even a third and then swing back round to the first. Our acronymic name for it was *Hug-me*. Hindi Urdu Gujarati Marathi English. Bombayites like me were people who could speak five languages badly and no language well. (*GF*, 7)

The ironic distance provided by the writer through the words of Rai Merchant, the narrator of the novel, unveils an almost autobiographical account of Rushdie and hints at the techniques of code switching commonly used by educated Indians. The "hug-me language" pictured by the character suggests the idiomatic composition of Bombay, a city re-built by the British but endowed with an Indian essence. Here the novelist emphasises the maternal 'hug' of Mumbai in a metaphor that inscribes the topographic representation into the bodily surface and celebrates the linguistic overlapping. Such curious fertility of dialects inscribed within the context of Indian English is exactly like a well-dosed blend of Indian pungent spices, another of Rushdie's skilled literary *masala* as we shall see afterwards, and provides the threshold leading to the treasure of narratives.

Agnes Scott Lageland[5] shows the different linguistic strategies adopted by the novelist to work out a new communicative dimension, such as borrowing Indian words, changing the spelling of terms, using atypical syntax, rhyming words or phrases, choosing names with puns or particular cultural assonances. Some words from Indian languages (especially those referring to food and clothes) remain untranslated and by now have entered English: delicacies like *seekh kababs*, *tandoori* chicken or *lassi* sound rather known to British and American readership, given the large communities of expatriates in the two countries. Another semantic field covered in Rushdie describes the religious lore (both Hindu and Muslim) with words like *guru*, *karma*, *mantra* or *mullah* and is used to reinforce a vernacular extension and to provide a meaningful context: this is particularly evident in both *Midnight's Children*, which is built upon the complex Hindu mythology and *The Satanic Verses* (1998), which initiates a revisionist discourse on Muslim values.

Rushdie has frequently commented on the use and diffusion of English across the subcontinent and more generally in former British colonies; in his vision, it has now become one of the official languages of the country, though endowed with its own peculiar independence from Standard English. By almost paraphrasing Raja Rao in his relevant Foreword to *Kanthapura* (1938), in which the father of modern Indian literature in English underscored the solid base for building the tenets of Indian English, Rushdie states that "Indian English, sometimes unattractively called 'Hinglish,' is not 'English' English, to be sure, any more than Irish or American or Caribbean English is."[6] Yet, English is not only considered a powerful means of communication throughout the world: it may also serve as an instrument to inscribe national consciousness. This stresses the fundamental importance of linguistically linking all the states of India and consequently "to conquer English may be to complete the process of making ourselves free" (*IH*, 17).

To explain the process of reformulating English, Rushdie reminds one that even his "mother-tongue, Urdu, the camp-argot of the country's earlier Muslim conquerors, became a naturalised subcontinental language long ago."[7] Unlike those writers who deliberately glossed vernacular words and expressions, Salman Rushdie displays a strategy of incorporating Indian words in his texts so as to reach a defamiliarising and yet 'natural' cohesion and coherence. Collocations and syntax then re-create what some critics once labelled as 'Babu English,' a language which is "stilted, bookish and flowery."[8] The classic *Hobson-Jobson Anglo-Indian Dictionary*, a pioneering text which was first published in 1886, explains the entry for Babu as "a term of respect attached to a name [. . .] and formerly in some parts of Hindustan applied to certain persons of distinction."[9] Given the diachronic perspective of the lexeme, which is sometimes still considered by the Indians as pejorative, it may be problematic to apply it to modern Indian fiction, although writers like Rushdie breach univocal definitions in order to subvert the sense of hierarchy and introduce the strength of irony. Such assimilated and reconstructed kind of 'english,' grafted onto the *deshi* frame of mind of educated society, proves to be the apt instrument to depict the Indian (imagined?) nation.

Hence we are shown the mechanisms of decolonising English, an operation which clearly touches on the political aftermath of Independence in India but reveals as well the new relation between languages and traditions. As a result, "it is inevitable that a nativization of English takes place,"[10] and in fact storytelling, a typical Indian oral activity, achieves excellent results thanks to this new 'Indian' language. Rushdie considers the ambiguous confines of the linguistic negotiation, one in which according to Foucault's analysis[11] knowledge and power interplay and affect the narrative mode as well: colonial English with its notion of imposed hegemonic control is thus substituted by the writer with a fluent, alternative tongue. In *Midnight's Children*, for instance, Rushdie enlarges the productive aspect of the English language, by including puns, rhymes, new coinages, and this is further reinforced by the echoes of a unchanged tradition rooted in classic Indian and eastern epics like the *Ramayana*, or the *Mahabharata*, or the stories of the *Arabian Nights*:

> Outside the washing chest, surrounded by people who seemed to possess a devastatingly clear sense of purpose, I buried myself in fairy-tales. Hatim Tai and Batman, Superman and Sindbad helped to get me through the nearly nine years. When I went shopping with Mary Pereira—overawed by her ability to tell a chicken's age by looking at its neck, by the sheer determination with which she stared dead pomfrets in the eyes—I became Aladdin, voyaging in a fabulous cave; watching servants dusting vases with a dedication as majestic as it was obscure, I imagined Ali Baba's forty thieves hiding in the dusted urns; in the garden, staring at Purushottam the sadhu being eroded by water, I turned into the genie of the lamp, and thus avoided, for the most part, the terrible notion that I, alone in the universe, had no idea what I should be, or how I should behave. (*MC*, 152-53)

The tone, though, is never elegiac or celebratory, but tends to be revisited in a sort of parody, almost a carnivalesque caricature of myths and legends juxtaposed to the modern heroes derived from vintage comics and popular shows. In the passage quoted above the narrator Saleem recalls the extreme fancy that moulded his childhood. Yet we ought to detect this type of masquerading not as a pure playful, merry activity but as the attempt to interrogate the value of identity, by indicating the beginning of a quest for the self.

The fantastic mode of narrating as a typical invigorating component of oriental storytelling also characterises in a marked way *Haroun and the Sea of Stories*, a sort of folk-tale dedicated to Rushdie's son, Zafar, whose source of reference is to be found in a nearly eponymous collection of stories, *The Ocean of the Streams of Stories* written in Sanskrit in the 11th century AD by Soma or Somadevi, a Kashmiri Brahmin. The metaphor of the ocean here described is characteristic of Indian classic literature with works like *Mantra-mahodadhi* (10th or 12th century), a Tantric devotional text, the *Chandombudhi* (16th century circa), a lyrical text in Kannada, or *Ghrta-sāgara*, a medicine account, probably dating from 17th century. In the ancient traditions of India, the practice of creating stories and reciting verses grants a cleansing effect and subliminally joins the author with the reader: it reinforces therefore the dialogic relationship that Rushdie builds from his exile.[12]

Obviously, Rushdie's language is also indebted to western textual strategies with explicit references to authors as diverse as Rabelais, James Joyce, García Márquez, Günter Grass and even Italo Calvino.[13] Experimental word-formation and postmodern clipping and/or truncation render his narrative a rich repository of literary quotations and technical devices. A common definition tends to establish a comprehensive umbrella, according to which magic realism conveys non-conventional methods of narrating and endorses the author to re-shape the world. Admittedly, the genre is close to the field of postcolonial literatures, given the peripheral location and is also used to describe writers from those countries which have painfully experienced colonialism and its aftermath. Actually the classification of magic realism originally refers to visual arts to indicate a movement of the 1920s, rediscovered in 1927 and 1945. However, through a combination of spell-binding techniques, it is adopted to treat cultural and literal phenomena and because of its ambiguous nature "is not only, as it is often described, out of partial tribute to the painterly origins of the term, a way of *seeing* [. . .] but also a way of *saying*: on a larger scale it is a way of telling a story; on a smaller scale, it is a way of showing 'reality' more truly with the aid of the various magics of metaphor."[14]

Magic realism then dictates a fictional strategy subscribed by novelists as different as García Márquez and Günter Grass. Such definition still remains problematic, and academics from time to time attempt to theorise new labels to inscribe a dynamic, abstract and yet concrete way of representing the world or worlds through the miraculous eye and pen of the artist. Saleem and Oskar, the messianic protagonists of *Midnight's Children* and *The Tin Drum* (1959) by Grass, share a common matrix before being projected into their whirling narratives; both of them are presented as deformed trickster-heroes, exiled to the margins of the world. In adapting the strategies of magical realism, the two authors opt for modes of narrating which are different from those of García Márquez: unlike what happens in *One Hundred Years of Solitude* (1967), the viewpoint of their novels is expressed via an intermittent, first-person fictional texture. Similarly the topographic representation of Bombay and Dazing is anchored to a precise map that defines the location and its characteristics. This is not the case of Macondo, a cartographic phantasmagoria dreamt by Marquez, a mental vision that functions on a symbolic level.[15]

Sometimes magic realism as a critical category has been accused to be a fallacious product, a spurious literal tendency to admix western realism and native 'magical' traditions. Observed as an organic metaphor, it is conceived as improbable child of West and East, though perhaps other approaches may be possible.[16] In an epic work like *Midnight's Children*, fantasy constitutes a guideline in the interwoven representation of Saleem and India. From the very title, it introduces the reader to the labyrinths of myth and magic in the subcontinent and subverts the probable to achieve the surreal. Fantasy as an application of magic realism corroborates telepathic noses, influences of the hands of clocks and time, or centuplicates the olfactory skills; in this respect, it nears the Rushdinian novel to the western contemporary canon, ranging from Patrick Süskind's *Perfume* (1985) to Peter Høeg's *The History of Danish Dreams* (1988). In its imaginative process of dramatisation, fantasy may be discerned in a tripartite manner with the verbal, episodic and structural categories.

The first type moulds the narrator's language and his penchant for word-plays. It consists of a crossing of linguistic confines and apparently discriminates the world of reality and the realm of dream: actually the two are conceived as complementary so that one cannot exist without the other. The episodic level of fantasy permits to establish connections between the main story, about Saleem's life, and the minor subplots. Miraculous characters like Shiva or Parvati[17] contribute to the cyclic development of the novel and their own adventures add new strength to the operative principle of fancy. Finally, Rushdie contrives a way to give coherence to the whole text by introducing structural fantasy. In its cohesive fragmentariness, *Midnight's Children* can also be read as a collection of fables: whether we substitute Scheherazade and Prince Shaharyar with Saleem and Padma we obtain an updated rendering of the *Arabian Nights*. Remarkably, the gender shift reduces the distance of the tradition and "is an acknowledgement of the changed times, values and circumstances that the roles are reversed in the present case; the man narrates while the woman listens, instead of the other way round."[18]

Rushdie's recent fiction is nearly akin to popular culture, whose sources include the world of TV, cinema, music and even the Internet. Such shapeless telematic framework evokes celebrities, so that for example Vina Apsara, the celebrated singer described in *The Ground beneath Her Feet*, reminds the reader of the queen of pop music Madonna; furthermore, her chauffeur narrates about a fatal car incident that might somewhat echo Princess Diana's tragic end in Paris in 1997[19] and, in this way, another intertextual reference with popular culture is set up. The incipit of the text witnesses this dual or plural characterisation and opens up a mythical and kitsch scenario, constantly sustained through the novel. Vina, leader of the group V.T.O. with her partner Ormus Cama, is scrutinised via the patchwork composition of heterogeneous materials and eventually evolves into a fading picture:

> Vina, to whom even strangers would come, following her star, hoping to receive redemption from her voice, her large, damp eyes, her touch. How was it that so explosive, even amoral, a woman came to be seen as an emblem, an ideal, by more than half the population of the world? Because she was no angel, let me tell you that, but try saying so to Don Ángel. Maybe it's just as well she was not born a Christian, or they'd have tried to make her a saint. Our Lady of the Stadiums, our arena madonna, baring her scars to the masses like Alexander the Great rousing his soldiers for war; our plastered Unvirgin, bleeding red tears from her eyes and hot music from her throat. (*GF*, 20)
>
> She was becoming notorious as an unashamed exhibitionist—a reputation that her largely absent Witch dress did nothing to disprove. To wear such a garment in Bombay could be dangerous, but Vina didn't care. She was an ornery loudmouth too. She appeared regularly on the covers of underground magazines, those new cracks in the media façade caused by the Western youthquake. By pouring out her rage and passion in those journals of narcotic typography, and posing pneumatically for their porno-liberal pix, she became one of the first sacred monsters of the counter-culture, an aggressive iconoclast, half genius, half egomaniac, who lost no opportunity to roar and suck and boo and preen and demolish and cheerlead and revolutionise and innovate and flash and boast and scold. (*GF*, 225)

The picture of the singer sketched here defines a postmodern *femme fatale*, an updated version of a bizarre Salome who is both a heavenly creature and a vampire courtesan. Like many diasporic (postcolonial, I would be tempted to say) characters, she continuously tends to oscillate between different worlds and cultural perspectives, lost in an eternal and ethereal quest for identity that could mitigate internal clashes.

Encyclopaedic knowledge is a critical category that sometimes seems to characterise the rambunctious narratives of Rushdie. Partially this derives from a typical tendency of Hinduism to classify, to construct typologies and enshrine chaos into a prescribed order: the *Kamasutra* for instance collects the different norms that mediate erotic behaviour. A postmodern box of memories, concepts and references opens up in Rushdie's writing whereas he abundantly induces on listing characters, items and details. This lingering movement carries the idea of multiplicity, of combining East and West, modernity and tradition. Simultaneously it permits a progressive erosion of strict social realism as magical interventions are made possible and can affect the plot and gives way to the mythical heritage: indeed, the author's "*magnum opera*, *Midnight's Children*, is characterised by an urgency to move beyond history for the purpose of finding out universal forces operating in the particular phase of time, which accounts for the extensive use of myths in it."[20]

NOTES

1. Salman Rushdie, "Minority Literatures in a Multi-Cultural Society," in Kirsten Holst Petersen and Anna Rutherford, eds., *Displaced Persons* (Sydney: Dangaroo Press, 1988): 36.
2. Philip Engblom, "A Multitude of Voices. Carnivalization and Dialogicality in the Novels of Salman Rushdie," in D.M. Fletcher, ed., *Reading Rushdie. Perspectives on the Fiction of Salman Rushdie* (Amsterdam-Atlanta, GA: Rodopi, 1994): 296.
3. Cf. Vijay Lakshmi, "Rushdie's Fiction: the World Beyond the Looking Glass," in Emanuel S. Nelson, ed., *Reworlding. The Literature of the Indian Diaspora* (New York and West Port, Connecticut: Greenwood Press, 1992): 49-155.
4. Traditional Indian literature chiefly consisted of poetry, and other forms of representation akin to theatre but the introduction of the novel is another consequence of the British penetration. However we should remember that the previous invasions from Persia, ac-

companied by the diffusion of Islam, imposed Persian as a sort of lingua franca and its literary influence lasted for at least five hundred years.

5. Agnes Scott Lageland, "Rushdie's Language," *English Today*, No. 45, Vol. 12, No. 1 (January 1996): 16-22.
6. Salman Rushdie and Elizabeth West, eds., *The Vintage Book of Indian Writing* (London: Vintage, 1997). See Introduction: xiii.
7. *Ibid.*: xii. xiii.
8. Agnes Scott, cited: 19.
9. See Henry Yule and A.C. Burnell, *Hobson-Jobson. The Anglo-Indian Dictionary* (Ware: Wordsworth Editions, 1996): 44.
10. Wimal Dissanayake, "Towards a Decolonised English: South Asian Creativity in Fiction," *World Englishes*, Vol. 4, No. 2, 1985: 234.
11. See Michel Foucault, *The Archaeology of Knowledge* (1969) (London: Routledge, 2002).
12. For a detailed analysis of the philological and historical sources, see Vidyt Aklujkar, "*Haroun and the Sea of Stories*: Metamorphoses of an Old Metaphor," *Commonwealth Novel in English*, Volume 6, Numbers 1 & 2, Spring and Fall 1993: 1-12. See also Jean-Pierre Durix, "'The Gardner of Stories': Salman Rushdie's *Haroun and the Sea of Stories*," in D.M. Fletcher, cited: 343-51.
13. Concerning the Rabelaisian matrix of Rushdie's works and the relationship with James Joyce, see Sadik Jalal al-Azm "The Importance of Being Earnest about Salman Rushdie," in D.M. Fletcher, cited: 255-92.
14. Patricia Merivale, "Saleem Fathered by Oskar: Intertextual Strategies in *Midnight's Children* and *The Tin Drum*," *Ariel*, 21: 3, July, 1990: 12. Author's emphasis.
15. However there are also similarities: the ending pages of *Midnight's Children* and *One Hundred Years of Solitude* sum up the themes previously exploited and evoke a sort of pessimistic prophecy, a warning for the generations to come.
16. Shaul Bassi, for instance, proposes to study Rushdie's 'special effects' by considering six areas of his narrative: "The fabulistic tradition of India, the anti-realistic tradition of the West, the rhetoric of English colonial India, the genre of ethnic (auto)biographies, the discourse of the body in a state of political emergency and the performative function of language and the literalisation of metaphor." See Shaul Bassi, "Salman Rushdie's Special Effects" in Elsa Lin-

guanti, Francesco Casotti and Carmen Concilio, eds., *Coterminous Worlds. Magical Realism and Contemporary Post-Colonial Literature in English* (Amsterdam, Atlanta, GA: Rodopi, 1999): 59.

17. In Hindu mythology, Parvati is the daughter of Himavan and Mena and mother of Ganesha and Kartikeya, while Shiva is depicted as the god of destruction and constitutes, along with Vishnu and Brahma, a holy trinity. Legends about his deeds are complex and riveting: after the death of his first wife, Sati, he is believed to have married Parvati. See M.L. Varadpande, *A Dictionary of Indian Culture* (New Delhi: Arnold Publishers, 1994) in particular: 103-4 and also 124-25. For the onomastic meaning, see also Maneka Gandhi, *The Penguin Book of Hindu Names* (New Delhi: Viking Penguin India, 1989): 281 and 368.
18. M.L. Pandit, *New Commonwealth Writing: A Critical Response* (New Delhi: Prestige, 1996): 48.
19. Rushdie dedicated an essay to the dramatic demise of Princess Diana in his collection of non-fiction, *Step Across This Line* (2002); he bitterly comments on the relationship between the idolised image of public personalities and the omnivorous interest of the readership of popular press. In this framework, he accuses not only the photographer's deplorable action but also the bulimic need of pictures, gossips and useless anecdotes stolen by paparazzi and broadcast the world all over. See "Crash," in *STL*: 118-21.
20. Nagesh Chaturvedi, "Indian Myths in Rushdie's *Midnight's Children*," *Language Forum*, Volume 19, No. 1 and 2, January-December 1993: 173.

Rushdie's Rhizomes: The One Thousand and One Narrative Techniques

> 'Though one thing you said is true . . . we had a great time in Mathews Street. I was happy there, happier than ever in my life. You people were all digging in to make a life here, all without a country. I joined in. I was one of you.'
>
> Abdullah Hussein, *Émigré Journeys* (p. 236)

In dealing with Rushdie's writing, I would like to try to apply an approach based on the idea of rhizomatic thinking, mapping and narrating.[1] The main critical instrument that I shall employ for my analysis is *A Thousand Plateaus. Capitalism and Schizophrenia* by philosopher Gilles Deleuze and psychotherapist Félix Guattari, which originally appeared in 1980 and was curiously divided into "plateaux" not chapters, a stratagem to underscore the idea of "germinal diffusion and rooted horizontal extension." Their focal attention was devoted to the notion of multiplicity connected with the image of the rhizome, specific of bulb-like plants. Originally the term comes from botany and indicates a horizontal, underground plant stem capable of producing the shoot and root systems of a new plant. The rhizome needs to be distinguished from the rootlets and is characterised by plagiotropism, the rapid growth at an angle to the vertical in response to a stimulus, and diagetropism, a diatropic response to the stimulus of gravity; diatropic, in this sense, refers to the response of plants or parts of plants to an external stimulus by growing at right angles to the direction of the stimulus.

Starting from a deconstructive look at the classic image of the book, which is constituted by the union of the taproot, a pivotal spine and the surrounding leaves, Deleuze and Guattari refuse the binary logic (by which one becomes two, two becomes four and so on) to favour an extension of lines, roots, thoughts. This system could be labelled as rhizomatic and constitutes the metaphor for a rapid growth, of circularity of interpersonal communication and cultural relations. By swapping notions and information, it composes a web-like structure; this is quite a familiar image in contemporary cultural studies thanks to the octopus-like expansion of the Internet but was anticipated with a good dose of courage by Deleuze and Guattari in the 1980s. According to the two scholars, the rhizome is "everywhere"; even animals may reveal some rhizomic features: rats and moles who build and live in their holes create a systematic wholeness, with intense acts of interplaying within a complex system.

In their theory on the potentiality of rhizome, they identify the following principles: connection, heterogeneity, multiplicity, a signifying rapture and cartography. Each of them can be appertained to Salman Rushdie's fiction and emphasis will be laid upon the notion of multiple identities, an attribute which appears to depict characters like Saleem Sinai or Gibreel Farishta. This sense of doubleness that seems to pervade throughout texts like *Midnight's Children* or *The Satanic Verses* and which contrives a series of oppositions (Saleem and his counterpart Shiva, Saleem's two mothers, Saleem's two countries, Saleem's various identities) could be viewed in terms of rhizomatic narrative structures. Amongst its features, the rhizome may assume several forms like ramified surface extensions in all directions, or bulbs and tubers under the ground; it flourishes on a subterranean level from radicals and roots and presents both useful products, like potatoes, and useless parts, like grass and weeds.

The first principle that we may adopt regards the idea of connection, which implies that any point can be connected to anything other, and unlike the linguistic tree *à la* Chomsky, for instance, which originates in a point and then starts a dichotomy, the rhizome can bestrew various interpretative systems and fields of knowledge. In Rushdie's fiction, this is exemplified in a chain of flashback and flash-forward movements that reconstruct the intricate web of

Saleem's story in a real "memory novel and therefore a semi-fantasy."[2] It is the very incipit of the text that emphasises the intricacy of narrative units and Saleem warns the reader about the confines between fiction and reality, myth and culture. In a decorated, apocalyptic style, Rushdie reveals the hypertrophic structure of his prose and specifies the role of the creative artist. Whether *Midnight's Children* is an allegory of India, the preliminary phase is to permit events to be transformed into a fluid, magical universe:

> And there are so many stories to tell, too many, such an excess of intertwined lives events miracles places rumours, so dense a commingling of the improbable and the mundane! I have been a swallower of lives; and to know me, just the one of me, you'll have to swallow the lot as well. Consumed multitudes are jostling and shoving inside me. (*MC*, 9)

Like a skilled botanist, a gardener-breeder of Victorian times who cuts and prunes trees and bushes and eventually provides them with a new 'shape,' the novelist is here concerned with a careful choice of words and images. Thus he deals with the question of form, a concept invested by drastic changes through befuddling postmodernism, by focussing on a fictional terrain that seems to explode in a primordial chaos. In fact the whole novel is grounded on "the anxiety of being split, of being divided down the middle, of being forced to recognise one's position on the cusp of either/or" [3] whereas the imagery refers to the Indian historic scenario and its compendium of meaningful events:

> As a people, we are obsessed with correspondences. Similarities between this and that, between apparently unconnected things, make us clap hands delightedly when we find them out. It is a sort of national longing for form—or perhaps simply an expression of our deep belief that forms lie hidden within reality; that meaning reveals itself only in flashes. Hence our vulnerability to omens. (*MC*, 300)

Rushdie accentuates the dreamy, unseizable nature of reality and in so doing sanctions the use of magic realism and the re-visitation of traditional narrative modes. His catachrestic use of mimetic representation requires a new definition and seems to suggest that actuality may even evolve into a new literary *topos*, in a writer's mind. The author lays emphasis on the dynamics of texts as discursive resources to involve the reader's attention in an active process, like the one dealt with in Umberto Eco's theories on narratology and intertextuality. With its main purpose to follow Saleem's pathway and draw a pungent allegory of India, the novel covers a progression of chronicles, but the deictic features may be intentionally incomplete; this is due to a specific strategy in which "hermeneutic gaps can range from very trivial ones, which are either filled-in automatically [. . .] or do not require filling-in (many gaps in the Bible), through various degrees of importance, to gaps which are so crucial and central in the narrative as to become the very pivot of the reading process."[4]

The formula of heterogeneity which ceaselessly establishes connections between semiotic chains, organisations of power, arts, sciences and social struggles can also be extended to the use of language(s); rhizomic narrative usually relies on the linguistic transformations, the mixture of patois, slangs and throng of dialects. In particular, *Midnight's Children* provides the linguistic dimension of India with an apt combination of English, Hindi and Urdu, plus some local expressions or words. A clear example is Padma, whose name indicates the lotus flower. The language spoken by Saleem's discreet wife reveals a vernacular influence through a peculiar syntax and this device gives colour to an otherwise nearly silent, absent character. The theory of the rhizome prescribes the absence of a mother tongue and favours an eclectic community of speakers using diverse languages: Indian English, to cite a metaphor of Deleuze and Guattari, may 'grow like stalks' and thereby cannot come to a standstill. Thus the language evolves and flows: in both *Midnight's Children* and *The Satanic Verses* we can investigate a rich literary *bric-a-brac*, endowed with a fervent combination of oriental/occidental constructs, including even a London-flavoured jargon.

Moreover, we note an evolution of the language which is exploited by virtue of a cinematic technique: the narrative tension is given cohesion, thanks to a suitable crosscutting that reduces, dilates and adapts historical moments and domestic episodes.

Multiplicity is another operative principle as rhizomes share no unity, no points or positions such as those found in trees. The chronicle revolving around quasi-magical Saleem regulates a web of stories intertwined like a complex mosaic. Even a marionette, in Deleuze and Guattari's vision, may be defined as a rhizomatic system because of the intimate binding of the strings that animate the puppet with the nervous fibres that guide the artist. The same imagery, anticipated beforehand in Dickensian fiction, occurs in the novel through the autodiegetic position of the protagonist, whose wife Padma "has started getting irritated whenever my narration becomes self-conscious, whenever, like an incompetent puppeteer, I reveal the hands holding the strings" (*MC*, 65).[5] When Saleem's miraculous powers are nearly extinguished, his family moves into Pakistan and in the 'land of the pure' his sister Brass Monkey takes up singing and acquires the role of a talented artist, known as Jamila. The boon of the girl concerns her voice and she is presented as an ideal, almost twin sister of Saleem because they had "exactly complimentary gifts" (*MC*, 315). From here, the author creates further ramifications of the Sinai family and, following the stylistic quality of multiplicity, sets in motion the classic storytelling of India. The intricate plots are further accelerated when we learn about the war between India and Pakistan to control Bangladesh in 1965. During the conflict, Saleem is victim of a pernicious amnesia that blots away his identity and name. Eventually he joins the Pakistani Army and goes through a series of adventures in the forests of Sunderbans, isolated from the rest of the country. He will be able to restore his past, thanks to Parvati-the-witch, "to whom midnight had given the true gifts of sorcery" (*MC*, 378).[6]

The process of saving Saleem's memory is activated by Parvati's magical arts and metaphorically reflects the effort of India trying to recover from its colonial past and seek for national consciousness after the painful episode of the Partition. Actually both India and Pakistan are treated in *Midnight's Children* and *Shame* (1983): whereas the former symbolises the tribulations of the former in a visionary way, the latter pictures through a distorted glass an anti-canonical, dark fable of modern regimes. The role of Saleem is central since in the text the debate about identity versus collective—the individual and the mass coincide in an obsessive multitude—is portrayed in the protagonist who is even allowed to undergo a process of disintegration and assimilation, almost a metaphysical scrutiny in order to be re-created:

> I no longer want to be anything except what who I am. Who what am I? My answer: I am the sum total of everything that went before me, of all I have been seen done, of everything done-to-me. I am everyone everything whose being-in-the-world affected was affected by mine. I am anything that happens after I've gone which would not have happened if I had not come. Nor am I particularly exceptional in this matter; each 'I,' every one of the now six-hundred-million-plus of us, contains a similar multitude. I repeat for the last time: to understand me, you'll have to swallow a world. (*MC*, 383)

Rushdie, through the mystic voice of Saleem, evokes and abridges the spirit of sprawling Indianness from its demographic hugeness to reach the single character who unveils a repository of actual and fictional identities. The author cunningly suggests the entire national sense of belonging and speculates on the meaning of historical circumstances. Yet Saleem's doomed fate looms and heads for a dramatic epilogue that stages in a parallel way all the violence of the Emergency, which invested modern India.

Given the loose and unseizable narrative frame, also the idea of a signifying rapture is present: the rhizome/writing could be broken, shattered at a given spot, but will start up again on one of 'its old lines or new lives.' It goes beyond a Manichean dualism and reaches a concept of interactivity, like the teeming existence of ants in an anthill or the reciprocal flirting of an orchid and a wasp. The anarchic structure of *The Satanic Verses* for instance alternates Saladin Chamcha's purgatorial quest through diabolic London with Gibreel Farishta's religious paranoia and glorious visions. Fixed in a cyclic conception of time, the two or more story-lines might be easily severed but eventually will re-connect and proliferate again, similar to a trailer. This type of novel, especially *The Satanic Verses* and *The Ground beneath Her Feet*, exploits a sort of *Gedankenexperiment*, an experiment of thought, that has to be repeated continuously before assessing the final result; in following the predicate of the un-linearity of time, Rushdie's peripatetic heroes or anti-heroes are compelled to move beyond spatial and temporal limits. The introduction of a plural discursive space constitutes the framework of Rushdie's writing and thereby "room is created for dialogue, shrill as it sometimes becomes, between innumerable, irreducible claims, visions, and ideologies, with no ultimate authority held in reserve by any of them that guarantees the outcome."[7]

Furthermore, in Saladin we find his peculiar ability to modulate many different voices and tones in order to perform all sorts of characters and even this polyphonic device is doubled by the presence of Mimi Mamoullian, Saladin's ventriloquist colleague. Similar to a grotesque version of wizards, they make a special couple. The whirling, comic style that permeates the presentation of the two conceals both echoes of traditional narratives (let us think about the *Arabian Nights* or the story of polyglossic Babel) and a multimedia universe bursting with MTV adverts and colourful quotations:

> Because he did have that gift, truly he did, he was the Man of a Thousand Voices and a Voice. If you wanted to know how your ketchup bottle should speak in its television commercial, if you were unsure as to the ideal voice for your packet of garlic-flavoured crisps, he was your man. He made carpets speak in warehouse advertisements, he did celebrity impersonations, baked beans, frozen peas. On the radio he could convince an audience that he was Russian, Chinese, Sicilian, the President of the United Nations. [. . .] With his female equivalent, Mimi Mamoulian, he ruled the airwaves of Britain, they had such a large slice of the

> voiceover racket that, as Mimi said, 'People better not to mention the Monopolies Commission around us, not even in fun.' [. . .] 'We should get married sometime, when you're free,' Mimi once suggested to him. 'You and me, we could be the United Nations.' (*SV*, 60)

Cartography (Saleem's face is described as a map) as a rhizomic code is provided through the operation of tracing and reproduction; the final result is a map that is open and connectable in all its dimensions: detachable, reversible, susceptible to constant modifications.[8] As a matter of fact, the author creates the major character by textualising an historical narrative and the organic metaphor of Saleem, whose distorted body should be representative of the whole country, stresses the literary/ corporal/ geographical space or surface. "Horn-templed, cucumber-nosed" (*MC*, 133) Saleem could perfectly fit in a *Wunderkammer* of a Renaissance prince, but he is also similar to the elephantine god Ganesh[9] because of the disproportionate, telepathic nose. His striking features constitute an allegorical portrait of India, created through Rushdie's literary surgery.[10] The body as personification of the nation is transformed into fictionalised material that may be symbolically 'kneaded.' In his precariousness, Saleem is sent to the anteroom of History and inscribed into the fate of the subcontinent. This procedure may even be accompanied by a revisitation of grand national figures: Rushdie has always praised the father of the nation Jawaharlal Nehru, but has strongly criticised Indira Gandhi's policy and consequently the novel "both undermines and presumes the possibility of history and it does so in order to encourage a self reflexiveness in the reader"[11]

However a cartographic/rhizomic representation of *Midnight's Children* should take into account not only Saladin's story-life but also the existences of the other Midnight's Children:

> The voices blabbed in everything from Malayalam to Naga dialects, from the purity of Lucknow Urdu to the Southern slurrings of Tamil. I understood only a fraction of the things being said within the walls of my skull. Only later, when I began to probe, did I learn that below the surface transmissions—the front-of-mind stuff which

> is what I'd originally been picking up—language faded away, and was replaced by universally intelligible thought-forms which far transcended words . . . but that was after I heard, beneath the polyglot frenzy in my head, those other precious signals, utterly different from everything else, most of them faint and distant, like far-off drums whose insistent pulsing eventually broke through the fish-market cacophony of my voices. [. . .] From far to the North, 'I.' And the South East West: 'I.' 'I.' 'And I.' (*MC*, 168)

The geographical and linguistic map that here Rushdie tries to sketch does not merely coincide with an uproarious repertory of idiomatic assonances and consonances ("polyglot frenzy"), but rather it endorses a broad perception of the subject, the nation and the self. Finally the Midnight's Children, who are endowed with magical powers, turn out to be bearers of new efforts and hopes for a better life. The psychoanalytical implication in this approach views the rhizome as the site of production of the unconsciousness that questions new desires of the individual. Actually only Saleem and Shiva possess supernatural powers: all the other members of the Midnight's Children conference seem to be a sort of freaks, or burlesque figures taken from an extravagant circus.

To conclude this short and incomplete introduction to rhizomatic discursive practices, I would recall how tree-shaped imagery has always dominated the western perception of reality and thought. Not only botany, but also biology, anatomy, theology, linguistics, even ontology and philosophy have been figured in visual representations of tree schemes or diagrams.[12] However the idea of thought ought to be imagined not as an arborescent construct but rather as a rhizomic spreading of reiterated items. Being similar to the ramifications of synapses, the rhizome carries no beginning or end and thus manifests itself in the middle of fragmentariness, between things, evincing its inter-being identity by virtue of an *intermezzo*: it is anti-genealogy. In fact, Saleem's schismatic family tree grows upon the idea of multiple parentage, with the roles of father (Ahmed Sinai, Nadir Khan, Wee Willie Winkie and William Methwold) and mother (Vanita, Amina Sinai and Mary Pereira) being multiplied in a diaphanous light. Whether the tree represents filiations, the rhizome is constructed via alliance and its literary fabric is made through conjunctions. The puzzle-like events or sequences of episodes catalogued in *Midnight's Children* would be not the 'coordination but the conjunction' of the story of Saleem Sinai and the account of Indian history from 1915 to the Emergency.

The same kind of reading could be applied to *The Satanic Verses*, whose narrative interstices show a sum of subplots: the picaresque adventures of Saladin Chamcha *and* the delirious experiences of Gibreel Farishta *and* the ethnic clashes in London *and* the legends of Ayesha and Mahound *and* so forth. The rhizomatic collage that we may detect in this kind of literature is symbolically evocative of the shattering and dispersal of identities that the experience of Indian diaspora implies. In his analysis of discursive practices, Foucault observes that "there must be a level (as deep as it is necessary to imagine it) at which the oeuvre emerges, in all its fragments, even the smallest, most essential ones, as the expression of the thought, the experience, the imagination, or the unconscious of the author, or, indeed, of the historical determination that operated upon him."[13] Thus, the analytic construction of Rushdie's novels interpolates the fictional text and the biographic detail in a jigsaw of discontinuous references that lies at the very core of post-colonial migration.

Rushdie's monsoonal writing has always displayed a preoccupation for the visual representation and its aesthetic constitution matches the writing with the optical perception. His novels benefit from influences of painting, photography and cinema in a variety of ways. The exchange of babies in their cradles, for instance, which brings out Saleem's destiny, is a typical cliché taken from Hindi B-grade films. Rushdie *en passant* turns to the use of ekphrasis, the narrative representation of a visual representation as well. The term, which encompasses a genre and a trope alike, betokens the confines between different artistic performances: the word and the image, the self and the other compete to obtain an independent space. However we should bear in mind that this ocular literary technique is quite sporadic in Rushdie: the main exemplification of ekphrasis occurs in *Midnight's Children* and regards the print of a Victorian painting hung in the room of young Saleem. Quite probably it is based on a real work, *The Boyhood of Raleigh* (1870) by Sir John Everett Millais. The writer, following the postcolonial paradigm of cross-cultural influence, deems the events figured in the picture and the life of Saleem dramatised in the text as parts of the same world. The synecdoche governs the dialogic relationship between the two spheres and discerns an imperial and post-imperial mode of staging (the Victorian picture *versus* Saleem's quasi-autochthonous narrative). Rushdie's astute device unveils what is hidden behind the canvas, that is the colonial age, and interrogates the pathway of history, in the improbable stories of the protagonist; this is made possible because visual and verbal arts meet in the postcolonial fiction.[14]

Ekphrasis, in its attempt to mediate diverse ways of perception, translates a feeling of anxiety, a dramatic confrontation between art and reality. Rather significant is the treatment of photography, especially in *The Ground beneath Her Feet* where Rai the narrator affirms that "a camera can see beyond the surface, beyond the trappings of the actual, and penetrate to its bloody flesh and heart" (*GF*, 80). It is an interior slippage between photography and narrative that permits the comprehension of the world and Rai seeks to come to terms with his multiple experiences and fractured identities by shooting photographs. It is also a way to exorcise death and the idea of the end, the dissolution of the universe. He then takes up the macabre habit of photographing funerals as an antidote for the omnivorous civilisation of the images in its greedy act of devouring:

> For a while I became a photographer of exits. It isn't easy to take photographs of strangers' funerals. People get annoyed. Yet it interested me that Indian funeral practices dealt so openly, so directly, with the physicality of the corpse. The body on the pyre or on the *dokhma*, or in its close-sewn Muslim shroud. Christians

> were the only community to conceal their dead in boxes. I didn't know what it meant, but I knew how it looked. Coffins forbade intimacy. In my stolen photographs—for the photographer must be a thief, he must steal instants of other people's time to make his own tiny eternities—it was the intimacy I sought to, the closeness of the living and the dead. (*GF*, 212-13)

The word and the image complete each other and predicate a reportage, an identikit of the self on the edge of time and history. The accurate description of the rites of death questions the integrity of man, his fear for ghosts and doubles. In Rushdie's mind, photography functions as a mechanism to chart life through symbolic death; this is Rai's function as narrator and photographer inasmuch as he is entitled to combine the word and the image, or "voice or vision, both finalised into a kind of writing, as shown by the Greek root of the word *graphein*,"[15] that characterises written narrative and photography. This aporia re-codifies the visibility of the body, witnessed in the pictures of Rai, and sustains a postmodern quest.[16]

NOTES

1. This section of my research is grounded upon the theoretical considerations expressed by Gilles Deleuze and Felix Guattari, in *A Thousand Plateaus: Capitalism and Schizophrenia* (1980) (London: The Athlone Press, 1988). I also employ the Italian translations: *Nomadologia. Pensieri per il mondo che verrà* (Rome: Castelvecchi, 1995) and *Rizoma*, with an Introduction by Franco Berardi (Rome: Castelvecchi, 1997).
2. Sushila Singh, "Salman Rushdie's Novels: Fantasy to Reality," *The Commonwealth Review*, Vol. 1, No. 1, 1989: 117.
3. Marc C. Conner, "*Midnight's Children* and the Apocalypse of Form," *Critique: Studies in Contemporary Fiction*, Washington D.C. (Crit), 38: 4, Summer 1997: 296.
4. Shlomith Rimmon-Kenan, *Narrative Fiction: Contemporary Poetics* (London and New York: Methuen, 1983): 138. To comment upon the narrative riddle of his text, Rushdie pointed out the intention to depict an open ending and in an interview he stated that he "was very interested in the idea of implying a multitude of stories

in one's structure, through which one picked one narrative path. There are stories you just happen to bump into and that you never see again, or stories that are just fragments of themselves and not completed," in John Haffenden, *Writers in Interview* (London: Methuen, 1985): 239. The quotation clearly recalls postmodern strategies and also illustrates the oeuvre of Italo Calvino: for instance *On a Winter Night a Traveller* (1979) employs such a principle at its peak whilst the reader is thrown into a sort of hyper-text that subverts traditional modes of narration.

5. The presence of the strings, fibres and lines of the rhizomatic perspective may also refer to the thread fabricated, measured and cut by the Fates or Parcae from the tradition of classic mythology. The three sisters Clotho, Lachesis and Atropos governed the birth, life and death of men, in their obscure and indecipherable will.
6. In Hindu mythology, Parvati is the daughter of Himavan and Mena and mother of Ganesha and Kartikeya, while Shiva is depicted as the god of destruction and constitutes, along with Vishnu and Brahma, a holy trinity. Legends about his deeds are complex and riveting: after the death of his first wife, Sati, he is believed to have married Parvati. See M.L. Varadpande, cited, in particular: 103-4 and also: 124-25. See also Maneka Gandhi, *The Penguin Book of Hindu Names* (New Delhi: Viking Penguin India, 1989): 281 and 368.
7. Philip Engblom, cited: 295.
8. The semantic study of Deleuze and Guattari envisages cartographic representations and idiosyncratically depicts a place like Amsterdam as a rhizomatic city, with no roots but with canals that stand for peduncles or stems. See Deleuze and Guattari (1997), cited, *passim*.
9. Elephant-headed Ganesh is the patron of intellectuals, writers and rascals alike. He is honoured in the month of Bhadrapada, between August and September and the major centres that attract pilgrims eager to participate in the rites and celebrations are Bombay and Poona. He presides over impossible deeds and is "known as the remover of obstacles." M.L. Varadpande, cited: 46.
10. "I was not a beautiful baby. Baby-snaps reveal that my large moon-face was too large; too perfectly round. Something lacking in the region of the chin. Fair skin curved across my features—but birthmarks disfigured it; dark stains spread down my western hairline, a

dark patch coloured my eastern ear. And my temples too: too prominent: bulbous Byzantine domes" (*MC*, 124).

11. Neil Ten Kortenaar, "*Midnight's Children* and the Allegory of History," *Ariel*, Vol. 26, No. 2, April 1995: 56.
12. In the West, the importance of the tree is comprised in the agricultural tendency to 'tame' the landscape, to cut forests and settle a community. Conversely, in the East we find the image of the steppe and the oasis, or desert: the model of cultivation, and by extension thinking, prescribes here the tuber, and the fragmentation of the individual. See Deleuze and Guattari (1997), cited, *passim*.
13. Foucault, cited: 27.
14. See Neil Ten Kortenaar, "Postcolonial Ekphrasis: Salman Rushdie Gives the Finger Back to the Empire," *Contemporary Literature*, The University of Wisconsin Press, Summer 1997, Vol. 38, Number 2: 232-59.
15. Carmen Concilio, "'Worthy of the World': the Narrator/ Photographer in Salman Rushdie's *The Ground beneath Her Feet*," *The Atlantic Critical Review*, Volume 1, Number 2, July-September 2002: 142.
16. Rushdie's passion for photography is blatant: in an essay titled "On Being Photographed," he records the experience of facing the camera eye, at Avendon's photographic studio. Judging his own photographic portrait, he cites the story of Faustus about the theft of shadows and images to tackle the discrepancy between artificiality and genuineness that photographed subjects are implicitly required to perform. See *STL*: 112-17.

Diasporic Lines

> . . . because fortunately after years of corporate synaesthesia (salt & vinegarblue, cheese & oniongreen) people can finally give the answers required when a space is being designed, or when something is being rebranded, a room/furniture/Britain (that was the brief: a new British room, a space for Britain, Britishness, space of Britain, British industrial space cultural space); they know what is meant when asked how matt chrome makes them feel; and they know what is meant by national identity? symbols? paintings? maps? music? air-conditioning? smiling black children or smiling Chinese children or [tick the box]? world music? shag or pile? tile or floorboards? plants? running water?
>
> Zadie Smith, *White Teeth* (p. 518)

Rushdie's theorisations of his notion of migrant identity and modern exile, extensively developed in a number of essays, form the central core of *The Satanic Verses*, which could be viewed as an example of world literature because, to quote Bhabha, "the truest eye may now belong to the migrant's double vision."[1] Although the novel unfolds, as always happens in Rushdie, a chain of various themes intimately connected, I shall take into account the salient role of the migrant and consequently dedicate my analysis primarily to Saladin Chamcha and Gibreel Farishta. It is vital in this respect to bear in mind that the author deals with the notion of diaspora as an engrossing rite of transnationalisation, a bypassing momentum that affects the postcolonial and postmodern condition of the man and the world.

Exile and migration have intensively influenced old and recent ages and re-shaped the geo-political configuration of the world:

their most devastating effects lie in the waves of migrants abruptly re-collocated in new social contexts. The pernicious aftermath of ethnic conflicts (let us think about the recent dispersion of peoples from former Yugoslavia) marks profoundly individuals who are deprived of their own identity and culture since they become alienated, nameless subjects in an incomprehensible scenario. *The Satanic Verses* may be read as a stigmatised precursor of Bhabhaian interpretations of migrancy, viewed as a cultural translation. The problem arises with the 'natural' connotation of 'untranslatableness,' that partially obscures the productive processes activated in the novel by all categories of émigrés, from 'vintage' migrants like Gibreel Farishta, to illegal refuges (like the grotesque figures kept at the detention centre) as well as first and second generation exiles. The hybrid contrast they create exfoliates the concept of 'pure identity,' which easily yields to racist fantasies and colonial memories.

We could observe the novel as a fantasist's attempt to witness the composition and significance of migrant communities in Britain and the imprint they carry through a process of transformation and thus what emerges concerns a chorus of characters that complete an intricate social jigsaw so that "to extrapolate a single coherent image from a common condition is to ignore the irreducible diversity and heterogeneity of this diaspora."[2] Minority cultures then ally together to construct a paradigmatic force of innovation bound to seek a new space in society. The most precise definition of the text is probably by the author himself, provided in an essay written in 1990 and which requires a full quotation:

> If *The Satanic Verses* is anything, it is a migrant's-eye view of the world. It is written from the very experience of the uprooting, disjuncture and metamorphosis (slow or rapid, painful or pleasurable) that is the migrant condition, and from which, I believe, can be derived a metaphor for all humanity. [. . .] *The Satanic Verses* celebrates hybridity, impurity, intermingling, the transformation that comes of new and unexpected combinations of human beings, cultures, ideas, politics, movies, songs. It rejoices in mongrelization and fears the absolutism of the Pure. *Mélange*, hotchpotch, a bit of

> this and a bit of that is *how newness enters the world*. It is the great possibility that mass migration gives the world, and I have tried to embrace it. *The Satanic Verses* is for change-by-fusion, change-by-conjoining. It is a love-song to our mongrel selves. (*IH*, 394; Author's emphasis)

Such harmonising vision of the writer accentuates in a semantic miscellany the key terms of the modern migrant's frame of mind that draw the coordinates we need to set the narratives of Saladin Chamcha and Gibreel Farishta, illustrious exponents of the diasporic condition.

The linguistic sphere and the figure of the migrant seen as an interpreter of 'Other' cultures are developed throughout the novel. To the admonishment that something may be lost in the translating process, Rushdie opposes the statement of the narrator of *Shame* who absorbs autobiographical echoes and simultaneously provides a context for the experience of the expatriate individual or writer: "I, too, am a translated man. I have been *borne across*. It is generally believed that something is always lost in translation; I cling to the notion [. . .] that something can also be gained" (*SH*, 29. Author's emphasis). The first-person narration indicates the practices of cross-cultural relationships as a privileged shrine of transferring cultures: this aspect will be further highlighted in *The Satanic Verses* which some critics have imagined as Rushdie's 'Passage to England.'

Through his peculiar intertextual modus operandi, the author seems to suggest that by staging the borderline condition of the émigré, the one who by antonomasia journeys across linguistic and cultural barriers, it is possible to detect several types of hybridity and mongrelisation. The congealed imagery of fixed memories and historical episodes is built up in the chapter dedicated to the prophetess Ayesha and distinguishes both the subject and the location, or rather the sense of displacement that accompanies the diasporic oscillation:

> Who is he? An exile. Which must not be confused with, allowed to run into, all the other words that people throw around: émigré, expatriate, refugee, immigrant, silence, cunning. Exile is a dream of glorious return. Exile is a vision of revolution: Elba, not St Helena. It is an endless paradox: looking forward by always looking back. The exile is a ball hurled high into the air. He hangs there, frozen in time, translated into a photograph; denied motion, suspended impossibly above his native earth, he awaits the inevitable moment at which the photograph must begin to move, and the earth reclaim its own. (*SV*, 205)
>
> Exile is a soulless country. In exile, the furniture is ugly, expensive, all bought at the same time in the same store and in too much of a hurry: shiny silver sofas with fins like old Buicks DeSotos Oldsmobiles, glass-fronted bookcases containing not books but clippings files. (*SV*, 208)

In Rushdie's grammar of migrancy, the photographic image acquires a fossilised status and becomes a signifier for the notion of home. The same concept is reiterated in *The Ground beneath Her Feet* where the protagonist Rai affirms that "photograph is a moral decision taken in one eighth of a second, or one sixteenth, or one one-hundred-and-twenty-eighth" (*GF*, 13).

While the text tends to be fractured into loosen narrative lines, an important role is played by Saladin Chamcha, a famous Bollywood actor who is condemned to tread upon a transformational itinerary. In this light, the discursive taxonomy of difference is employed to depict the 'corrupted' body of the immigrants, beset by a cultural shock in the 'foreign' country. Monstrousness as a metonymic device to signify the mark of otherness instils into Saladin a satanic, weird appearance, anticipated in the epitaph of the novel quoted from Daniel Defoe's *The History of the Devil*, which confirms Rushdie's comparison: Satan himself is a traveller, an immoral pilgrim and in the end a parodic counterpart to the modern immigrant. However, the devilish character that derives from a long and composite tradition is "Blake's devil, or Bulgakov's; and the voice is ultimately Beckett's voice, the furthest we can go in reaching back from the origins of consciousness."[3] Stylistically the leitmotif of transformation that Rushdie employs to draw the diasporic context has a highly intertextual origin and results in the outlandish portrait of metamorphosed Saladin. The horrible mutation—the character is now covered with air, boasts a long tail and is incredibly tall—is clearly indebted to specific models spanning from Kafka to classical authors,[4] through the sorrowful story of Elephant Man, exposed to public derision as a circus trophy.

The political criticism and indignation for racist abuse is viewed not in the representation of a nearly 'traditional' demon, but rather in the most freakish nature of the character, humiliated by the surreal trinity, or *trimurti* of the Indian tradition, composed by Stein, Novak and Bruno, the immigration officers, and kept under arrest in a dystopic detention centre. The technique of metamorphosing characters, previously exploited in *Midnight's Children* with special reference to Saleem, is again at work here in the tribulations of Saladin who is now surrounded by curious creatures—the immigrants forced to live in a nightmarish world, which reminds one of the violence that reverberates in Anthony Burgess' *A Clockwork Orange* (1962). Being one of them, the 'manticore,' or man-tiger, lists the unfortunate prisoners and comments upon their native land:

> The manticore ground its three rows of teeth in evident frustration. 'There's a woman over that way,' it said, 'who is now mostly water-buffalo. There are businessmen from Nigeria who have grown sturdy tails. There is a group of holidaymakers from Senegal who were doing no more than changing planes when they were turned into slippery snakes. I myself am in the rag trade; for some years now I have been a highly paid male model, based in Bombay, wearing a wide range of suitings and shirtings also. (*SV*, 168)

The absurd, gothic atmosphere is meant to assemble a horde of postcolonial outcasts; it is also an instance of a revitalised colonial practice of locating overseas territories and cities like Nigeria, Senegal, and Bombay on an imperial map, in the Kiplingian sense of duty of the white man's burden to civilise and therefore control hegemonically such agencies of radical newness and possible disorder.

Significantly, the episode spins around the question of language as a tool of power. The communities of migrants, downgraded into a subcategory of behemoths by the non-realistic modes of narration, are marginalised and deprived of any acts of speech and naming. Voiceless subjects, they are considered 'creatures' from exotic lands and suffocated within a racist project. Saladin, despite the solidarity shown by his sad companions, feels alienated and weakened because of the segregating mechanisms of the West. Hence we gather a sense of failure from both the pioneering experience of diaspora and the fallacious dream of a united community that annihilates the migrants because the authorities of the detention centre "they describe us. [. . .] They have the power of description, and we succumb to the pictures they construct" (*SV*, 168). This very image lies at the heart of the intolerant British reaction towards immigration and illustrates the process of racial discrimination introduced by stereotypes. The individual is then substituted in the collective consciousness by an impermeable, monolithic icon of otherness or foreignness; as a result, identity turns out to be constructed through language. In the process of establishing a dialectic relationship between the immigrant and the local, Rushdie has identified three types of disruptions experienced by the exile: the loss of roots, the linguistic clash and the social re-settling. Starting from the actual meaning of the Greek verb metaphor ('to carry over'), the novelist formulates a visionary definition of such individuals because "migrants—borne-across humans—are metaphorical beings in their very essence; and migration, seen as a metaphor, is everywhere around us" (*IH*, 278-9)

From this perspective stems the character of universality of migration, as a human experience that binds together all nations regardless of time. The novelist substantiates his quintessential credo by viewing memory not only as a site of accumulation but of mediation as well, an agency of coming to terms with one's self. The salient image of Saleem pickling memories in jars as if they were tasty chutney ingredients coincides with the nurturing of the identity of an individual, and by extension of a nation. The private and the public stands offer the chance to see common men as chroniclers at work: they record personal biographies and national histories and in thus doing they take into account the notion of memory, which will be further emphasised through the immigrant's exposure to the dilemma of the diaspora, of the double belonging and ethnical and urban re-shaping.

The clash with the host country—the Indian expatriate approaching Britain exemplified in the quasi-mythic vignette of Saladin and Gibreel 'falling from the sky' after the hijacking of the Boston, the aircraft named after one of the Gardens of Eden—questions the winding path of memory, its ability to mould pictures in the collective frame of mind and its closeness to the perilous voyage to the West. Rushdie maintains that the "past is a country from which we have all emigrated, that its loss is part of our common humanity" (*IH*, 12) and the consequent feeling of temporal/physical displacement allows a speculation on the potential recreation of the past with reference to the open space of the present and the misty atmosphere of the future. The astounding encounter with the 'elsewhere world' produces an unstable ego of the character and interrogates both personal and social identity, cast on the matrix of hybridity. The process of transnational cultural formation, encapsulated in the diaspora, spans from the anglicised persona to the virulent fundamentalist and acquires the coordinates of a conflict (ethical, social or generational). As Bhabha has illuminated, such tension is located at the borderline between cultures and gives rise to the dynamics of hybridity.

In this context Rushdie's characters work out a mimic resistance to the hegemonic modes of subjugation articulated by immigration policies. Identification is given a prominent role in the processes of migrating penetration and is basically achieved through the use of imitation and recreation, the former as a tool of colonial heritage with the mirage of British education for Commonwealth citizens and the latter as a protection towards the post-imperial assimilation. We should consider the historical premise as it is staged in the colonial narration, one in which the tendency to imitate the accent, lifestyle and customs of the coloniser sometimes turns into a comic, kitsch scene of aping. However, as Bhabha admonishes, the critical category of mimicry that we observe here in operation does not merely embody a process of appropriation or parodying but forges an ambivalence that juxtaposes similarities and differences:

> Mimicry is, thus the sign of a double articulation; a complex strategy of reform, regulation and discipline, which 'appropriates' the Other as it visualizes power. Mimicry is also the sign of the inappropriate, however, a difference or recalcitrance which coheres the dominant strategic function of colonial power, intensifies surveillance, and poses an immanent threat to both 'normalized' knowledge and disciplinary powers.[5]

The basic instinct concerns resemblance, as the colonised expresses the inner fantasy to become like or similar to the coloniser but will always assert his peculiarity and difference. Mimicry then can also evoke a fear or menace behind the reproductive and mirror-like aspect in the overshadowed and ambiguous relationship between coloniser and colonised. Mesmerised by the imposed, fake myth of white superiority, the colonised feels compelled to define himself as a marginal subject; consequently he will be accommodated in a minority discursive space, far from the metropolitan centre, and imprisoned in a periphery that is frequently imagined as a menacing sign of otherness, marked by the 'exotic' difference that 'denies' the idea of community and belonging.

When he seeks to escape, he may deploy the survival tools of mimicry or recreation, exactly like Gibreel Farishta when he conceives London as the city to be "tropicalised" and fantasises about the introduction of exotic trees (coco-palms, tamarind and banyans) or birds (peacocks and cockatoos). The vengeful transformation set in motion by the migrant, son of a minor god, goes beyond the narrative trope of magical realism, and in the end contaminates popular culture as well, in particular the performative act of playing music and clubbing. The London-based inter-ethnic scene is celebrated through the social rites of gathering, toasting, rapping and rhyming. It is a connection of Caribbean sounds and African references that create an urban multicultural milieu. In the novel, for instance, the deejay Pinkwalla,[6] whose real name is Sewsunker Ram, is the catalyser of groups of migrants and his interaction with the audience at the Club Hot Wax reveals the union of 'racialised' (postcolonial) subjects. Needless to say, as in the typical style of Rushdie, all names bear a symbolic aura. This parodic globalisation of topographies presents the character of metonym by bringing to light the one part of the whole cultural mosaic (geographical references as representations of postcolonial countries) and by introducing mockery, another term extensively used by Bhabha.

Equipped with such devices, the characters that emerge from *The Satanic Verses* have to compromise their own identity and negotiate a limited cultural space. Indeed, the migrant's reaction may oscillate between a painful process of identification and a denial of the unknown culture. The two protagonists of the novel perform such a tension and become paradigmatic of conflicting positions. Postmodern, urban Saladin Chamcha decides to conform to the rules of his new social location whereas Gibreel Farishta, bewildered in his schizophrenic state, refuses to accommodate the English way of thinking and searches for a shelter in his mystical visions. Notwithstanding, the narrator himself stakes a claim to their single identity since the two characters share a common background and energy. They make up the same cultural construct—a picture of Janus actually—and interplay in the moment of social and linguistic transformation:

> Should we even say that these are two fundamentally different *types* of self? Might we not agree that Gibreel, for all his stage-name and performances; and in spite of born-again slogans, new beginnings, metamorphoses—has wished to remain, to a larger de-

> gree, *continuous*—that is, joined to and arising from his past; that, he chose neither near-fatal illness nor transmuting fall; that in point of fact, he fears above all things the altered states in which his dreams leak into, and overwhelmed, his waking self, making him that angelic Gibreel he has no desire to be;—so that his is still a self which, for our present purposes, we may describe as 'true' . . . whereas Saladin Chamcha is a creature of *selected* discontinuances, a *willing* re-invention; his *preferred* revolt against history being what makes him, in our chosen idiom, 'false'? And might we then not go on to say that it is this falsity of self that makes possible in Chamcha a worse and deeper falsity—call this 'evil'—and that this is the truth, the door, that was opened in him by fall?—While Gibreel, to follow the logic of our established terminology, is to be considered 'good' by virtue of *wishing to remain*, for all his vicissitudes, at bottom an untranslated man.—But, and again but: this sounds like, does it not, dangerously like an intentionalist fallacy?—Such distinctions, resting as they must on an idea of the self as being (ideally) homogeneous, non-hybrid 'pure,'—an utterly fantastic notion!—cannot, must not suffice. (*SV*, 427. Author's emphasis)

Rushdie confronts Saladin and Gibreel not solely as symbols of dichotomy but he tapers them as combining elements of the same human mechanism, and to enhance the value of the key term hybridity he postulates the presence of a mongrelised self in the consciousness of the migrant, opposed to the mirage of purity, a mental fallacy.

Like in a futurist painting where lines double their trajectory and find themselves shattered into infinitive segments, in the text we encounter "two men, Gibreelsaladin Farishtachamcha, condemned to this endless but also ending angelicdevilish fall" (*SV*, 5).[7] Their cathartic descent onto the British alien land from the hijacked plane insists on the sameness of the ego and forecasts the mutability or dismemberment of the self: a bifurcate path awaits Rushdie's diasporic characters. Their choices taken within a spectrum of negotiations shape the limits of hybridity and build up a new sense of being. Tantalised by the efficiency and commodities of the West, they face up to a theatrical world, one in which living and settling coincide with learning roles and lines. While approaching the much desired destination, the immigrants roam throughout the globalised 'supermarket or archive' of identities[8] where the codes of behaviour are constantly re-written, and contribute to the procedures of connection and alteration.

In other words, the writer indicates that the notions of race, class and identity perceived as monolithic categories have to be reinterpreted and redefined as crossings or borderlines. This critical vocabulary, which again refers to Bhabha's analysis, should also include the failure of unmediated multiculturalism and fake cosmopolitan strategies. The racial alienation that segregates the migrant from white metropolitan society seems to be well rooted and exacerbates the relation with new communities from former colonies. The tension that arises from this unstable social scenario disintegrates the unlikely translating processes, by which different cultures could establish meaningful links. Actual references in the form of deictic features anchor the textual discourse to the recent history of Britain, so that the image of the 'river of blood' summons forth the controversial figure of Right Wing leader Enoch Powel,[9] who in 1968 clearly expressed his racist opinions on the question of immigration and whose political message was restored during the years of Thatcherism.[10]

Provided such an harsh context, the immigrant may be tempted to look back to his native land, but this desperate cry for help cast *à rebours* is bound to break over the walls of memory and thus "when, after realising the impossibility of his fusion with the Other world that he had so much idealised, the diasporic man returns to reappropriate his former space, he is painfully aware that the territory of origin is not an entirely different place."[11] The impossibility of inclusion into a circumscribed canon, a condition that stresses anew the migrant's liminality, demonstrates how the West operates ideological mechanisms of cultural control so that London may become an urban jungle where dangers are more frequent than in remote India.

Whether Saladin's exploration of the metropolitan space grows into a parable of the modern migrant wandering across the post-modern city, in Gibreel's case, a mystical quest projects visions of identity through an hallucinating kaleidoscope. The character percolates in a limbo peopled by angels and in the end identifies himself with the archangel Gabriel. The core topic here is the way in which the fervent religious credo brought by migrants is presented and accepted in the western world. Rushdie's affair and Khomeini's *fatwa*[12] are well known and inscribe both the public author and the private persona in a discursive and cultural debate that conjugates the religious interstices of the relation between West and East as expressed through the multi-faceted diaspora.

Rushdie's "crime," according to Islamic accusatory, lies in his linguistic pastiche that rearranges the structure and tradition of the Koran. The 'Arab sections' of the text are built upon the figure of the Prophet, but the name chosen by the author, Mahound, was coined in the medieval times and works as a pejorative epithet. The character is sketched in problematic and ironic light, and even his monotheistic faith is sometimes challenged and besmirched by a possible establishment of a pantheon that may include three ancient goddesses: Lat, Mannat and Uzza. Also the context of polygamy is altered, so that Mahound awards himself a harem of twelve wives and restricts the number for his adepts. Then the prostitutes of Jahila, a place name that means 'ignorance,' are named after the twelve consorts of the Prophet. All these elements of revision seem to mix Islam with signs of corruption, and the sacrilegious act of juxtaposing the mark of Satan with the holy book cannot be accepted by the Muslim in his utmost integrity. The very problem of 'misnaming' is exacerbated again since it is perceived as an attack towards a community. Hence stems the nature of blasphemy which should be regarded as a strategy of staging intercultural confrontations, in Homi Bhabha's view. The critic highlights the notions of blasphemy and translation, and we could address the question of the literary form in terms of Rushdie's choice of the novel (updated by a postmodern whimsicality), which is at odds with the genre of classic poetry of Muslim tradition, one in which the artist's imagination can build other worlds.

Within the oriental traditional context, the poetic genre is expressed through the recitation of the *ghazal* (lyrical love poetry), written in Urdu, Pakistan's official language nowadays. This literary phenomenon is non-autochthonous, being introduced by the invasion of Persians and thus functions as a linking wheel between the Arabic (Muslim) culture and the Indian environment. In the subcontinent, Islam also gives birth to the genres of *kawwali*, which is licentious oral fiction and *baed-bari*, or debate. Feroza Jussawalla believes that the novel reinforces the references to such typology because Rushdie does not sustain a crusade in favour of secularism and a Muslim backdrop may be an important constituency of one's cultural essence and personal identity. However she indicates a further literary creation, the *dastan-e-dilruba*, representing a love song for the beloved, to tackle *The Satanic Verses* since "in the Indo-Mughal tradition, love for one's religion, whether Hindu or Muslim, is expressed as love for a beloved, both in lyric poetry or longer oral narratives."[13]

Rushdie borrows the *dastan* genre from skilled storytellers of long-gone Persian tradition and emphasises both the oral narration and the fantastic element. For instance, the prophetess Ayesha may be regarded as a *pari*, a typical winged creature from these poems. She is the protagonist of incredible episodes and walks around the city of Jahila "dressed in golden butterflies" (*SV*, 235). As the language superbly reflects the inclusion of spells, bewitching events and uncanny characters, one should distinguish postmodern strategies of re-writing historical episodes or compiling exercises in magical realism on the one hand, and the Muslim perspective of this type of tradition on the other. The metaphor of the *dastan* observed as a "love letter" from Rushdie to Islam calls for a close scrutiny since it has to be located within a specific context, that is Islam in India. This determines both the characters that emerge from *The Satanic Verses* and the approach towards the issue of religion. Rushdie, born to a Muslim family, plays the role of an atypical spokesperson of a complex community and witnesses his relationship with Muslimism on the backdrop of India. His characters illuminate this hybrid nature and function as the outcome of different peoples in diverse ages across Indian history.

Following Bhabha's premise, we should note that the condemnation of Rushdie comes from his attempt to debate the historical circumstances of birth of that religion: in other words, it is the author's revisionist imprint that interrogates cultural (and thereafter political) structures:

> Blasphemy is not merely a misrepresentation of the sacred by the secular; it is a moment when the subject matter or the content of a cultural tradition is being overwhelmed, or alienated, in the act of translation. Into the asserted authenticity or continuity of tradition, 'secular' blasphemy releases a temporality that reveals the contingencies, even the incommensurabilities, involved in the process of social transformation.[14]

Blasphemy becomes the taxonomic stance of the difficulty of translating cultures, in which religion is given a significant role. It is this very quality of 'in-betweenness,' this lack of the Word, that establishes the identity of the migrant and unfolds an opaque dialogic space. Bhabha's theory contrives a permutation of words and crystallises the verb 'to blaspheme' with the meaning of 'to dream.' Furthermore, in a different perspective, Sara Suleri revisits the episode of the miswriting of the godly word, by moving from an Islamic context into an historicised speculation and stresses that blasphemy "generates a language of cultural questioning that allows the author to throw up a pair of Muslim hands at the incongruities that impel his discourse, and to elucidate the similarities between the idioms of betrayal and loyalty that history has imposed upon a post-colonial world."[15] Following such line of enquiry, it may also be possible to observe Thatcher's London and western racism as further examples of the enlarged concept of blasphemy.

The agency of blasphemy should then be re-located within a wide variety of cultural and textual strategies that the novelist employs to challenge the margins and the confines of translation by activating a propulsive force to exceed boundaries. Life and literature mirror the uncertain territory that surrounds the man and the migrant and fills them with a feeling of panic or anxiety. The ambiguity of the present retrieved by the past grows from the fear of the future and records an ongoing social transformation:

> The 'newness' of migrant or minority discourse has to be discovered *in medias res*: a newness that is not part of the 'progressivist' division between past and present, or the archaic and the modern; nor is it a 'newness' that can be contained in the mimesis of 'original and copy.' In both these cases, the image of the new is iconic rather than enunciatory; in both instances, temporal difference is represented as epistemological or mimetic distance from an original source.[16]

The rhetorical question that disturbs the reader concerns the possibility to detect the field of migrant relationships by commencing with an historical gaze onto the life of Mahomet and the birth of the metaphorical religious glue that keep together different peoples. And yet the untranslatable nature of the intercultural encounter explains the origins and sources of the stamina of the migrant and affects the performative capability.

Rushdie imagines the dream-like events pivoting around the Prophet as a link between a secular present and the tradition of holy texts: incessantly the world dreamt by Gibreel is shifted into the text and creates a space of constructive comparisons. Dream is the instrument to intertwine different narrative structures and, through its misty, borderless dimension, work out themes of modernity and tradition, which recuperates either echoes of postmodern tendencies or time-honoured issues. According to Joel Kuortti, three types of reverie can be distinguished and they include the level of revelation, the level of cultural contact and the level of fictionality. The first one scans the notion of revelation in our present, secular world and could be interpreted in a double perspective: while Gibreel's mental creations are classified as products of schizophrenia in the western world, the Islamic assessment has to refer to the Koran and cannot contemplate a rational vision. The level of cultural contact which functions as a vehicle of diaspora is performed by Gibreel and Saladin and their uneasiness attached to the condition of the migrant. Chamcha is said to have an "obsession to the conquest of Englishness" (*SV*, 256), but his great expectations will be destroyed by the gloomy, nightmarish portrait of London. Finally, on the level of fictionality, the visionary representation of the two characters confounds any attempts to fix a logic. In Saladin's fiction, the overwhelming strength of chaos is made relevant because "at first, these dreams were private matters, but pretty soon they started leaking into the waking hours, as Asian retailers and manufacturers of button-badges sweatshirts understood the power of the dream" (*SV*, 286), whereas Gibreel is even given the privilege to meet God, albeit he is still doubtful about the whole episode: "What struck him most was that the apparition was balding, seemed to suffer from dandruff and wore glasses. This was not the Almighty he had expected" (*SV*, 318).

However, fictionality operates also with reference to linguistic patterns: the most problematic keywords are 'fundamentalism,' cited to define Islam, and 'secularism,' employed to depict the West. The text shows how both may be frequently misunderstood and endowed with different meanings because of the large semantic area they cover nowadays. The western Eurocentric perception, which is still characterised by an hysterical rejection of the Other, relies on the use of the plural term 'fundamentalisms' connected with an orientalist gaze. Yet the noun should be paraphrased as a "complex set of oppositions converging in the term 'fundamentalism': the etymological history, the political superimposition, and the ideological accommodation."[17] We can relocate the thorny issue of fundamentalism in the cultural space of identity, one in which individuals struggle to achieve a self-definition: this is precisely what animates Saladin and Gibreel too. In the end, all their flabbergasting episodes, their journey into the unknown and the lingering memory of Bombay head for a speculation of innermost awareness, of belonging and being. Salman Rushdie in so doing moulds a textual discourse that penetrates the fields of fiction, (inter)cultural confrontation, revised historiography, ethnic origin, and fanciful psychodrama.

The cultural contact aforementioned, with all its implications of religious outburst and postcolonial affirmation, shapes Rushdie's shorter fiction as well: the collection *East, West*, which appeared in 1994 and includes some stories previously published in journals and reviews, immediately witnesses the synthetic encounter of two worlds. The very title, divided and/or linked by a comma, also depicts the three sections into which the nine stories fall: 'East,' 'West' and 'East/West.' In his project of investigating the intermingled relationship between Occidental and Oriental viewpoints and the result of diasporic hybridisation, the author employs the genre of the short story: this choice allows creative writing to efficaciously combine in a straightforward matter contemporary themes, on the backdrop of political and social satire.[18]

In particular the stories aim at levelling the preconceptions of the mental constructs of East and West and at challenging all kinds of holiness, not only in a religious sense but also with a mundane and postmodern spirit. Rushdie inverts the biased image of the 'orientalised' subcontinent and 'modern' West and demolishes the blind veneration of sacred objects (Islamic relics as well as ritzy commodities) via a deconstructive process. "The Prophet's Hair" unfolds a religious background and recalls an actual event that occurred in 1963: the prophet Muhammad's hair, housed at the Hazar Bal Mosque since the 18th century, disappeared and was eventually found the next month. In the tale when the Muslim moneylender Hashim discovers the stolen vial containing the precious relic, a miracle invests his life and his passion for collecting Indian antiques is turned into a strict adherence to Islamic practices. The discriminating condition of *purdah* is introduced for his wife and daughter, all books, except the Kuran obviously, are banned and then burnt, and as a consequence the whole family adopt a severe, parochial behaviour. In spite of the moral purity implied in the profession of faith, Hashim continues his activity of usury and regularly visits his favourite prostitutes. His son Atta and his daughter Huma try to restore their family balance and hire a professional thief to purloin the prophet's hair, jealously guarded by Hashim.

A sequence of venturesome facts follow. However, the focus should not be put on the religious lore or Islamic strictness but rather on the metaphor of sacredness attributed to objects. The adoration of the prophet's hair contravenes the purity of the rite and blurs the worship of God. The short story reveals an iconoclastic aspect, one in which the relic becomes a surrogate and shifts into the order of simulacra; thus it ought to be regarded not as an attack towards religion or the intimate relation between state and Islam in Oriental countries, but rather as an assessment of how fetishes are drawn from variegated typologies (mystic, but also mundane or even 'commercial'). This mania, which evaluates earthly things enormously, afflicts both East and West: it produces totems and idolises individuals. Jean Baudrillard's meticulous analysis of simulacra could be adopted as a way to scan the images or fetishes that permeate the entire volume. In his cold theory of a nameless void that substitutes God, he interrogates himself about what lies behind the mask:

> But what becomes of the divinity when it reveals itself in icons, when it is multiplied in simulacra? Does it remain the supreme power that is simply incarnated in images as a visible theology? Or does it volatize itself in the simulacra that, alone, deploy their power and pomp of fascination—the visible machinery of icons substituted for the pure and intelligible idea of God? This is precisely what was feared by Iconoclasts, whose millennial quarrel is still with us today. This is precisely because they predicted this

> omnipotence of simulacra, the faculty simulacra have of effacing God from the conscience of man, and the destructive, annihilating truth that they allow to appear—that deep down God never existed, that only the simulacrum ever existed, even that God himself was never anything but his own simulacrum—from this came their urge to destroy the images.[19]

The pivotal position of the fetish works via the 'supermarket ideology' and in a globalised world invests everything; the idea of holiness originally rooted in an ecumenical context cannot survive from this postmodern elaboration of pictures, fragments and forms. Even the godly rank is overthrown and therefore relics become commodities, pieces of a large collection of simulacra. This operation is particularly evident in the West where, according to the narrator of "At the Auction of the Ruby Slippers," "we have witnessed the auction of the Taj Mahal, the Statue of Liberty, the Alps, the Sphinx" (*EW*, 98). The selling out of symbols implies the desolate wasteland of a sick contemporaneousness, where ideas (and heritages too) are downgraded into goods that will be launched onto the globalised market of status symbols and fake roles.

The processing of identities also constitutes a main theme in the tale "The Courter," set in 1960s London. The young narrator belongs to a family of Indian refugees and presents a gallery of curious characters: besides the different members of his family, dominated by a violent and authoritarian father, we find Mary, his Indian Catholic ayah, Mecir, a skilled chess player from an East European country, and two wealthy and ambiguous maharajas—the Prince of P and the Prince of B. As usual, Rushdie's style emerges in the making of nicknames that the narrator punctually assigns to everyone: Mary is called Certainly-Mary or Aya Mary (by dropping an 'h' in the Anglo-Indian word), Mecir is rechristened Mixed-Up and Sir Charles Lutwidge-Dodgson, a posh, aristocratic family friend, becomes "the Dodo."

The story alternates a comic register with dramatic occurrences, so that the title alludes to the linguistic incomprehension between Mary and Mecir: the woman is not fluent in English while the man cannot pronounce certain letters because of a stroke that has paralysed his mouth. It is quite plausible then for a porter like Mecir to become a "courter" and we observe here the first instance of transformational identities. However the two use the game of chess as a substitutive language and their wooing goes on. The narrative frame is grounded on a symbolic switching of gestures and identities that generates a false, rosy world; pop culture, comic puns, the game of chess seem to furnish a fabulous, blissful scenario and yet this mirage of great expectations in Britain abruptly has to come to terms with reality and episodes of violence mark the social conflict within the diasporic context. Even music, which reverberates throughout the text with lyrics to popular songs, turn out to be a simulation, a carousel that hides the actual condition of the individual and the migrant, in particular, not only from the subcontinent but also from elsewhere. In this light, the text also foreruns symbolically instances of mass migration from Eastern Europe and admonishes about the reshaping of present-day society.

The competition for identities and alternative selves is shaped by all the lodgers of Waverly House who yield to the fascination of the West and in the narrator's mind, the place appears as a

> seething mass of bad marriages, booze, philanderers and unfulfilled young lusts; of the Maharaja of P—roaring away towards London's casinoland every night, in a red sports car with fitted blondes, and the Maharaja of B—skulking off to Kensington High Street wearing dark glasses in the dark, and a coat with the collar turned up even though it was high summer; and at the heart of our little universe were Certainly-Mary and her courter, drinking chimpanzee tea and singing along with the national anthem of Bedrock. (*EW*, 190)

This quotation does not only function as a collage of various icons and metonyms of West and East but indicates the processing of identities, the intertextual connection of the two cultures; Rushdie's tactical manoeuvre consists in eroding a cohesive image and cultural wholeness. No character is immune to this syndrome: even the princes who are expected to behave aristocratically show customs and vices of the West and speak in a rather cinematic language.

Every single element of the story conceives a meaning or allusion so that the game of chess, practised by various characters, may mirror the colonial heritage and the techniques of losing and winning a new unique identity. The example is found in connection with Field Marshal Lutwidge-Dodgson, who cannot accept to be defeated by the young protagonist and thus rejects him. The act of imposition is also performed by the narrator's father. The boy, whose fondness for Mary is obfuscated by an Oedipus complex, detests the paternal figure and strives to re-create an ideal family. The ambiguity that saturates the human relationships in the tale is also evocative of the intertwined bonds established between a metropolitan (glittering) space and a progressive diaspora. The author reinforces his disillusionment with the much-praised intercultural harmony by orchestrating Mary's return to Bombay and providing the narrator with a British passport. Eventually the woman repudiates both her lover and the dream of an English life:

> So it was England that was breaking her heart, breaking it *by not being India*. London was killing her, *by not being Bombay*. And Mixed-Up? I wondered. Was the courter killing her, too, because he was no longer himself? Or was it that her heart, roped by *two different loves*, was being pulled both East and West, whinnying and rearing, like those movie horses being yanked this way by Clark Gable and that way by Montgomery Clift, and she knew that to live she would have to choose? (*EW*, 209. Emphasis added)

Analogously the boy wonders about his condition and plans his future tactics; being now a British citizen allows him to formulate a new perspective. While his father decides that the family has to move into Pakistan, he remains in London. But his catharsis into a new type of Englishman is accompanied by doubts and shadows and inaugurates the discursive location of immigrant communities: "But I, too, have ropes around my neck, I have them to this day, pulling me this way and that, East and West, the nooses tightening, commanding, *choose, choose.* I buck, I snort, I whinny, I rear, I kick. Ropes, I do not choose between you. Lassoes, lariats, I choose neither of you, and both. Do you hear? I refuse to choose" (*EW*, 211. Author's emphasis). The narrator's dilemma should not be considered as a lack of responsibility, a childish hesitation, but rather the frail and ambiguous territory of the self, in which the Bhabhaian in-betweenness of diasporic individuals and their allowance to occupy multiple cultural spaces prevail and question the future.

In its complex simplicity and windy linearity, two examples of oxymoron that we need to illustrate Rushdie's short narrative, the concept of hybridity is reiterated and given a further significance: it refers not only to the relations between the former coloniser and the displaced immigrant, but expands its borders and, as Rudolf Beck suggests, in this collection of stories "hybridity, mélange and hotch-potch serve to undermine ideological certainties of *any* kind, and to resist *any* sort of appropriation."[20] As a matter of fact, Rushdie is not interested in offering superficial comments upon the condition of the modern émigré or elaborating on rules of immigration policy. In his role of an artist, he deploys the word to browse the deeper levels of reality in a fantastic mode: he enhances the stylistic form by deconstructing rigid cultural entities and building up symmetrical narrative patterns.

NOTES

1. Homi Bhabha, *The Location of Culture* (London and New York: Routledge, 1994): 5
2. Martien Henmarde Dutheil de la Rochère, *Origin and Originality* (Berne: Peter Lang, 1998): 93
3. Damian Grant, *Salman Rushdie* (Plymouth: Northcote House, 1999): 84
4. Indeed the conversation between Chamcha and Muhammad Sufyian is based on the interpretation of the metamorphosis according to Lucretius and Ovid. Their theories constitute the dichotomy of

viewpoints on the notion of diaspora and migration that the text takes over. In *De Rerum Natura*, Lucretius holds that in the process of transformation, the self not only changes its forms but alters its nature too, in a drastic way. Conversely, the position of Ovid expressed in the *Metamorphoses* regards the immutability of the self since solely the external shape may mute, like "yielding wax" (*SV*, 276). Both Sufyia and Saladdin (and implicitly Rushdie too, as we have previously seen) agree with the latter to justify the odd mutation and the episode is formulated as an interlude constructed on the word 'wax,' after which the disco mentioned later on is named. Furthermore, the writer broods on the arduous process of literary translation, which is a key theme in the entire novel: his rhetorical strategy brings back to modern time the classic authors through translation.

5. Homi Bhabha, cited: 86.
6. The curious epithet may be rendered as "pink (or white) fellow" and denotes the tension of parody in delineating ethnic characters. Concerning the technical aspect of *wallah* or *walla*, "this Hindi word has entered the speech of some British Standard speakers but it is much more frequently used in Indian variants of English and in compounds where it would not occur in BS, such as box-wallah (commercial traveller), police-wallah, rickshaw-wallah, OUP-wallah," Paroo Nihalani, R.K. Tongue and Priya Hosali, *Indian and British English* (New Delhi: Oxford University Press, 2000): 190.
7. The fall as a literary device is characterised by a biblical origin but influences contemporary authors too, since it can be read in different ways and contains salient metaphors of modernity. Rushdie ironically takes for granted the fall of the British Empire, and by extension of western culture, as well as the fall of men into a post-modern feeling of void. However the sense of the end that emerges from the fall is accompanied by the instinct of birth or rebirth and alludes to the pattern of cyclicity (let us think about the myth of the phoenix): in the opening of the book, this motif is celebrated through Gibreel's refrain: "To be born again [. . .] first you have to die" (*SV*, 3) and by nearly borrowing Christ's words, the author accentuates a compulsory stage prior to the transformation and changing of identities (from a religious, social or mental viewpoint). The idea of resurrection is shared by both Rushdie and

Joyce because it "suggests that the cultural fall resulting from our loss of faith in the past is a fortunate and liberating one that opens up a variety of exciting possibilities for the future," M. Keith Booker, "*Finnegans Wake* and *The Satanic Verses*: Two Modern Myths of the Fall," *Critique—Studies in Contemporary Fiction*, Vol. XXX, No. 3, Spring 1991: 195.

8. See Aijaz Ahmad, *In Theory* (1992) (London: Verso, 1994).
9. Such dreadful expression comes from a speech delivered in the April of 1968 in which Powell strongly criticised the development of a new race legislation that extended protection to the black community. See Paul Gilroy, cited: 45-51 and 104-9 in particular.
10. The then Prime Minister Margaret Thatcher, a central exponent of British political or racist intransigence, is mercilessly lampooned in the character of Mrs. Torture. A colourful description reads: "'Torture. Maggie the Bitch.' Oh. 'She's radical all right. What she wants—what she actually thinks she can fucking *achieve*—is literally to invent a whole goddam new middle class in this country. Get rid of the old woolly incompetent buggers from fucking Surrey and Hampshire, and bring in the new. People without background, without history. Hungry people. People who really *want*, and who know that with her, they can bloody well *get*.'" (*SV*, 269-70. Author's emphasis).
11. Geetha Ganapathy-Dore, "Mapping Continents: the Journey Home in Salman Rushdie, Michael Ondaatje and Bharati Mukherjee," *Commonwealth Essays and Studies*, Vol. 17, No. 1, Autumn 1994: 5.
12. The novel was published in September 1988 and banned in India in October 1988, while Ayatollah Ruhallah Khomeini's (death) sentence in the form of fatwa was broadcast on Radio Teheran on 14 February 1989. See Lisa Appignone and Sara Meitland, eds., *The Rushdie File* (London, 4th Estate, 1989). A long negotiation was run by the governments of Britain and Iran and led to the suspension of the *fatwa* in 1999. It comes as no surprise that when we deal with *The Satanic Verses*, we have to contemplate a discourse on the idea of authority (political, religious or of other nature) and national and transnational contexts (banning the text in India and across the Islamic world, book burning and riots in Bradford). It is also a debate on the author's permission to break narrative conventions and shape new literary forms. In this sense, Rushdie's case,

darkened by the reaction of the various Muslim communities, becomes also the public sphere for contesting the law on the backdrop of fundamentalist hotbeds. However it is worth remembering that Islam and religious fanaticism were not born out of the blue after the publication of the novel.

13. Feroza Jussawalla, "Rushdie's *Dastan-e-Dilruba. The Satanic Verses* as Rushdie's Love Letter to Islam," *Diacritics*, vol. 26, No. 1, Spring 1996: 54. Specifically the *dastan* genre belongs to the Persian heritage and pictures a dramatic scenario, in which the sad lover bemoans the absence of the loved; instead the Arabic culture that permeates the *Arabian Nights*, a text frequently cited or hinted at in Rushdie's writing, relies on the use of *qissa*, a briefer, full of verve form. Rushdie, according to Jussawalla, has a predilection for the *dastan*, an apt genre to conquer the beloved one over an entire night but subtly adds a tone of a complaint. The final result is a lament for the impossibility to achieve the beloved—here a metaphor for Rushdie's Islam—due to his "ambivalent postcolonial relationship and his Indianised secular Muslim attitudes": 67.
14. Homi Bhabha, cited: 225-26.
15. Sara Suleri, "Contraband Histories. Salman Rushdie and the Embodiment of Blasphemy," in M.D. Fletcher, cited: 224.
16. *Ibid.*: 227.
17. Joel Kuortti, "Intercultural Identification and Salman Rushdie's *The Satanic Verses*" in R.K. Dhawan, ed., *Writers of the Indian Diaspora* (New Delhi: Prestige, 2001): 64.
18. See Stefano Manferlotti, "East or West? Le due culture nella narrativa breve di Salman Rushdie" in M. Billi, ed., *Voci sull'India e dall'India. 1947-1997* (Viterbo: Sette Città, 2001): 87-103. In his analysis of the story "The Prophet's Hair," the critic underscores the revisitation of tragedy (the Elizabethan form in particular), whose gore essence is here diluted into a tragicomedy.
19. Jean Baudrillard, *Simulacra and Simulation*, trans. Sheila Faria-glazer (Ann Arbor: The University of Michigan Press, 1994).
20. Rudolf Beck, "Close Encounter of the Third Type: Salman Rushdie's Short Story Cycle *East, West*," *Anglia—Zeitschrift fur Englische Philologie*, Band 116, Heft 3, 1998: 379 (Author's emphasis).

Coda: Literary Curries (Postcolonial or Postmodern Recipes?)

> That sound, though not the words, remains still with me, lodged in a corner of my brain where such things live. And along with that, the smell! As the hour came, the men would undo the knots of their bundles and spread the cloth on the ground. Inside would be thick roti folded foursquare which they open out to lay on the cloth, revealing a lump of mango achaar wrapped in the centre, a spot of chutney made of pounded green chilli and salt, sometimes a little earthen cup half-full of daal with a lid on, other times nothing but the roti which they would eat with lassi given them in brown earthen bowls by the blacksmith, who had a pitcherful of it by his side. [. . .] The smell was not of anything, not of gas from the burning coal nor of sparks from the hot iron nor of sweating bodies nor achaar nor leaves of fresh coriander floating on top of the daal. Neither it was a mixture of all these. It was the smell of heat—of hot earth and bodies black with toil but at rest, nor hurried, willing as if for an unbroken passage of days and nights, bullocks, ploughs, crops, the sun. This smell had a shape in my mind and it was the shape of my father because he had built and owned the hut and for me it was all there was left of him.
>
> Abdullah Hussein, *Émigré Journeys* (p. 38)

The notion of food as a taxonomic device employed to describe a cultural context has illustrious examples in different literatures, spanning from Proust's traditional *madeleines* to Isabella Allende's *Afrodita*, a work that literally 'melts' together actual recipes with fiction, but Rushdie's literary use of dishes highlights a manifold project, one in which the author introduces the notion of migration, with food being a pivotal element to convey culture in migrating communities and social groups. As a matter of fact, textualising food becomes a discursive practice that seems to characterise expatriate writers, from Manzu Islam to Monica Ali.[1]

Frequently we observe certain broad categories such as Indian or Asian food represented as forms of imagined cuisine, or *commensalité* in anthropological terms, which not only constitute a powerful instrument of social bonding (the making, offering and sharing of food as an act to join together individuals and communities) but also witness cultural and ideological relationships. In this context, food seems to belong to an 'invented' tradition as demonstrates the example of Farrukh Dhondy's *Bombay Duck* (1990). From the very title, the author adopts what Australian linguist Kate Burridge terms as "culinary camouflage," namely "language that disguises, distorts, deceives, misleads, inflates, obfuscates—language that makes the unpalatable seem palatable, the negative seem positive, the unpleasant seem attractive, the ordinary seem extraordinary."[2] In the novel, the writer in his daring attempt of lexicalization coins a new category, "chop suey," which dilates the sense of perplexity and displacement of the individual split between the mythical past hanging in the labyrinths of memory and the overcoming of the space of identity. Within this arena of negotiations, the notions of tradition and modernity, life and imagination are manipulated and thereafter the self remains puzzled and isolated: "Chop Suey is when you've bought something to whose authenticity you cannot attest. Usually because you're ignorant. Usually because the vendor has contrived to culturally mug you!"[3] The original or invented traditions of food comprise both chutney, which indicate a mixture of vegetables, fruits and spices, and curry, which may cover a broader semantic area.

Chutney is a well-known Indian sauce which has now become a quite popular dish available in the West as well. First we should make a distinction between the (original) Indian chutney and the

Anglicised version, commonly sold at British supermarkets. On a metonymical level, the former projects a gaze upon the past, within the archaic system of food taboos whereas the latter, usually translated with 'relish,' unfolds a globalising operation, a link between the West and the East based on the idea of assimilation, and also a product offered to please the migrant community. It is an abridging word, in the sense that it conveys a sense of being and belonging, whereas in the migrant's fantasy it suggests sharing the same ideal *commensalité*. Conversely, following an orientalised interpretation, it stands for the intra-ethnic entertainment imagined by the West. The entry in the *Hobson-Jobson Anglo-Indian Dictionary* records its Hindustani origin and reads: "A kind of strong relish, made of a number of condiments and fruits, etc., used in India, and more especially by Mahommedans, and the merits of which are now well known in England."[4] It is a definition that in its general terms testifies to the popularity of Indian food abroad since the 19th century and alludes to the complexity of the relationship between not only two countries, but between two heterogeneous cultural factions as well awkwardly divided and linked by the historical experience of colonialism.

In a narrative context, food in its colourful presentation becomes a purposeful vehicle able to communicate cultural values and interior tensions. In *Midnight's Children*, Rushdie holds the renown Indian recipes as figures of speech with Proustian-imbued echoes and adopts a strategy that modifies the text and the traditional world vision.[5] Indeed the recipes of chutney require a list of ingredients which are "raw materials, obviously—fruit, vegetables, fish, vinegar, spices" (*MC*, 460) but the sense of the metaphor inscribes the idea of History, juxtaposed with the mundane level of life, into the magical jars of the tasty sauce. In particular the novelist deals with green chutney, Mary Pereira and Saleem's treasure, as an engrossing metaphor of maintaining memories, with thoughts being treated as if they were precious ingredients of a never-forgotten recipe. Before deconstructing the salient images of the text, we ought to build a thematic parallelism between creative writing and gastronomy. In Book One, Saleem, whose smell perception has been made supernatural by the powers of the midnight miracle, offers a curious self-portrait, one in which his roles of (unreliable) narrator and extravagant cook coincide:

> Rising from my pages comes the unmistakable whiff of chutney. So let me obfuscate no further: I, Saleem Sinai, possessor of the most delicately-gifted olfactory organ in history, have dedicated my latter days to the large-scale preparation of condiments. But now, 'A cook' you gasp in horror, 'A khansama merely? How is it possible?' And, I grant, such mastery of the multiple gifts of cookery and language is rare indeed; yet I possess it. You are amazed; but then I am not, you see, one of your 200-rupees-a-month cookery johnnies, but my own master, working beneath the saffron and green winking of my personal neon goddess. And my chutneys and kasaundies are, after all, connected to my nocturnal scribblings—by day amongst the pickle-vats, by night within these sheets, I spend my time at the great work of preserving. Memory, as well as fruits, is being saved from the corruption of the clocks. (*MC*, 37-38)

This stylistic connection classifies the protagonist's position, in its unique idiosyncratic nature that controls both the boons of literacy and food preparation. It is a permutation of the symbolism of the cook as a maker then: the erudite art of choosing the proper ingredients is accompanied by the predisposition to narrate stories, to select temporal circumstances and dramatise them. The final aim of such operation is to encapsulate history, to construct a multilayered archive of perceptions and warnings held together by a communal consciousness. It is a complex recipe therefore that sometimes reveals a bitter taste as it also evokes the painful experience of the Partition and ethnic conflicts that struck communities, villages and countries, India and Pakistan, Hindus and Muslims. Rushdie's eccentric subtext—the connection between the time-honoured cuisine of India and the mechanisms of fiction—bespeaks a radical judgement of "that generation of politicians who seem to have been pickled in immortality" (*MC*, 327): they are held responsible for persecutions and corruption, and thus perceived as polluting ingredients in the making of history. Hence stems the necessity to preserve memory and update the awareness of a nation pictured in a continuous metamorphosis.

The image of the writer in the guise of a cook needs to be illustrated by Rushdie's parodic and humoristic character. It is not a sacrilegious plan to downgrade the artist's work, to reduce the epic of India with its glorious corollary of deities and rites to a burlesque analogy; on the contrary, it is a way to break untouchable notions of historical fixity. In his ambitious attempt to draw a fictional portrait of modern India and unearth sorrowful episodes of the country, Rushdie needs to re-set the genre of the novel in order to allow allegory to manifest itself.

Spiced chutney emblematises through a pungent sweet-sour taste the delicate space of negotiation that the author collocates into his writing. The surreal rhetorical question that Saleem poses—"Why, at this crucial instant, when all manners of things were waiting to be described [. . .] did I introduce a mere condiment into conversation?" (*MC*, 208)—actually encompasses the paradigms of narrating insofar as food shifts the focus from the moral level to the mundane and in thus doing it opens a discourse based on the irony of language. In this light, it is added to a network of signs that erode the status of the text as artifice. Rushdie's textuality is re-codified in a perpetual motion between an ethnic act of locating origins and a transnational construction of the notion of diaspora. In the process of creating clusters of meanings, it also projects Indian culture in its core essence by enunciating the relative prescription of the treatment of food.

We have to comprehend that "the gastronomic metaphors for art become metaphors for history"[6] because the power of chutney lies in the possibility of scrutinising scattered sequences of historic modules. Furthermore it mediates a position of ambivalence or compromise, one that seeks to limit the verbosity of a critical debate concerning difference and assimilation, or globalisation we would say in our age. Rushdie's procedure of chutnification of history as a textual strategy of cohesion goes beyond the boundary of prescriptive norms of *halal* and *haram* food, in an eastern context. According to these two dietary categories of the Muslim code of behaviour, it is possible to draw a line of division respectively between what one is allowed to eat and what is forbidden. The image is further elaborated by the author so as to underscore the totemistic heterogeneity of constructs referring to East and West. The discriminating principle, implied in the dichotomy of Saleem's delirious perceptions, refers to a strict sense of Muslim belonging but is treated parodically by Rushdie who organises his text by the modes of fantasy. Thanks to his magical nose, Saleem detects events and things and formulates what he calls "the science of nasal ethics":

> Sacred: purdah-veils, halal meat, muezzin's towers, prayer-mats; profane: Western records, pig-meat, alcohol. I understood now why mullahs (sacred) refused to enter aeroplanes (profane) on the night before Id-ul-Fitr, not even willing to enter vehicles whose secret odour was the antithesis of godliness in order to make sure of seeing the new moon. I learned the olfactory incompatibility of Islam and socialism and the inalienable opposition existing between the after-shave of Sind Club members and the poverty-reek of the street-sleeping beggars at the Club gates. (*MC*, 318)

Rushdie elaborates on the quintessential Hindu habit of compiling catalogues and applies it to a Muslim point of view—we should not forget that he belongs to an Indian family with an Islamic background. The outcome consists in a cultural wholeness that forges a handbook of rules.

However this is not just a sharp device of separation justified by the contrapositions of *halal* and *haram*. In fact, Rushdie's move leads to the concept of chutnification of history. The narrator is endorsed to constitute a tripartite focalisation through the use of the organic metaphor: the historical acknowledgement of India, the collage of teeming communities of the subcontinent and the entangled narrative text draw an analogy that is also a reflection on discrepancy. One could properly term this a "food isotope."[7] Saleem admits that errors may be possible in his recording of histories but this is also a confession of the author who has to look for new instruments for narrating. Saleem's mock autobiography interferes with the genre of the novel and this hybrid clash postulates the presence of lexemes as spices. Nonetheless it is safer to recall that the fear of pollution in the Muslim world and the dietary prescriptions for each caste amongst the Hindus determine the choice of food and inscribe a closed frame. It is an attempt to regulate social structures that the author borrows to weigh his language and shape the text, in a process that is next to the identity crisis in postmodern literature:

> My special blends: I've been saving them up. Symbolic value of the pickling process: all the six hundred million eggs which gave birth to the population of India could fit inside a single, standard-sized pickle-jar; six hundred million spermatozoa could be lifted on a single spoon. Every single pickle-jar (you will forgive me if I become florid for a moment) contains, therefore, the most exalted of possibilities; the feasibility of the chutnification of history; the grand hope of the pickling of time! I, however, have pickled chapters. Tonight, by screwing the lid firmly on to a jar bearing the legend *Special Formula No. 30: 'Abracadabra,'* I reach the end of my long-winded autobiography; in words and pickles, I have immortalized my memories, although distortions are inevitable in both methods. We must live, I'm afraid, with the shadows of imperfection. (*MC*, 459)

As the quotation shows, an atmosphere of misgiving permeates the narrator's voice and foretells the tormented period of the Emergency with its endless domestic horrors. By citing indecipherable images pertaining to the symbiosis of life and writing, Rushdie darkens the lyrical or comic tones with mirthless premonitions.

The idea of food is usually combined with chromatic assonances that ideally insist on the colours of the Indian flag, but from a *deshi* or national sense of community we should register a shift into a domestic environment which is, in the Hindu case, highly organised through hierarchies. In the crowded picture of the traditional household, the woman administers food and churns gluttonies but her position of power, so to speak, has to be confronted with the Sanskrit notion of *pativrata*, one that institutionalises the roles and duties of a husband and a wife. It is not a mere question of the allotment of spaces within a domestic extension, but rather the redefinition or even imposition of predetermined identities, so that the woman is located on a lower rank. Whereas the patriarchal Indian society tends to weaken and subjugate the feminine condition, Rushdie destabilises stereotypical forms of identification and dramatises female figures in a double vision: because of their biological nature women are creators of manhood and simultaneously may turn into destroyers of life. The nourishing aspect, witnessed by the act of looking after or feeding children, is annihilated in the character of the Widow, modelled on Indira Gandhi, and loaded with raucous scorn.

In spite of her liminality, traditionally associated with her gender and her condition of widowhood, she actively participates in the political and historical revision of India. Having pulled down a gendered division and ripped the *zenana*, the segregating metaphorical screen that separates women from men, the Widow subverts a given status and acquires a mythical and monstrous image, close to the representation of powerful Durga and merciless Kali. On the ground of a lunatic, modernist syntax, Rushdie portrays the Widow as a bearer of death, a nightmarish banshee who is accused of having introduced an irrational, disastrous policy.[8] Conversely, the female trio of Naseem, nicknamed Reverend Mother, Mary Pereira and Amina assumes the kitchen drudgery, and the elaboration of their recipes of lime chutney, mango pickles and cucumber kasaundies conveys an alchemic echo that interpolates the presentation of food in everyday life with rhetorical stratagems. And when the table is laid, we are shown "fish salamis of stubbornness and the birianis of determination" (*MC*, 139) as well as the pickles of Mary, that are believed to have the "power of making those who ate them subject to nameless uncertainties and dreams of accusing fingers" (*MC*,

139). The nourishment of a nation is evoked in a potion of 'spicy' words and metaphors that encompass the destiny of men.

However, I would like to reflect on the lexical potentiality of "curry," a term that Rushdie seldom adopts in his writing, but which looms as a marker of emigration throughout contemporary Asian fiction in English. The word suggests at once an alien cultural background, being eradicated from the fervid Indian cultural soil, and therefore expands towards a wider social and political dimension: literatures of the diaspora appropriate this kind of discourse and meditate on the notion of translation of cultures. The enormous popularity of curry houses in Britain records historical, cultural and social connections and endorses a paradoxical view that conceives Indian curries as part of the British cuisine or introduces invented recipes to titillate the western palate. The introduction of curries and Indian food in general is pictured in Manzu Islam's *Burrow* (2004), in which the novelist provides a semi-historical account dating back to Georgian times when a Scottish serviceman keen on Bangladeshi food returned to Britain but "in the town the rumour spread that an evil curry spirit had possessed him."[9]

Differently, a section of a documentary titled *The Great British Asian Invasion*[10] broadcast on Channel 4 in 2004 relates the presence of curry houses and restaurants in England to Dean Mahomed, an expatriate who was shampooing surgeon to the Prince Regent and ran a sauna and massage parlour in Brighton. He gingerly opened the first Indian restaurant in 1809 and this pioneering example of culinary Orientalism gave birth to an unexpected sociocultural phenomenon bound to a huge success in modern times. Here we recognise the urban rites of "going for an Indian" and "Friday curry night" as common experiences in British contemporary everyday life.[11]

Let us focus on the morphological aspect of the word curry, which betrays a foreign or at least doubtful origin, and a defamiliarising quality since it percolates on a binary division between the colonised and the coloniser. The definition of curry is worth quoting at full length:

> From the Tamil word *kari*, a term for black pepper, derives the Indo-Anglian curry, which has come to symbolize Indian food for the western. The term originally denoted any spiced dish that accompanied south Indian food and was first referred to, using the term *caril*, by Correa as early as in AD 1502 and by Garcia da Orta sixty years later. Later the word curry was greatly widened in usage to include a liquid broth, a thicker stewed preparation, or even a spiced dry dish, all of which appear in turn in a south Indian meal, each with its own name. Colonials like Mrs. Eliza Fay served 'curry and rice' as a matter of course in AD 1780 in Calcutta.[12]

The term now indicates a blend of spices but the meaning is further extended through a web of linguistic resonances and the blind interstices of translation cannot affect its impenetrability, one that is outlined in the pragmatic endorsement of the word itself. Rushdie mentions the "curries and meatballs of intransigence, dishes imbued with the personality of the creator" (*MC*, 139) and highlights the osmotic relation within the integral metaphor. Consequently, we may identify the literary essence of the word with Rushdie's response *à rebours* dogmatic western literature: his postcolonial (or to a certain degree postmodern) recipe coincides with this bespreading of curry onto diasporic fiction and constitutes, to borrow Rushdie's words again, "the impregnation of food with emotions" (*MC*, 330).

In our ambitious paraphrase, we should attribute the blundering plural value of curry to postmodernism and assign chutney to postcolonial literatures. The process of curryfication is thus linked to the globalisation of the world in its attempt to homologate or conceal local cultures. As a speculative device of expressing new ways of being Indian in the West, the cultural sphere of curry may also activate a system of references (the global in the local and *vice versa*) in the reshaping of contemporary world societies and "this is why symptoms of visibility, such as [. . .] the naming of curry as a national British cuisine, can seem so significant."[13] Idiosyncratically this opposition of curry and chutney leads to the discussion of postmodernism in Rushdie's oeuvre. Despite some explicit references to the western (both realistic and fantastic) modes of writing, his novels feature substantial differences and receive influences from various sources. They express their own peculiar Indian context and therefore withdraw from a Eurocentric perspective. A very innovating point resides in the fact that now, in Rushdie's texts, it is possible to undermine traditional issues of castes, patriarchal family circles and the marginality of womanhood. The ideology of history for the benefit of corrupted politicians, for instance, is bitterly debunked and *Midnight's Children* dramatises the epos of the nation. Postmodernism and postcolonialism are two critical categories that may share some elements which establish different approaches to literature. From the very name, postmodernism gives predominance to the vision of time and its chronological assumptions, unlike postcolonialism which is preoccupied with cultural hybridisation and linguistic transformations. In spite of their resemblance, the two categorisations differ notably, especially in relation to the re-writing of the western canon, the revision of history and the use of metafictional style.

Rushdie's well known catchphrase about the Empire 'writing back to the centre' elucidates this counter-response of postcolonial authors who subvert imposed literary norms. In his re-collocation of the terms of argument and re-moulding of characters, they affirm their identity by virtue of mixing cultures, idioms, and traditions. On the other hand, postmodernism relies on the accumulation of themes, in a chaotic game of Chinese boxes, that corrodes the textual unity. It is an overflowing of symbols and metaphors that surround the open ending of the postmodern novel. This difference of meanings further marks the role of the individual: whereas postmodernism bemoans the death of the self (and the author) and the void of history, postcolonialism foregrounds the rise of the character from the periphery of the plot and the desire to constitute a national heritage of memories for the future generations. Concerning history, the postmodern novelist perceives a feeling of mislaying that crystallises the individual. *Dies irae*: it is a nebulous crisis and no alternative versions of history are possible. Conversely, the postcolonial author recuperates the mnemonic treasure and with the help of supernatural devices or magical realism speculates on the notion of belonging and collective identity, filtered through personal histories and domestic discrepancies. Finally, we should observe the metanarrative vein, or the Scheherazade syndrome in Stephen King's words, which affects both postcolonial and postmodern literatures. The postmodern author interpolates the frayed plot and its subplots with a meditation on the efficacy of writing and the ruining of the word. The ghost narrator oscillates nervously among the roles of *scriptor*, *compilator* and *auctor*. On the contrary, for the postcolonial author, the narration speaks of an entire country: Saleem is India, India is Saleem. The chiasmus sustains a literal metaphor and a corporeal image; hence the postcolonial preoccupation of the relevance of the body and food. Different viewpoints, different results: the postcolonial and the postmodern play hide-and-seek in the field of world literature and literary criticism has the task to decipher unexplored trajectories.[14]

NOTES

1. I have discussed the theme of food in diasporic literatures in "The Reinvention of Tradition: English/Banglish Dishes and Diasporic Texts," in A. Monti, M. Goglio, E. Adami, *Feeding the Self, Feeling the Way, in Ancient and Contemporary South Asian Cultures* (Turin: L'Harmattan Italia, 2005): 216-31.
2. Kate Burridge, *Blooming English* (2002) (Cambridge: Cambridge University Press, 2004): 220-21.
3. Farrukh Dhondy, *Bombay Duck* (1990) (New Delhi: Penguin India, 1999): 242.
4. *Hobson-Jobson*, cited: 221.
5. See Alessandro Monti, "Chutnifying the Text: a View on the Split of Synchronicity and Literary Globalisation," *The Atlantic Literary Review*, Volume 2, Number 2, October-November 2001: 190-201.
6. Patrica Merivale, cited: 18.

7. See Stefano Manferlotti, *Dopo l'impero* (Naples: Liguori, 1995) especially: 33-35.
8. At the beginning of the section titled "At the Pioneer Café," the loathsome otherness of the Widow explodes in a dichromatic vision of a dystopic future: "High as the sky the chair is green the seat is black the Widow's arm is long as death its skin is green the fingernails are long and sharp and black. [. . .] Now only she and I and no more screams the Widow's hand comes hunting hunting the skin is green the nails are black towards the corner hunting hunting while we shrink closer into the corner our skin is green our fear is black and now the Hand comes reaching" (*MC*, 208). Rushdie explains the polychromatic patchwork that characterises the Widow as a remembrance of the green-skinned wicked witches of the East and West from the film *The Wizard of Oz*, which he saw in Bombay during his childhood; see "Out of Kansas," *STL*, in particular: 18. For a discussion on the position of female characters in the novel, see K. Purushotham, "Rushdie's Images of *Bharateeya Nari* in *Midnight's Children*," *Kakatiya Journal of English Studies*, Vol. XIII, 1993: 90-103.
9. Manzu Islam, *Burrow* (Leeds: Peepal Tree, 2004): 205.
10. *The Great British Asian Invasion*, written by S. Manzoor and broadcast on Channel 4, on 20 October 2004. Contributors include M. Syal, A. Malik, S. Bhaskar, B. Gulati, H. Kureishi, K. Guru-Murthy, R. Rich and R. Hammer.
11. "No Saturday night pub-crawl would be complete without a visit to the local Tandoori or Balti restaurant. And when the English go on holiday abroad, the food they most miss, according to the latest surveys, is not fish and chips or steak-and-kidney pie but a proper English curry." Kate Fox, cited: 301.
12. K.T. Acharya, *A Historical Dictionary of Indian Food* (New Delhi: Oxford University Press, 2001): 58.
13. Sandhya Shukla, cited: 9.
14. For the much debated question of the relationship between postmodernism and postcolonialism, I shall limit myself to indicating Elleke Boehmer, *Colonial and Postcolonial Literature* (Oxford: Oxford University Press, 1995), especially the section titled "The postmodern and the postcolonial," in the sixth chapter: 243-50. See also Cameron Richards, "Postmodernism or Postcolonialism Tomorrow? The Relevance of a Dialogic Framework for Postcolonial Criticism," *SPAN*, Special Issue, Vol. 1, October 1993: 65-74. Concerning postmodernism in Indian narrative in English, see Viney Kirpal, "Postmodern Strategies in the Indian English Novel," *Littcrit*, No. 43, Vol. 22, No. 2, December 1996: 21-33.

Hanif Kureishi in the Intimacy of Writing

The Artist Complete

> I lay on the poet's divan and saw the green and brown patches on the ceiling. The patches of mould were dancing in intricate geometric patterns. I couldn't take my eyes off them because the sudden loops of their curves and the crisscrossing play of their lines were etching the passageways through which so many had come to map the new city. Armies of men, women and children marched shoulder to shoulder like columns of ants. Undaunted, they pushed their way through the mazes, but many lost their way through the mazes and floated on the deep pools of their toils to arrive at the golden city they had mapped in their dreams.
>
> Syed Munzurul Işlam,
> *The Mapmakers of Spitafields* (pp. 83-3)

Hanif Kureishi appears today to have been moving cunningly between the genres of the novel, the short story, drama and cinema. Hence, considering such a rich cultural background, one has to face the question of definitions and trying to encapsulate the author into one single canonical category will inevitably turn out to be reductive and limited. Kureishi's diasporic and postcolonial connotations cast a further complexity for the cultural debate on his work. The "almost English" writer has shown, through the genesis of his fictional and cinematic characters, a plurality of approaches towards not only literature, but also cultural issues whose roots deepen into countries as diverse and remote as England and India or Pakistan, leading to alternative results in the process of 'imaging the nation.'

Thus, a new type of society seems to give rise to the contemporary quest for identity and present the revisited notions of 'Englishness,' detached from stereotypical images of post-imperial grandeur. The author's perception and provoking affirmations of 'being English,' epitomised by the ground-breaking incipit of *The Buddha of Suburbia* (1990), works as a key to comprehending the intercultural forces and historical agencies that have reshaped and moulded British society over the last decades. Whilst the process of decolonisation and the struggle for independence of the overseas colonies date back to the end of the Second World War, what Kureishi speaks of is the hybrid legacy and postmodern vision of the historical results of such salient events. The fruition of the oeuvre of Kureishi is redeemed from easy labels, absorbing migrant and local elements, depicting a multicultural London, inhabited by immigrants and dropouts, in the partial shadow of the Indian heritage. A double position, then, given the peculiar nature of in-betweenness which forges this new sense of belonging.

A few biographical details help to trace Kureishi's social milieu and diasporic reference. Born in December 1954, in Bromley, Kent, his genealogic extraction shifts between Pakistani and Indian family links; the author himself uses the two geographical terms confusingly but as important signs that make up his faceted background. His father Rafiushan belonged to a prestigious Muslim family of Madras and moved into the United Kingdom in 1947, while his relatives settled in Pakistan after the Partition. Given such premises, Kureishi holds a peculiar status on the literary scene: on the one hand, he restores Asian reminiscences, for instance in the figure of the urbanised Buddha selling New Age doctrines in his most known text, a carnivalesque interpreter of the western commercial and secular gaze onto the East; on the other, he collocates his writing into the traditional English canon, ranging from the *Bildungsroman* to the 'state of the nation' theatre.

If the style of Kureishi seems to be unsophisticated, not bearing the characteristics of the postcolonial wave that brought about a flowering of authors from Commonwealth countries, we may consider his choice of different techniques and genres as a wide polyphonic strategy to express meanings and explore realities. Far from incorporating Hindu or Urdu terms, this kind of prose tends to absorb slang and colloquial expressions, but the nature of the medium employed (montage for the films, theatrical devices for drama, episodic construction for novels) brings a multiplicity of registers, for these means of communication constitute particular 'languages' that create artistically and shape the word in a manifold perspective.

Therefore the biographical context for Kureishi is made even more complex by having an Indian father and an English mother: sharing a sense of being a second-generation migrant led him to elaborate on new reflections on nationhood, fully aware of the post-imperial phase of social and political globalisation. Yet, his family bonds proved to be a salient metaphorical arsenal, with many of his characters being shaped to different degrees on his relatives, on his parents and sometimes on himself. Karim Amir, for example, the protagonist and narrator of *The Buddha of Suburbia*, is of mixed-race, bringing personal memories of the author himself, who as a boy had to cope with English small-town racism. The sense of 'con-fusion' that characterises Karim's vision is a typical quality of Kureishi's character-making, which intertwines notions of social class, nationhood, political awareness, gender identities. This explosive blend of categories allows to explore new insights and depicts Thatcher's 1980s and the globalised 1990s. The cultural richness and variety of Kureishian personages also serve another purpose: namely to provide social and racial minorities with adequate voices. In fact, the author's British/Pakistani/Indian parentage finds a location in an ethnic and religious minority contained within an immigrant minority, outside mainstream society. This occurs because the double roots of Kureishi's family are shared between Britain and the Indian subcontinent.

Several interviews with Kureishi have revealed his concern with the idea of national identities seen as a hybrid product of social transformations that are taking place in modern Britain:

> But being British is a new thing now. It involves people with names like Kureishi or Ishiguro or Rushdie, where it didn't before. And we're all British too. . . . But most of critics in England don't understand that. So there isn't any understanding of Britain being a multicultural place. They think that I'm, let's say, a regional writer or writing in a sort of subgenre. They think writers like [me] are on the edges. We are still marginalized culturally. . . . They don't see that the world is now hybrid.[1]

By affirming his much-discussed and provoking Englishness, or Britishness whether we consider the above-quoted passage, in the same terms mouthed by Karim at the beginning of his first novel, Kureishi subtly promotes a reshaping of English society, one in which new identities are struggling to emerge. Such complex process of 'home-making' goes beyond the simplistic geographical divisions that pose the cartographic representations of England and the Indian subcontinent on the world map, and foregrounds a series of transnational relations because "the two countries, Britain and Pakistan, have been part of each for years, usually to the advantage of Britain" (*MBL*, 38). It is this circuitous relationship that predicates new instances of being and questions the traditional and monolithic idea of national states and fixed identities. The stern admonition that arises from his critical writing points to the expansion of cultural horizons and pulls down schematic boundaries built by racist and intolerant migration policy: "It is the British, the white British, who have to learn that British isn't what it was. Now it is a more complex thing, involving new elements" (*MBL*, 38).

The cultural change and challenge brought about by immigrant flows should remind one of the fictionalised and carefully constructed idea of monoethnic states. Benedict Anderson's view of nations as "imagined communities" postulates a process of formation based on cultural instances[2] rather than a pre-existing entity.

This applies to Kureishi's re-imagining of British social stratification, and in order to develop his thematic articulation, the author adopts more than one literary vehicle, ranging from drama to short stories.

Kureishi's literary career began within the theatrical milieu when he was commissioned by the Royal Court Theatre to write a play and there he met actors, playwrights, directors and artists. Corroborated by his father's fondness for literature and the vibrant atmosphere in which he suddenly found himself immersed, Kureishi adopted theatre writing as a main tool to analyse the changing social stratifications of England. It was probably 'easier' to treat and challenge thorny, difficult topics when they were staged, rather than narrated in novels, and the textual reinforcement of Kureishi's plays aimed at striking the audience. Indeed, as Keir Elam affirms, "in its 'incompleteness,' its need for physical contextualization, dramatic discourse is invariably marked by a performability, and above all by a potential gestuality, which the language of narrative does not normally possess since its context is described rather than 'pragmatically' appointed to."[3] The author's aesthetics of performing had a strong connection with 'fringe' theatre, off-Broadway productions that radically undermined the pillars of an institutionalised theatre (and traditional culture as well). In 1980, *The King and Me* opened at Soho Poly, followed by *The Mother Country*, staged at Riverside Studios. The year 1981 was prolific too, with the opening of *Outskirts* at the Royal Shakespeare Company Wardenhouse Theatre, *Tomorrow-Today!* (again at Soho Poly), and *Borderline*, at the Royal Court. Amongst other issues, racial discrimination and ethnicity were also handled in 1983 with *Birds of Passage*, which shows influences from British playwrights such as David Edgar, who as an exponent of the innovative radical drama of the 1970s and 1980s started introducing the ethnic element, for instance in *Destiny* (1976) and *Our Own People* (1977).

By the mid-1980s Kureishi had embarked on a film-writing adventure, moving gradually away from the world of theatre: "I stopped being able to find a tone or style to accommodate my voice or themes. I didn't feel comfortable writing plays anymore: I didn't know what sort of plays they should be; and the challenge of that doubt didn't stimulate me" (*PO*, xx). Yet his repertoire is still complemented by a new elaboration of styles and genres, which focus on intimate portraits of individuals. In fact, Kureishi's turning to cinema shows a line of continuity with his experience in drama: *My Beautiful Laundrette* (1983) was originally conceived as a play, while both *Sammy and Rosie Get Laid* (1988) and *London Kills Me* (1991) return to social engagement and interests in urban and racial clans. In spite of the great success achieved by his 1983 film, Kureishi's art could not fit properly into the cinematic medium for the role of the screenplay writer in film-making might be reduced or affected by the choices of the director.

Such restrictions led him to experiment other forms of storytelling. Hence, at the turn of the 1980s, the publication of *The Buddha of Suburbia* (1990) marked Kureishi's own endorsement of the novel: aware of a modified intellectual scene, he restored his old dream of becoming a writer.[4] Therefore, he organised his mode of discourse in a highly thematic manner, drawing on a plurality of genres and subgenres: *The Buddha* for instance may be regarded as a *Bildungsroman*, a homage to pop music, an ethnically-oriented saga and a 'condition of England' novel. Kureishi's subsequent exploration of fiction incorporated influences from writers as diverse as Malcolm Bradbury and David Lodge, though *The Black Album* (1995) still centres on the conflicting questions of migrancy, fundamentalism and Britishness. In his more recent production, Kureishi works out personal details in his stories, collected in *Love in a Blue Time* (1997) and *Midnight All Day* (1999), nearing almost autobiographical writing. The social realism that permeates his tales sometimes gives way to experimental narrative, in which a surrealistic tone shapes hermetic characters and moods, once again on a rich western literary backdrop that encompasses Gogol and Calvino.

The humoristic short story "The Penis," for instance, offers an ambivalent response towards conventional narrative structures and draws hints on the theatre of the absurd and classic Russian writers. In Gogol's tale "The Nose," published in 1836, the escape of the protagonist's nose starts a series of Gargantuesque adventures which, in psychoanalytical terms, embody metaphors and allegories of power. Kureishi too, who as a university student read the Russian classics extensively, adopted irony to present a peculiar 'protagonist.'[5] To sustain his refusal of the techniques predicated by magical realism so often employed by postcolonial writers, Kureishi revises his social realistic norms to approach a caricature of modern life in experimental terms. In this story, the sexual organ of a pornographic actor decides to begin its own solo career by severing from the man and escaping in order to concentrate on serious drama; this is how it challenges the man: "'I want to play Hamlet,' said the penis. 'No one has quite understood the relationship with Ophelia. You could be my assistant. You could carry my script and keep the fans away'" (*MAD*, 214).[6] Yet the striking image does not concern the member's plans to achieve a respectful artistic position (perhaps a satirical stroke against over-celebrated actors and artists in general), but rather emphasises the lack of reactions that all the characters have towards the 'moving organ' that defeats all physical laws and wanders around London. The only effect of the whole absurd story is that it cannot be 'morally accepted' in parochial England: Alfie, the protagonist of the story who mysteriously finds the 'living object' in his pocket, and his wife agree that such scandalous oddity is against the rules of good behaviour, not against the laws of nature! The woman then points out the need to eliminate it because "'my mother's coming for lunch! Get it out of here'" (*MAD*, 208).

To gain access to a larger audience as well as respectability, Kureishi methodically introduces a postmodern coherence, though his writing may be seen as an antidote to his strong cynical view of the world and not as a mere exercise in style. The intertextuality shown via the exponents of Russian literature—Chekhov is another central source of inspiration, along with European authors (Strindberg, Ibsen, Joyce but also Maupassant and Berkoff)—further betrays Kureishi's location in the (apparently) mainstream canon of British and western literature, mediating the transition from the implication of postcolonialism to the inclusion in the 'new' national literature, largely enhanced by the writers of immigration. Kureishi's recent production does not record an abundance of rhetorical devices: on the contrary, sometimes the language employed may even sound banal or formulaic, but actually it disguises an anatomy of feelings behind a barrage of bitterness, profanity, coldness and obscenities. Considering the diversity and heterogeneity of texts by Kureishi, no easy identification is possible, though, according to Moore-Gilbert, "his works recognise the postmodern in the name of the diasporic (and postcolonial) by adopting some of its modes, conventions and epistemological perspectives to migrant experience, an encounter which cannot but expose the putative Eurocentrism of postmodernism."[7]

The same autobiographical dimension, with a more intense emphasis, marks thoroughly his recent narrative, like the novella *Intimacy* (1998), the play *Sleep with Me* (1999), which opened at the Royal National Theatre (Cottesloe), the novel *Gabriel's Gift* (2001), and the collection *The Body and Seven Stories* (2002). All such works are inscribed into a self-conscious line of enquiry that probably coincides with the literary maturity of the man/writer. Juvenile attempts to illustrate a vibrant London life, injected with confused sexual experiences, drug use, pop culture, fragments of Asianness and ethnic self-affirmation are now substituted by an inner exploration of new themes, which broaden the horizon of the author in his search for identity. The fictional soil of Kureishi's narrative highlights a progressive manifestation of pessimism, which dominates the plots of his stories, while the intensity of feelings evokes a deeper analysis of psychological attitudes, a trait quite common in classic Russian literature as well.

Kureishi attributes a stance of great freedom to the craft of novel writing, but simultaneously he deeply roots it in the traditional British canon; that is why, although the diasporic reference of Indian issues is consistent, his view of the novel is close to the English tradition. The main model here is Dickens, whose portrait of London, not only as a city, or a *locus* of past grandeur for us, but also as a cluster of variegated mankind encompassing all social strata, dominates *The Buddha of Suburbia* and will also pervade throughout the screenplay of *London Kills Me*. The conventional manner of narration is updated with postmodern taste and the registers are grafted onto a variety of cultural forms that include 1970s music, the glitter of fashion and bohemian arts. The frenzied tone shifts from the social to the grotesque, from the surrealistic to the comic, in a pure Dickensian style, in which the denunciation of tainted lives is carried out by means of irony. The dialectic between the city centre and the outskirts provides the ideal setting for Karim who faces, like Pip, the protagonist of *Great Expectations,* a farcical (and somehow perilous) peregrination across the metaphoric heavy 'scaffolding' of a wicked London.[8]

A complex scenario of British connections then, as Kureishi the novelist abundantly infuses his writing with educated citations and the spirit of post-war fiction and working class consciousness too. *Lucky Jim* (1954) by Kingsley Amis, *Billy Liar* (1959) by Keith Waterhouse and *Saturday Night and Sunday Morning* by Alan Sillitoe (1958) are just a few of the many titles that can be quoted, but the actual revolutionary aspect of all recent British fiction lies in the multicultural dimension that has brought on the literary scene authors like Salman Rushdie and Buchi Emecheta. Kureishi's verve also derives from such privileged position, though his narrative does not easily yield to the challenge of postcolonial re-writing. His postmodernism-oriented adjustment imbues his unique writing, so that "neither Zola nor Dickensian sentimentality can be usefully invoked to describe the hard core form of the new realism of the novel based on societal conceptions far removed from those of the earlier works."[9] His act of re-mapping the fictional territory of the novel indeed is loaded with literary charisma, pungent irony and irreverent vocabulary.

The same strategy is applied to a large section of his production, and in its deconstructive aspect, it affects the framework of realism. Furthermore Kureishi's storytelling sometimes shifts into a certain form of metafiction intersected within the text and marks the intrusion of either the author or the character. Following a definition by David Lodge, metafictional rules "flatter the reader by treating him or her as an intellectual equal, sophisticated enough not to be thrown by the admission that a work of fiction is a verbal construction rather than a slice of life."[10] By adopting a first-person narration, especially in his shorter fiction, Kureishi interpolates viewpoints and moods, while speculating on the nature of writing itself. This also allows him to express a deep cynicism in a nearly existentialist frame. Notably, the clarifying example should be observed in the story "With Your Tongue down My Throat," from *Love in a Blue Time*, where Nadia and Nina, two stepsisters who have the same Indian father, provide their points of view in a mirror-like fashion, forging and reworking family ties. Towards the end, the entire fictional construction begins to crumble, so that the actual nature of the narrating voice is revealed:

> Hello, reader. As I'm sure you've noticed by now, I, Howard, have written this Nadia and Nina stuff in my sock, without leaving the country, sitting right here on my spreading arse and listening to John Coltrane. (And rolling cigarettes). Do you think Nina could have managed phrases like an 'accent as thick as treacle' and 'But the curtains are well and truly pulled here' and especially 'Oh, oh, oh'? With her education? So all along, it's been me, pulling faces, speaking in tones, posing and making an attempt on the truth through lies. And also, I just wanted to be Nina. The days Deborah and I have spent beating on her head, trying to twist her the right way around, read this, study dancing, here's a book about Balanchine and the rest of it. What does she make of all this farce feeding? So I became her, entered her. Sorry. (*LBT*, 103)

Howard, the mother's partner, confesses his deceitful plan and his words sound like a therapy that should cure the sickness of the inner self. 'Authoring' and the doubling of characters (Howard/ Nina in their ventriloquist account of 'double worlds,' like India and England) do not only point to Kureishi's idiosyncrasies, but evolve into a degree of aporia, simultaneously highlighting the difficulties of representing the world through the agency of words ("an attempt on the truth through lies" is the key phrase that challenges the mimetic constitution of literature).

To Kureishi, the action of giving voice to the text, by impressing an ontological state to the narrator in a composite and illusory game of Chinese boxes, also implies depriving the author of authority. This only apparent paradox leads to a privileged location that coincides with the artist's eye. As a result, writing becomes an exorcising practice that demolishes dogmatic barriers and enlarges the horizons of the self. In his ultimate chronicle, Howard is allowed to include obscene references and his justification pivots on the fact that "it's my job to write down things that happen here and because I have a rule about no material thing being sacred" (*LBT*, 104). And the answer to the rhetorical question of the narrator ("what does that make of me") juxtaposes storytelling with a certain extent of imposed voyeurism, one in which readers are forced to share a common point of view in a subtly disturbing atmosphere: "I feel like that old spy, a dirty betrayer just with a loudspeaker, doing what I have to" (*LBT*, 104). Reporting events and elaborating on plots metamorphose into a duty and stand as Howard's final response to life and artistic legacy.

Intimacy returns to the obscure pessimism and accurate introspective enquiry of the previous texts and their 'written orality,' an oxymoron that characterises the recent production of Hanif Kureishi. In this novella, the reader is forced to share a deep immersion into the meditations of Jay the protagonist, who decides to leave his wife and children, after a matrimonial crisis has turned his home into a sort of domestic hell. Apart from a series of autobiographical elements, the text expands the author's reflections on narration and contrasts them to the idea of a (mock) testimonial, one in which Jay the protagonist conceals his own identity and voice: "I will not be returning to this life. I cannot. Perhaps I should leave a note to convey this information" (*I*, 3). He is still not aware of the fact that his account is the notorious note he cites, the meditative blade that tears him apart. This reflective aspect of his diary focuses on the close relationship between word and action and exalts the pragmatic function of narrative: "Because words are actions and they make things happen. Once they are out you cannot put them back. Something irrevocable will have been done, and I am fearful and uncertain. As a matter of fact, I am trembling and have been all afternoon, all day" (*I*, 4). When the character anticipates the plan of his escape, his writing resembles a confession reported on a journal, and the tone is clouded by the internal frictions that testify to the struggle between the word and the text, echoing Derrida's investigations on the word given by God and the epistemology of Man and his philosophy. The word and the text bear a disturbing effect and instil a sense of temporality that inevitably reminds one of man's caducity: "I turn out the lights and find myself climbing the stairs to the boredom. What am I doing? If this is my last night here, if these are, indeed, the final hours, hadn't I better get packed and ready? Soon I will be dead. Is it really the last night? No, no, no, never. Not really I was only entertaining myself" (*I*, 76). The prison of the mind turns out to be a labyrinthine artifice but evokes a nihilistic and fierce gaze onto the self.

Yet all Jay's aphoristic revelations indicate a narrative voice which is not reliable. The protagonist, who works in the visual media on television scripts and adaptations, recognises his present tendency towards self-description and introspection: "I am more of an engineer than an artist, although as I become more accomplished I find myself putting more of myself into the stories than formerly" (*I*, 46); nonetheless he cannot deny the interfering autobiographical quality of his writing and, by doing so, we are confronted with an overlap between narrative and (fake) biography. Jay's cold-eyed scrutiny transforms the writer ("the artist") into the technician ("the engineer"), but this tactic is not meant to reduce the author's vision; on the contrary, it emphasises a bitter tone and a descriptive character. Obviously even the most objective attempt to represent reality in a mimetic manner is, to a certain extent, fictionalised through the lenses of the unreliable narrator, whose long-established tradition in English literature includes examples as diverse as Chaucer's Wife of Bath, Conrad's Marlow and the butler Stevens of Ishiguro's *The Remains of the Day*.

Interestingly, there is little space devoted to Jay's Indian descent; the only noticeable point is remarked in his cynical demolition of sentiments, in a fashion that nearly touches on misogyny. He evokes the concept of *zenana*, namely the condition of discrimination of Indian women as a symbol of his detachment from the world: his Indian connection is re-invented and used as a weapon to confirm the individualism of his ego. This trait reaches its climax in Kureishi's dark treatment of the notion of family, criticised in the previous works in which the social networks and the construction of relations are eroded and turned upside down. But it is this text in particular that deeply lacerates the human and narrative net of individuals, fictions, biographies and stories. There is a passage which is worth quoting at length:

> In India they don't seem to put the same emphasis on romantic love. Couples copulate when necessary and get on with their separate lives. In Lahore my uncle lives in one part of the house with his sons, three brothers, male friends anyone else who feels like staying a couple of years. My aunt, the daughters, female servants, and the children, live in another part. They meet, at times but there is no funny business. (*I*, 79)

Jay is not concerned with his Asian roots, and childishly views the segregation of women as a system to protect himself from the chance of embarking on too complicated relationships. Before his eyes, his wife Susan is perceived as the culmination of tainted relations, because she is unable to live in a detached way, independently, to build up her own private emotional zone. Yet one may question whether Jay's boastful words carry the brutal honesty of masculine psychology, or should be read as part of Kureishi's actual crisis that devastated his family life. Susan may sound as an alias of Tracey Scoffield (Kureishi's former partner and editor at Faber) but there are a lot of dissimilarities too; the novel covers the entire relationship between the two characters but concentrates on one sole night as the ideal point from which looking back to the past and detecting thoughts are explicitly part of the author's intervention. This again signals a perpetual crossing between the confines of writing, by enriching fiction with clear biographical elements.

Nonetheless, several newspapers sharply attacked the author and criticised his attitude to mixing real episodes from his controversial relationship with the former partner and his creative writing. In a 1999 interview Marianne Macdonald coined the definition 'literary villain' for him and identified the writer's career as the real epicentre of his life. The journalist affirmed that "his passions are primarily his writing, then himself, then his children,"[11] establishing thus a rank of values that betrays her bitter critique of the novelist. In her opinion, Kureishi rejects the idea of human bonds and destroys the current vision of couple life; even children are not given a better treatment and are not safe from his will to desecrate (the article refers to his twin children too). *Intimacy* then could possibly be interpreted as Kureishi's most personal and profound investigation into the notion of contemporary masculinity, one in which central issues like love and marriage are painfully analysed.

NOTES

1. Cited in Kenneth C. Kaleta, *Hanif Kureishi. Postcolonial Storyteller* (Austin, Texas: University of Texas Press, 1998): 7.
2. See Benedict Anderson, *Imagined Communities: Reflections on the Origin and Spread of Nationalism* (London: Verso, 1983). The author insists on the 'imagined' aspect of the community/nation be-

cause the cultural unity of a people cannot coincide with a fixed and actual coherence in the constellation of families and the individual is very unlikely to meet or even see all the other fellow-members. In Anderson's definition, "all communities larger than primordial villages of face-to-face contact (and perhaps even these) are imagined. Communities are to be distinguished not by their falsity/genuineness, but by the style in which they are imagined": 6. Therefore, we should turn to the results of diasporic cultural practices in which members of the same group are engaged in detecting the first germs of national consciousness and concept of belonging.

3. Keir Elam, *The Semiotics of Drama and Theatre* (1980) (London and New York, 2002, 2nd Edition): 129.
4. "When I was fourteen, I made up my mind to become a writer. It was the first major decision I'd made, the first time I was aware of having a whole life and not just a succession of days" (*PO*, x).
5. The Italian novelist Alberto Moravia too employed a similar narrative strategy with the expropriation of authority, performed by a metonymic device, in his *Io e lui* (1971), a text with postmodern overtones that creates a burlesque and disturbing atmosphere. The novel functions as the comic revisitation of the Pryapus-based myth and incorporates Freudian echoes of culmination.
6. Curiously, a veiled pun is here introduced to reinforce the relevance of the practice of writing and the authority of narrative voices: the central noun phrase 'the penis' could be easily deconstructed as 'the pen is,' so that claims of fictionalisation are established, within a parodic link between the 'pen/is' and the text mentioned in the quotation.
7. Bart Moore-Gilbert, *Hanif Kureishi* (Manchester and New York: Manchester University Press, 2001): 31.
8. Moreover, the literary coordinates that assimilate Kureishi to Dickens are grounded on the "minuziosa corrispondenza fra aspetto esteriore del personaggio e sua dimensione psicologica, della disavventura picaresca spinta talvolta sino al limite della verosimiglianza," Stefano Manferlotti, *Dopo l'Impero,* cited: 164; ("The meticulous similarity between the exterior aspect of the character and his psychological dimension, the Picaresque mishaps sometimes pushed up to the limit of verisimilitude," my translation).
9. Alamgir Hashmi, "Hanif Kureishi and the Tradition of the Novel," *Commonwealth Novel in English*, 6: 1 (Spring-Fall, 1993): 57.
10. David Lodge, *The Art of Fiction* (London: Penguin, 1992): 207.
11. Marianne Macdonald, "Acts of Betrayal," *Night & Day*, 4 April 1999: 21.

Relocating Kureishi's Families in the 'New Mother Country'

> Should he just call it quits and go back to Bangladesh? If his parents had been alive, it would have been natural for him to go back; perhaps he would never have come to England in the first place. Strange that he hadn't thought about his parents for years. [. . .] He never dreamed about his father, but often fantasised that he was alive, and that he comes face to face with him in the street of a strange city. Although his father does not recognise him, walks past him, and disappears into the crowd, he feels happy because he knows that his father is still alive.
>
> Manzu Islam, *Burrow* (pp. 32-33)

In the academic debate on postcolonial literatures, the term homeland, or 'mother country,' is generally used to refer to Britain, drawing on the construction of Englishness as an element of hegemonic coherence, imposed across the different dominions and sections of the Empire. Such overused label seems to lose its original significance in the present re-interpretation of critical approaches, but it should also remind one of the centrality of parental roles and generational positions as metaphors to stage cultural forces. John Thieme, working on the vocabulary notably established by Edward Said, highlights the difference between 'filiative relationships' and 'affiliative identifications' in his introduction to the notion of re-writing classic English texts. It is a narrative strategy adopted by postcolonial authors who re-read and re-construct the English canon, imposed *de facto* during the heyday of colonialism throughout the Anglophone world. Such relationship features the rejection of colonial parental figures and operates new literary genealogies.

After the acceptance of Freudian theories, the western modes of thinking, as well as means of literary transmission, have dealt with and moulded the centrality of the system of the family (and human relations in general) in the Oedipus complex, whereas feminist criticism has tried to revise this viewpoint by focussing on female segregation. Yet on the postcolonial scenario, the cultural agenda becomes more complex, within an ambivalent sphere of values: "narratives of mother-loving and father-killing tend to obscure the complex discursive networks produced by displaced and multiple ancestries; maternal genealogies may offer preferable alternatives, especially if the colonizer has been constructed as masculine and, as is often the case, the colony as inert female space, but this model also tends to simplify."[1] The adoption of such techniques results in the response of writers from postcolonial countries, but as in the case of Kureishi, who is profoundly affected by the duality of a peculiar sense of belonging, the hybrid aspect of the narrative shapes the numerous metaphors of the family, which in the author's intention link together places (the rural Indian subcontinent and industrialised England) and individuals (immigrants of the first generation are confronted with their own anglicised sons and daughters).

In the Asian, and African, frame of mind, social models of organisation like the concept of the extended family are central, and postcolonial literatures thematise them and operate an ironic revisitation. The extended family, sometimes called 'joint family' in Indian English, for instance, is somewhat included and disassembled in Kureishi's novels, too; this strategy highlights a deregionalisation and a metaphoric extension and interplay of peoples and countries (Britain, Pakistan and India), with the result of a new hybrid being created. Furthermore, the constant recycling of characters (for example Karim Amir and Charlie Hero, who had been minutely shaped in *The Buddha of Suburbia*, occasionally reappear in *Gabriel's Gift*) offers an amplification and precise analysis of the family and its social links. In Kureishi's imagery, however, the family is not a quiet social institution, but rather it functions as a site of tensions, which calls into question the policy of integration and relationship between different communities or generations. Often the family network endorses a relation with the physical space, opening a series of binary oppositions: on a macro-level, Britain is opposed to Pakistan or India, whilst on a micro-level, it is London versus the suburbs or small towns, conventionally based on the margins of society.

The family theme is pivotal in *Borderline*, first performed at the Royal Court Theatre, London, on 2 November 1981, where British Asians and English characters tackle and challenge conventions. The 'suburban' aspect and traditional circumspection of some immigrant families, rigidly antithetic to the British neighbourhood, loom as an impasse, though the anxiety to break family connections and escape from claustrophobic outskirts marks the migrant character of the second generation. The Pakistani family of Amina, now settled in suburban London, includes the father Amjad, who is well integrated into British society, and the mother Banoo, who views the status of émigrés as a suffocating condition of imprisonment. Also Haroon, Amina's boyfriend, feels the weight of his situation, although in self-ironic terms:

> Amina: When your exams are over get to college in London. It's not far.
>
> Haroon: Not far enough. I really need to smash the connection and everything.
>
> Amina: We've got on for so long. (*PO*, 100)

The father and daughter relationship is dictated by a traditional scheme, so that Amina and Haroon have to keep their love affair secret, in the manner of modern and postcolonial Romeo and Juliet or westernised versions of Majnu and Laila, the protagonists of the ancient Islamic/Persian romance. Amjad, the possessive father, strictly watches over her daughter and even plans her future, trying to 'save' her life from the moral corruption of England: "'We mustn't let our daughter be influenced by these westernised children. You'll have a shock one day Banoo, if you catch her kissing a boy. I'll marry her soon'" (*PO*, 107).

The issue of arranged marriages, a perennial preoccupation for patriarchal Indian families, symmetrically affects other characters as well: Yasmin, a scornful, young girl who belongs to the Asian Youth Movement, suggests the same theme and recalls how her father's will to marry her off becomes a cultural statement, a line of divide. In her dry and bitter tone, Yasmin reports the events of her marriage and points out her father's device, a hunger strike to persuade the rebellious girl to marry the chosen husband (the same strategy will be employed again in *The Buddha of Suburbia*). The following image, which is introduced by the slightly declamatory tone of Yasmin, unfolds a deceleration of the action and carries a reflection on the imposition of strict traditional customs, in a decadent scenario, where actual shabbiness mirrors the disintegration of social values:

> Yasmin: I had a father like yours.
> Haroon: We've all had 'em. You're no freak of nature, Yasmin.
> Yasmin: He arranged a marriage for me. I kept refusing. He began to starve himself to death.
> Haroon: Jesus.
> Yasmin: Yes. He preferred death to being laughed at by his relatives. So eventually I relented. I can still remember his joy—he trembled like a leaf—though he was so weak, his bones poking through his flesh. And the room stank of shit because he hadn't moved from his bed. I know now if he'd died it would have been better for us all. Now as far as they're concerned I'm dead.
> Amina: I didn't know you'd been married.
> Yasmin: I don't regard it as a holiday period.
> Haroon: What happened then?
> Yasmin: What happened?
> Anwar: Haroon.
> Yasmin: I'm no longer married to a man. I have understood . . . one or two things about things. (*PO*, 116)

Whether the family networks appear to be soundly centred around the figure of the father holding a position of primary significance, Yasmin's lines set up for a denunciation against patriarchal customs.

The family motif is also employed by the playwright to provide an emotional space for the other central theme of *Borderline*: the experience of the migrant community and the tools of integration and transformation operating within British society. In the case of Ravi, the newly arrived migrant, for instance, the intrusion of memory sharply marks his coming to England. Humiliated, grief-stricken and disappointed by the fictional dream of a wealthy Britain, he has to face up to a further delusion from his only friend Anil, but eventually is sheltered by Susan, a liberal journalist interested in Asian cultures. The intolerant and provincial reaction of Britain makes Ravi think of his "mother's face, her greedy face slobbering at the thought of England. My sisters, sewing, sweating at the thought of me returning with good things for them" (*PO*, 121). The migrant's mirage and his great expectations also take on a sense of regret, confronting a glorious past: "My father drove the English from India. He heard Gandhi speak, he was proud" (*PO*, 121), but Ravi is soon forced to understand that his heroic father cannot be considered a model in such a depressing human context.

As Amina's parents, Amjad and Banoo are given two oppositional roles: the man, in spite of his autocratic decision, feels integrated in England and does not fear the racist assaults and abuses that periodically take place whereas his wife is depressed by the constant insults and bricks thrown into their house. Nonetheless Amjad, an exponent of the *nouveau riche* class, clings to his belongings and admonishes sad Banoo: "I don't want to be loved by your relatives. I want the kitchen decorated. I'll send you to Pakistan for a holiday after the court case" (*PO*, 106). To some extent, particularly in the character of Banoo, we are displayed two principles of Indian traditional norms that regulate the proper woman's conduct working at odds: whereas her passive and lapsed role underscores the condition of the loyal wife completely devoted to the care and nurturing of the husband (*pativrata*), the merging of her identity with that of her husband (*atmasamarpana*) is treated superficially because the woman always idealises her homeland and thus secretly and subtly shifts away from Amjad's sphere.

In spite of the difficulties they are living through, Amjad insists on the unity of his household ("We are one family" [*PO*, 127]) and, with reference to his daughter, restores old ties: "I will make sure my Amina is looked after by her husband. Our family in Pakistan don't like her working" (*PO*, 127). Amjad's oscillation between the role of the westernised, integrated émigré and the time-honoured, fatherly figure of firm authority prescribes the typical double process of characterisation established by Kureishi, based on the notion of liminality. Amjad represents the element of unity, matching together the Pakistani culture and modernity, a stereotype of welfare and peace that also actually clashes with the Right Wing propaganda promoted by Enoch Powell. Though the bitter awareness of displacement is watered down and rendered mild by Amjad's enthusiasm for the technologically advanced country, peculiarly this character also functions as the bearer of old, traditional values, which are no longer possible (or even allowed) in the configuration of the human re-mapping of Britain. Therefore, he is doomed to die following a sort of rite of passage, which through the means of destruction and death opens new perspectives. The demise of the head of the family may be viewed as a sacrifice for the younger generation to spread and flourish:

> Amjad: No. I want a doctor.
> Banoo: Are you sure?
> Amjad: Do what I say. (*to Amina*). Go to the phone box. I understand nothing about my family but I understand when I'm dying. (*PO*, 157)

Amina, who inherits Amjad's last legacy, decodes the sad event as the inevitable act of growing up, of turning into adulthood, which finds a suitable location in the new family, where the mourning ceremonies are permitted in the 'other' country (Pakistan):

> Amina: I spent a month in Pakistan for my father's funeral.
> Haroon: I know that.
> Amina: My mother stayed there. I belong here. There's work to be done. To make England habitable. (*PO*, 158)

The manipulative power of Amina's deictic references ("there"—"here") rises in order to signal a new scale of values. This type of parallelism establishes a polar contrast between the two countries and in binary terms accentuates the positions of the 'centre' and the 'periphery,' the West and the East. Such lexical choice and rhetorical strategy suggest that, in the Thatcherism-shaped England, individuals have to struggle to re-imagine the inner cohesion of a new society. Amina has come into strife with her parents over marrying a pre-chosen boy, but after violating this taboo and the death of Amjad, she decides to take action, obliquely seduced by the Youth Asian Movement. She is allowed to live on her own in Britain only with the condition of being looked after by an elderly relative sent from Bradford, a symbolic and geographical fragment of the Indian immigration in Britain. Banoo instead returns to her country to reach her private shelter and defeat the restriction of identity that marked her life as an immigrant.

Therefore, in Kureishi's fictional world, fathers are turned the spotlight onto as carriers of mixed meanings, bulwark of traditionalism and propensity towards innovation. The writer's personal experiences and biography contributed to shaping characters, though such operation was sometimes highly criticised by his own relatives. Nonetheless, the father and son relationship remains a fundamental issue in his work: Karim and Haroon, in *The Buddha of Suburbia*, clearly remind the reader of Kureishi himself, a mixed-race Englishman living in suburban England, with a father who passed onto him his own love for books and his own literary ambition. The author's father indeed was "a domineering but also a dominant man. . . . He imposed himself on you. He was also an interesting man to write about. . . . My dad was a civil servant for all of his life, but he used to write. He used to write very early in the morning. He'd write from five-thirty."[2]

Further evidence concerning the primal role (in both biographical and narrative terms) of Kureishi's father appears from the memoir *My Ear at His Heart* (2004), whose subtitle "Reading My Father" matches the exploration of the family's roots and memories with some reflections on the idea of writing, for both Kureishi and his father. The book features a series of beautiful black and white photographs of several members of the Kureishi family and questions the legacy of recollections and feelings, whilst the shadows of the past give way to the doubts of the present in a nostalgic manipulation of narratives. The stories written by Kureishi's father have "turned out, in my retelling, to mean more than he thought they meant. [. . .] But this is the fate of any form of expression and what happens to parents as they turn into the myths of their children" (*MEHH*, 194-95). The author deftly tries to restore memories and rejects illusionary dreams or mirages of myths so as to reconsider a surplus of meanings: the figure of his father, the purpose of being a writer and the Indian background.

Before turning to his novels, though, it is still worth noting that the problematic question of family relations regards both Asian and British characters: *Birds of Passage*, which is evidently indebted to Joe Orton's *Entertaining Mr. Sloane* (1964), is based on the act of usurping and disintegrating the domestic space, with the consequent neutralisation of the head of the family, operated by an Indian student. The family who put him up will be subtly subjugated by its guest, and become the victims of a process of 'revenge' decolonialism since the text also functions as an allegory of imperial conquests overturned through and mocked by an Indian point of view.

Asif, the newly arrived lodger, disguises his ambitious plans within the prospect of attending the Imperial College; paradoxically, by entering the United Kingdom, he becomes a pilgrim of the new economic 'yuppyish' faith tendencies, introduced under the government of Mrs. Thatcher, which is imbued with a strong degree of individualism: "You have to make money, that's all" (*OP*, 198) is his motto, a guideline to achieve his goals. However, as always in Kureishi's storytelling, a generous dose of irony prevents creating stereotyped characters and the influence of different playwrights emerges in "the attempt to adopt elements of the absurd to a more explicit exploration of questions of social justice and morality than is characteristic of Beckett."[3] The language betrays the echo of Joe Orton, the playwright from Leicester, and at the same time is refined, aphoristic and colloquial, trying to evoke a feeling of decadence and entrapment (which hints at *Waiting for Godot* too) and a paralysis of time and events.

The house is expropriated by the cunning immigrant who then plays an authoritarian role, excluding or overturning the traditional family scheme. Talking about the building, the Pakistani self-appointed businessman declares: "It's perfect for conversion into two flats. That'll mean work and money. Because structurally the place will have to be altered. In the meantime I've got eight Indian students moving in" (*PO*, 210). Parodically Anif's plans, which anticipate other immigrant entrepreneurs sketched in *My Beautiful Laundrette*, fit perfectly into the bourgeois rise of Right-winged Britain and reach their climax with the following statement: "Despite dizziness, this house is the beginning of my empire. Hold this, someone. I think I'm going to be an expansionist" (*PO*, 215). The notion itself of the English family, along with the postcard-image of the typical suburban detached house, surrounded by well-kept gardens, is bound to change: here Kureishi makes a ridicule caricature of the fear felt by parochial Britain dealing with Asian or African émigrés by imagining a grotesque 'invasion' from former colonies.

A similar focal point is elucidated by Salman Rushdie in a fundamental 1982 essay titled "The New Empire within Britain," but unlike Kureishi, who chooses to employ irony as his main tactic, the Rushdian analysis is meticulously based on historical accounts and points out inner contradictions of the celebrated multiculturalism across Britain:

> It sometime seems that the British authorities, no longer capable of governing a new community of subject peoples of whom they think, and with whom they can deal, in very much the same way as their predecessor thought of and dealt with 'the fluttered folk and half-child,' who made up, for Rudyard Kipling, the White Man's Burden. (*IH*, 130)

Like Asif, who praises his father ("He was a pilot in the RAF. They gave him the MBE" [*PO*, 185]) and simultaneously stresses his detachment from rural Pakistan, Karim too has a high opinion of his father, though he cannot approve of his decision to leave Margaret Amir, his English biologic mother to join extravagant Eva. In Karim's eyes, Haroon not only represents the beloved father but also lays claim to a position of cultural superiority that overthrows or redeems the sense of frustration that burdens immigrants:

> Like many Indians he was small, but Dad was also elegant and handsome, with delicate hands and manners; beside him most Englishmen looked like clumsy giraffes. He was broad and strong too: when young he'd been a boxer and fanatical chest-expander. (*BS*, 4)
>
> Dad had always felt superior to the British: this was the legacy of his Indian children—political anger turning into scorn and contempt. For him in India the British were ridiculous, stiff, unconfident, rule-bound. And he'd made me feel that we couldn't allow ourselves the shame of failure in front of these people. (*BS*, 250)

The picture delineated by the narrator is in stark contrast with the image of the English mother, perceived as a marginal character, who desperately tries to shy away from the tumultuous experiences of Karim and the enthusiasm of Haroon for 'informative mysticism,' grounded on a messy contamination of Buddhism, Sufism, Confucianism and Zen. Margaret Amir is described as a plain woman who, in a very English way, cares for the family's privacy (she always pulls the curtains to seal her household activities from the external gaze) and anonymously turns to drawing, TV watching and cheap books as the only ways of entertainment:

> Mum was a plump and unphysical woman with a pale round face and kind brown eyes. I imagined that she considered her body to be an inconvenient object surrounding her, as if she were stranded on an unexplored desert island. Mostly she was a timid and compliant person, but when exasperated she could get nervy aggressive, like now. (*BS*, 4)

Once again, we may detect distant autobiographical elements in Kureishi's images of womanhood and mothers, although the author feels rather jealous and reserved about his mother's life.[4]

The father's role is well illustrated and produces a sort of friendship that involves Karim while sponsoring New Age cultural meetings and mystical conquest of London. On the other hand, the mother's function branches off and competes with Haroon's mistress, the posh, stylish and flamboyant Eva, the British icon of 'marketing ethnicity.' Seduced by the substitute mother, Karim interpolates a double family life, with his father and Eva, in their London-bound mission of converting the English to oriental philosophies, and Margaret and Allie, his brother, on the suburban scene, who further marginalize their metropolitan space. A partial exception is Allie's immersion into the world of fashion, in which he probably finds a way out from static life, thanks to the vivid and flashy clothes.

Whilst in *The Buddha of Suburbia* Eva (the mother figure) and Margaret (the actual, biological mother) constitute examples of double characters that dot Kureishi's narrative, in the short story "With Your Tongue down My Throat," Nina and Nadia may embody a split, double identity:

> 'Your father had a wife in India,' Ma says wincing every time she says *father*. 'They married when they were fifteen, which is the custom over there. When he decided to leave me because I was too strong a woman for him, he went right back to India and right back to Wifey. That's when I discovered I was pregnant with you. His

> other daughter Nadia was conceived a few days later but she was actually born the day after you. Imagine that, darling. Since then I've discovered that he's even got two other daughters as well.'
>
> I don't give my same-age half-sister in another country another thought except to dislike her in general for suddenly deciding to exist. Until one night, suddenly, I write to Dad and ask if he'll send her to stay with us. I get up and go down the lift and out in the street and post the letter before I change my mind. That night was one of the worst and I wanted Nadia to save me. (*LBT*, 64)

The unexpected revelation of a stepsister for Nina conveys a disturbing effect, and yet is accompanied by a sentiment of reconciliation, in order to re-unite the family, and the self. Stylistically tortuous, the first person narration turns out to be grounded on an unreliable voice: indeed the whole story is charted by Howard, the mother's lover. But the seminal originality lies in the duplicity of characters, Nina and Nadia, and places, Britain and India. In fact, the symbiotic relationship between Nina (and her mother) and Nadia displays an ambiguous nature and unveils insights into the psychology of the characters. Nina is simultaneously attracted by and hostile towards Nadia, perceived as a part of her own cultural heritage, along with a desire to come to terms with her origins: "Ma and I watch this sweetie compulsively, wondering who she is: so close to us and made from my substance and yet so other, telling us about Dad with an outrageous intimacy we can never share" (*LBT*, 67).

The bond between extrovert, crass Nina and timid, coy Nadia appears blurred and (apparently) culturally untranslatable, affected by a psychological taunting. Nonetheless, at this narrative junction, the writer delves into the complexities of the relationship and works out Nina's empathy to express the complicated reciprocity that seems to operate here. The critic Alladi Uma affirms that within the context of Indian womanhood "sisters having dissimilar or contrary view can empathise with one another; they can still express oneness and fight against a common foe."[5] It is exactly the case of Nina and Nadia, almost twin sisters who mutually complete and sustain each other in order to rescue their inner selves. The English girl scans the Indian girl seeking a salvation from her wretched life experience imbued with doping, squatting and marginality (the "foes" evoked by urban decay). Her recently discovered Indian connection equips her with a new energy and self-consciousness that leads to affirm her ethnic diversity: "Becoming enthralled *by this new me* now, exotic and interior. With the scarf over my head I step into the Community Centre and look like a lost woman with village ways and chickens in the garden" (*LBT*, 69. My emphasis). This technique of imitation, or self-discovery, has been worked out in postmodern fiction in its effort to dismantle conventional representation of reality through the speculative use of art. In Linda Hutcheon's investigation, "quests in postmodern literature lead to *quest*ions, not answers. There are always excuses, alibis, elsewheres."[6] Therefore Nina's crisis reflects a plurality of voices: the girl(s), the actual narrator and the author interrogate the modes of writing and their expansions.

The adoption of a double perspective characterises several stories by Kureishi and in the case of "Face to Face with You," now collected in *The Body and Seven Stories* (2002), it even acquires eerie tones, *à la* Edgar Allan Poe. Ann and Ed are curious to meet their new neighbours, but when the newcomers move into the upstairs flat they are struck by incredible coincides: the belongings, tastes, furniture and aspect of the new couple are similar to theirs, and even the names of the other couple are Ann and Ed. The cold introduction of fragmentation is actually camouflaged as a banal, trivial event, but it slowly evolves like in a horror story: "Once in a pub in which there were many mirrors, Ed thought he saw Ed from upstairs sitting behind him. Thinking he'd seen the devil, he stood up and rushed out, gasping and gesticulating at nothing [. . .] he saw pieces of his own face swimming in the darkness, like bits of a puzzle being assembled by God, and he had to close his eyes" (*BSS*, 153). In a complex narrative structure, the author confuses the reader on purpose in order to scan the relationships of the two characters: by projecting their experiences, dreams, wishes and doubts onto other bodies, they actually question themselves and their sense of identity. In their reciprocal bond, they cannot distinguish the ego and the other, and this story of divided selves highlights the perception of innermost feelings. Ed, conversing with a colleague at work, wonders about his odd experience: "Suppose they were not only quite similar, but were—how shall I put it?—exactly the same. It's as if they're the originals and you're only acting out their lives" (*BSS*, 150). Kureishi uses the device of doubling characters and viewpoints, in a split dimension of sameness and fragmentation, to focus on the schizophrenic and problematic pathway of the man and the character: the curious gaze on the outside returns inside and painfully seeks unsaid truths concerning existence.

To return to Haroon, it is interesting to note that "fathers represent the public aspect of maturation"[7]; in fact, Karim's father evolves as a character and from time to time receives either support or disapproval from his son. Eventually, Karim's stage of self-formation drives him away from Haroon, though significantly the title of the novel hints at the father,[8] not the son! The father and son relationship could also be regarded as a feature of the *Bildungsroman*, a genre that poses the ground for the entire plot of *The Buddha*: the list of literary references (which derive from the western canon) is long and includes Voltaire's *Candide*, Twain's *Tom Sawyer*, Gosse's *Fathers and Sons*, and Salinger's *The Catcher in the Rye* amongst the others.

Paradoxically, the depressing sentimental crisis of the novel anticipated actual events of Hanif Kureishi's life: after experiencing fatherhood in 1993 with the birth of two twins and just one year after his fortieth birthday, the writer had to face the end of his marriage. However a new relationship, with Monique Proudlove, was started in 1995 and led to the birth of a son in 1998. The media and the popular press largely tried to ostracise him, and his dismay and a disheartening tendency gradually filters through his recent production, particularly in *Intimacy* and *Sleep with Me*. The feeling of instability that Karim perceives conveys a paradigm of erosion for all the characters that emerge from the text; like the disintegrating Victorian houses and shabby estates pictured in the novel, all families are seen in their fading aspect: husbands and wives separate, children keep away from parents, couples split up and are substituted by unlikely relationships.

Karim's family is the example *par excellence*: Haroon leaves his timid wife Margaret to join his mistress, Allie remains with his mother, Charlie frequently disappears and then returns to play the role of the prodigal son, while Karim (partially) follows his father's steps but does not abandon his mother, who moves into another house and starts her life again by looking for a new partner. Karim therefore finds himself wondering around Haroon and Eva's house, his previous house and Auntie Jane's place (where Margaret is put up), in a desperate quest for a steady barycentre. The poetics of his trebled spaces unfolds an inner struggle and ambitions that are mirrored in the 1970s pop culture and acquires a personal dimension that leads Karim to sever all his family's ties. In part, Charlie is a model, but chiefly the young mixed-race protagonist has an orbital movement towards his father and then the 'two mothers' alike. His acting experience and his pioneering approach to the 'big cities' (London and then New York) challenge traditional family links and establish a new self-made notion of identity, in which the component of Britishness and Asian roots melt together into a consciousness whose manifesto surfaces in the incipit of the text and elaborates on a re-vindication of identity of the new Englishmen, "born and bred, almost."

Another trait that characterises the father and son relation comprises an illumination of gender discourse, where maleness is seen in its competing aspect. Both Karim and Haroon have a strong personality and their virility is emphasised by several elements. The son's outlandish clothes and hippie frills and the father's meditation with training and physical exercises equally move towards the affirmation of sexual-related identities and male predominance. Yet in Karim's case, a confused sexual orientation and the generational conflicts carry a blurring effect. The character's degree of ambiguity adds another ingredient to Kureishi's revised recipe of sexual relations, which is much more than simply tackling the gay issue, already suggested in *My Beautiful Laundrette*. Haroon may reproach his son's ambiguous friendship with Charlie Kay, but also his own adulterous attitude confines him to the margins of social acceptability. Furthermore, Karim's attraction to his friend does not furnish a mere indication of alternative sexual orientation, but rather it goes beyond strong male bonding and interconnects with the self-construction, the *Bildung* aspect of the whole novel.

In his peculiar position of postmodern Everyman, joining the East with the West, the suburbs and the city, fine arts and pop culture, Karim shifts between sexual roles as well and interrogates his own ego. Thus a restricted sexual categorisation cannot bind him to a single definition: Karim has to undergo a subtle catharsis to express his frame of mind. In her overview of Foucault's theories, Tasmin Spargo clarifies that "the fracturing of the myth of a unified and unifying gay and/or lesbian identity can be seen as a product not simply of differences of personal and political priorities but of basing politics on identity."[9] Karim's confused sexual behaviour shows a narrow path among gender positions and depicts a chaotic perception of interpersonal relations, a feature that is shared by most characters of the text. This general directionlessness erodes social conformity and intensifies the novel's confused atmosphere. The gender innovation and transformation of society that took place in the 1970s underscores this vision and offers considerable models, such as popular icons, for instance from the world of music like David Bowie, who is frequently cited in the book. In this revolutionary climate it is clear that relationships "are transgressive and based simply on instinct"[10] and surface not just as a compelling impetus to violate rules. As a matter of fact, the terms that Karim uses to dictate his sexuality converge on the declaration (and exploration) of his own identity and transcend a pure physical reaction; Kureishi is not concerned with the sexual exploitation of characters, but rather with the reflection on human individuality.[11]

The father's name for Karim is a signifier and a signified, and the story comes full circle as both the beginning and the end of the novel feature the two characters. In the Bhabhaian analysis, the significance of the name is linked to the migrant's condition and "no name is yours until you speak it; somebody, the circuit of signs, gestures, gesticulations, is established."[12] Though the focus and the perspective are mainly set on the son, the father exhibits a significant role too. By the end of the book, Karim suspects that Haroon's 'orientalistic' masquerade does not wish to unsettle firm convictions or carry a discursive finality, in a revitalised vocabulary of mysticism. Nonetheless, the novel ends with the reunion of father and son and their reciprocal gaze charts the consequences of their behaviour. Haroon decides to resign from work and publicly announces he will marry Eva, while Karim is given an important part in a new nationwide soap opera. His future might include rosy prospects, but a sense of incompleteness seems to threaten the boy's life. London, which used to be the capital of a huge Empire and now is a commercial metropolis, is defined as "an old city," swallowed up by the frenetic modernity in its urban squalor. Furthermore, England is said to be "a tiny island" and Karim's thoughts are mixed: "I felt happy and miserable at the same time." Then he recognises that, in spite of all his fragmentary adventures, he still has to comprehend the dynamics of life and continue his personal quest, now split from his family and armed with his own will and determination only.

In *The Black Album* too, the father and son theme is marked by gender connotations but the confrontation that Shahid the protagonist has to carry out with his father is interposed throughout memories, because we are informed that the father is dead. Papa (we are not told the real name) praises Chili, the eldest son, and his virility, and even competes with him for manhood predominance; instead Shahid, the younger son, is described as 'bookwormish,' and his interest in culture and literature are often mistaken as a 'feminine side.' As we learn from the beginning, Papa died of a heart attack, so that all the details about him transpire as reminiscences. However his ghost-like presence hangs in Shahid's and Chili's memories and underpins the gendered, androcentric vision. Papa had a penchant on toiletries and grooming, and showed his sons how to be elegant, fit and appeal to girls. With the purpose to erase a weak or effeminate attitude, this attitude reinforces his male position in a hierarchical frame:

> Papa took his sons personally to the shops, ensuring that both he and they had the finest clothes. Even as his sons made faces at each other in the mirrors of Burtons the Tailors, he and the manager turned the fat books of clothes squares, patterned and plain, like scholars peering into manuscripts. Papa would return, several times, for adjustments—always the trousers were too long—before deciding, after interminable consideration, which tie and waistcoat were slightly wrong for the suit. At home, he took Shahid and Chili, scrapping and pinching the flesh. (*BA*, 53)

Papa's quasi-mania for fitness, health and smart clothes is matched with Chili's sexual appetites and vaguely reminds of Allie's fondness of fashion, though here its aim centres on wooing, whereas Karim's brother simply seeks a sophisticated way to express his uniqueness. Karim too, who benefits from the atmosphere of the vibrant 1970s, adopts dressing as a strategy of affirmation, but he also imposes a personal vision, modelled on hippie icons and punk images.

After Papa's demise, Chili himself acknowledges Shahid's metamorphosis: talking to his younger brother, he affirms: "'You're starting to look good, more healthy. Getting rid of glasses, the contact lenses and all . . . that shorter haircut . . . you've become less womanish. You look quite determined. You were always such a cry-baby. I s'pose you're nearly a man now. Papa would be pleased'" (*BA*, 42). Chili is in fact aware of the marginalisation that Shahid has suffered within the family. However the isolation and suffocation of the younger son are accompanied by his brilliant intelligence and curiosity, a characteristic that, in spite of his father's insults

("You bloody eunuch fool" [*BA*, 52]), Papa had always recognised in secrecy because according to Chili, he had "always admired your brains" (*BA*, 42).

Whether in Lacanian terms the name of the father incarnates the power of language, the moulding of discourse and the birth of the word, by concentrating on marginal characters (sons in particular) Kureishi undermines established conventions. His outcast protagonists, Karim and Shahid, have to modulate the encounter/clash with the Other, moving along the spectrum of ethnicity, gender boundaries and class-consciousness. They revisit customs and fight archetypal structures in their own speculation about human nature. Postmodernism (and feminism) provides the author with its analytic dismantling of texts, images and fashions. Indeed, Shahid's sentimental relationship with her college teacher Deedee clings not only to a revisitation of gendered roles and social positions but also to the dynamics of sexual power. The teacher and the student, the woman and the boy furnish a dual arena of confrontation reinterpreted inasmuch as Shahid's cross-dressing calls into question stereotypes and feminism-articulated lines of thought.

In conclusion, we have noticed how Kureishi's deconstructive and criticising approach to the notion of fatherhood, and more generally of the family, can be extended to his whole production. The story "Goodbye, Mother" for example serves, with its frequent shifts of time and place, as a plea to skim human relations of different binary opposition: mother/son, husband/wife, father/daughter. Commencing from the very incipit ("If you think the living are difficult to deal with, the dead can be worse" [*BSS*, 161]), which sounds like a threatening epigraph, it supports a painful investigation into the extended labyrinths of memory and family ramifications. The bitter-sweet relationship between Harry and his mother unfolds a domestic void and intensifies a sick solitude. The visit to his father's tomb implies a direct gesture of digging up into the past and the present and a collision with his own mother. However Kureishi seems to mitigate the protagonist's aporia at the end of the story ("He thought of Father under the earth and of Mother watching television; he thought of Alexandra and his children. He was happy" [*BSS*, 205]) because he employs epiphanic events to shelter his character by granting a wider consciousness. Consequently it is possible to observe that "many of Kureishi's tales also register Chekhovian moments of low-key revelation, which galvanise their protagonists towards self-renewal."[13] In its ultimate aim to achieve what Roland Barthes theorised as 'zero degree writing,' these short stories communicate with modern man and speak of his nervous fragility.

Sometimes the father figure is substituted by palliative images of uncles, as the Indian tradition would require; examples are provided with Uncle Nasser in *My Beautiful Laundrette*, Uncle Tippo in *The Black Album* and even in *The Buddha of Suburbia* with Uncle Ted, the white character married to Karim's Auntie Jean. The relationship can be claustrophobic, as in the case of Papa and Omar in Kureishi's first screenplay, in which the son must take care of his alcoholic father; the boy's dignity is humiliated by a restricted role, marginalized even in his own family and reduced to a sort of servant. Yet, in spite of Papa's rough ways, the father's love is expressed by the fact that he wants to convince Omar to start university and therefore build a sound career for himself. During a phone conversation, Papa and Nasser talk about Omar, and here the focus concerns the traditional enthralment and distancing of children in the Indian frame of mind:

> Papa: He's on dole like everyone else in England. What's he doing home? Just roaming and moaning.
>
> Nasser: (*VO on phone*) Haven't you trained him up to look after you, like I have with my girls?
>
> Papa: He brushes the dust from one place to another. He squeezes shirts and heats soup. But that hardly stretches him. Though his food stretches me. It's only for a few months, yaar. I'll send him to college in the autumn. (*MBL*, 52)

Papa's affection may be rough but it is brusque but sincere, and at the end of both the screenplay and the film, he will move out of his self-confined shelter to rescue his son. He will even play the part of the benevolent father with Johnny, Omar's ex-fascist friend. The same model is used by Kureishi to mould the character of Haroon, portrayed with a series of lights and shadows, contradictions that contain a humane reflection. Uncle Nasser's position, instead, prescribes a moneymaking sort of dictatorship in the family structure, based on exploitation.

Not all uncles are characterised negatively: Ted offers an alternative, changing point of view that is oppositional to that of his wife, Auntie Jean. The two, who have been nicknamed "Gin and Tonic" by Karim, belong to the section of white characters of Kureishi's literary family and their scope is dramatised by the western approach towards Asian immigration. Auntie Jean displays a false liberalism and hypocritically excoriates Haroon's extra-marital relationship; on the other hand, Ted strives to comprehend his brother-in-law's crisis. Indeed when Eva and Haroon settle in central London, Ted turns up at their house and actively collaborates with them to redecorate the house. The phase of restoration of dismissed buildings (pulling down old walls and erecting new divisions, painting and changing rooms) metaphorically alleges the impulse of a new family, shrugging off stale notions to shed light on the enhanced and revitalised figure of the father and the man.

Kureishi's style considers a progressive corrosion of relations which cannot be concealed behind stereotyped images. In *Sleep with Me* (1999), Julie childishly dreams of a steady family life ("The family is a point you can live from. I like ordinary, everyday life . . . laying the table, being in this house, choosing furniture" *SWM*, 49) but she cannot hide a deep sense of frustration and powerlessness. In the comment of her friend Sophie, human relationships and families are once again perceived as physical objects, sick dwellings, in a 'demonisation' of bonds. The metaphor carries a striking isolation and reduces the identity of characters:

Julie: Yes . . . a little . . . I've always wanted a family . . . to disappear into.

Sophie: That's the mistake, though—thinking you can find everything there . . . Families, if you don't mind me saying so, are mental hospitals. (*SWM*, 49)

The same kind of gloomy dislocation and pessimistic estrangement seems to haunt Kureishi's personal background when, in his non-fiction, he tackles the concepts of family and home. What emerges from his approach regards the inevitable impossibility of social relationships, of knowing properly, or at least coming to terms with, one's family, parents and self: "In the end, of course, you can never leave home. [. . .] One thing you do see, though it takes a lifetime to understand it, is that a human being—your parents and then yourself—is profoundly unknowable. I have about father, after all this, the feeling you can only have after knowing someone for a long time: that you don't know him at all, really" (*MEHH*, 197).

A partial correction to this devastation of human connections arises from *Gabriel's Gift*, in which a mellifluous tone strives to depict a moralistic modern fable. The protagonist, after the death of his beloved twin brother, decides to contribute to the reconciliation of his divorced parents. The young boy's expectations, sustained by a magical boom, a sort of supernatural contact with his brother, have to struggle with a fierce reality. In the post-yuppies era, Gabriel's Dad is a former musician of the 1970s, whereas the mother is a disillusioned woman. The whole story is blurred by some happy ending rhetoric, and its plain characters fail to alleviate the somnolent atmosphere of the narrative. Although the text bears remote echoes of the migrant community and quickly provides sketches of London, this type of writing does not have a subversive scheme, but rather it poorly offers a banal story, domesticated to please the western taste, perhaps relying on a sense of literary populism. Yet, the diasporic theme has always been given primary significance in Kureishi's work and has changed through time.

NOTES

1. *Postcolonial Contexts* (London and New York: Continuum, 2001): 11. See the whole introductory chapter for a general overview of parents, sons and orphans that emerge from postcolonial texts.
2. Kenneth C. Kaleta, cited: 181.
3. Bart Moore-Gilbert, cited: 59.
4. "My mother was important in my life too. But she is important to me privately. I don't feel that I particularly want to write about her, for others to read about her." Cited in Kenneth C. Kaleta: 189.
5. Alladi Uma, *Woman and Her Family. Indian and Afro-American: A Literary Perspective* (New Delhi: Sterling, 1989): 78.
6. Linda Hutcheon, *The Canadian Postmodern* (Toronto: Oxford University Press, 1988): 182. Author's emphasis.
7. Kenneth C. Kaleta, cited: 189.
8. Regarding the decline and fall of the myth of fatherhood in western culture, I would highlight the theory elaborated by Luigi Zoja in a recent volume *Il gesto di Ettore. Preistoria, storia e attualità e scomparsa del padre* (Milan: Bollati Boringhieri, 2003) which draws on the tradition of myth. The eclipse of the father figure is experienced by the hero of the *Iliad* Hector who, hidden by his armour, is not recognised and thus rejected by his own son: Astyanx, in fact, misinterprets the paternal hug because of the threatening aspect of the martial father and shies away. However the essay underscores the dual role of the hero, a father who typifies both force and tenderness, generosity and stiffness. The notion of fatherhood as a fragile cultural and social construction, opposed to the role of the woman, as a biological symbol of caring motherhood, moulds the metaphor of the cuirass as a means of protection. The decadence and metamorphosis of the fatherly imagery features the "terrible fathers" like Hitler and Stalin, the "fathers-friends" in recent times and the "base fathers" exemplified in the great tradition of the 19th century novel (see Dostoevsky, for instance). My reading of Kureishi's fathers is also grounded on such terms and stresses a series of the scattered identities: Haroon, Papa, Parfez, even Jay are characterised by a certain sense of ambiguity, restlessness, lost of confidence, pictured in their personal confrontations and intense competitions with their sons.

9. Tasmin Spargo, *Foucault and Queer Theory* (Cambridge: Icon Books, 1999): 33.
10. Richard Allen, "Men Need History. V.S. Naipual, Barry Unsworth and Hanif Kureishi," in Nilufer E. Bharucha and Vrinda Nabar, ed., *Postcolonial Indian Literature in English* (New Delhi: Vision Books, 1998): 227.
11. "And Charlie? My love for him was unusual as love goes: it was not generous. I admired him more than anyone but I didn't wish him well. It was that I preferred him to me and wanted to be him. I coveted his talents, face, style. I wanted to wake up with them all transferred to me" (*BS*, 15). Karim's evaluation of his affection for Charlie is structured from an egotistical point of view and envious self-imagined notion of gender. Of course, the young age (to some degree a late puberty) of the character ought to be taken into consideration, and towards the end of the novel, Charlie's sexual performances do not rouse or affect Karim. "I realised I didn't love Charlie anymore. I didn't care either for or about him. He didn't interest me at all. I'd move beyond him, discovering myself through what I rejected. He seemed merely foolish to me" (*BS*, 255). Though he still has not completed his quest, Karim is now able to ponder on his past and judge his life pathway. His 'in-progress' building of identity has shown a process of growing into manhood which discards teenage sexual yearnings and opts for compromised choices.
12. Homi Bhabha, "The Vernacular Cosmopolitan" in Ferdinand Dennis and Naseem Khasan, eds., *Voices of the Crossing* (London: Serpent's Tail, 2000): 142.
13. Bart Moore-Gilbert, cited: 159.

Postcolonial Everyman: From Migrancy to Hybridity

> Only a little away from me sat the Indian bus driver in his blue uniform, but for some reasons I thought of him as 'Asian,' and he became for me mysterious and unclassifiable. At each stop, he greeted kindly old ladies in a hearty English manner, 'Hullo, dear! It's lovely day, innit?' and later bid them inimitable farewells. 'Have a nice day, dear!' but the way he was more English than the English was very Indian, and there was something surprising about his utterances.
>
> Amit Chaudhuri, *Afternoon Raag* (p. 35)

The persistent emphasis on migrants in Kureishi's works matches with his preoccupation to introduce a new concept of national identity. As I have pointed out earlier, the author is deeply concerned with the dynamics of transformation that have affected British society, and therefore strives to go beyond obsolete definitions. Nationalism, he seems to suggest, now belongs to the past because a huge 'global village' is substituting social settings: large cities represent the main sites of such dramatic innovations. The ethnic component in Kureishi is problematic insofar as it emphasises both the centre and the margins, England and the subcontinent, and poses questions to the self. The writer recognises the Indian background, which is a seminal narrative source in many of his works, and yet breaks every conventional literary label. Unlike postcolonial novelists, who adopt the notion of counter-discourse to challenge the monolithic canon (re-writing classic texts is paralleled by the introduction of new perspectives and themes, as in *Jack Maggs* by Peter Carey or *Foe* by J.M. Coetzee) and who subvert standard English by employing regional idioms, Kureishi's prose concentrates on the individual, sustaining an investigation into the human personality which enlarges the scope of his writing.

Kureishi affirms that "I'm not really writing about Asians as a category . . . we are all people. I don't think because [a character] is Asian, I have to be reverential. That would be ridiculous."[1] Indeed, as the analysis of his (meta)narrative family tree has showed, little of the Indo-Pakistani heritage emerges from his oeuvre. There are plenty of echoes, hints, but paradoxically he seems to suggest that migrants should operate a double, cathartic process for accepting and changing mainstream society in order to acquire visibility and respect. *The Buddha* for instance launches New Age enthusiasm mistaken for or disguised as a symbol of Asianness onto the 'global western market' of identities, in which the struggle for endorsement is always competitive. Furthermore, Kureishi went to Pakistan only twice, in 1983 and in 1984, and his visits turned out to be a pregnant encounter with the ancestral land.

Approaching Pakistan was a highly symbolic journey across the contradictions of a double sense of nationhood. In fact, in spite of his sense of detachment from the rural local reality, where an almost feudal social, political and religious hierarchy disintegrates freedom and the creative spirit ("In England I was a playwright. In Karachi this meant little. There were no theatres; the arts were discouraged by the state—music and dancing are un-Islamic—and ignored by practically everyone else. So despite everything I felt pretty out of place." [*MBL*, 17]), Kureishi tries to track down the fine culture of the Asian country, its thirst for knowledge, its critical interrogation and sound fondness for books.[2] Back to England, Kureishi's confused sense of belonging orients his writing towards the new immigrant communities, now mainly associated with urban and suburban locations. Obviously, this interest stems from his own condition of migrant of second generation, but it is also intensified and made more complicated by his own identity crisis. Thus the diasporic characters that mark his narrative reiterate the revised concept of being English and his own meditation on the British context, rather than a dialogic relation with the subcontinent. Kureishi himself corrects his statements ("From the start I tried to deny my Pakistani self. I was ashamed. It was a curse and I wanted to be rid of it. I wanted to be like everyone else." [*MBL*, 9]), which he elaborated during his childhood, when he had to experience racial abuses and ethnic discrimination. The key idea that moulds his storytelling and thinking concerns the birth of a new national consciousness that takes into account the effects of immigration and reformulates old paradigms of belonging.

The migrant figure challenges the pure process of assimilation and starts an insidious journey across the narrow social strata of England; like a postmodern and postcolonial Everyman, he investigates his quest and shifts from the subcontinent to the former imperial centre, from the periphery to the heart of the city. Moving across boundaries assumes a symbolic significance, a pathway to improve the conditions of life, through a 'compulsory' harsh pathway, in the attempt to move up the social ladder. Thus we should compare Karim with Everyman, a typical character of the early forms of English drama, an allegorical personification that functioned as an *exemplum* during the later Middle Ages.[3] The theological perspective that constitutes the theme of this type of play implies the notion of the journey as a sort of purgatory, a dire experience which will be rewarded with the access to Heaven the ultimate salvation, shrugging off the threatening burden of vices. Similarly the immigrant has to move and complete his peregrination to conquer a sense of identity; the intense irony of Kureishi lies in the essence of the émigré character who seems to be reduced into a stereotyped passive role, whose threatening otherness is rejected by society. Karim, being the clear example of Everyman-based migrant, dreams of London and orchestrates his process of formation nearly bearing in mind an ashamed or disturbed concept of the ego ("I am often considered to be a funny kind of Englishman, a new breed as it were, having emerged from two old histories" [*BS*, 3]), so as to fulfil his expiatory rite.

To corroborate the recognition with Everyman, Kureishi's style highlights the oddity of his main characters, like Karim, "a suburban maverick with a saucy tongue,"[4] Shahid, 'the Muslim atheist'[5] or Parvez, the westernised father in the tale "My Son the Fanatic," collected in *Love in a Blue Time*: they could all be classified as parodic versions of the anti-hero, a dislocated Picaro, a Falstaffian knave that oscillates in a pendulum-like movement between the sociological representation of minor communities and the mainstream cultural debate on globalisation.

The young Anglo-Indian boy moreover longs to be an actor, and this tendency to play a part emphasises the immigrant's construction of identities; discussing the production of Kipling's *The Jungle Books*, in which Karim has been cast, his theatre director comments on the status of the expatriate refugee: "What a breed of people two hundred years of imperialism has given birth to. If the pioneers from the East India Company could see you. What puzzlement there'd be. Everyone looks at you, I'm sure, and thinks: an Indian boy, how exotic, how interesting, what stories of aunties and elephants, we'll hear now from him. And you're from Orpington" (*BS*, 141). In spite of such affirmations, the orientalised construction of Mowgli is based on imposed models: Karim has to use a disguise to stage the prodigious boy and his skin must be darkened with some make-up cream. This proves that English racism, in its various forms, operates a subtle transformation of the body and the skin through a humiliating procedure with the intent to adopt social modes of discriminating races and cultures. The discursive representation of the ethnic body, which is a leitmotif in Meera Syal's writing too, defines the colour of the skin as the indelible mark that characterises, protects and wraps the self. In psychoanalytic terms, skin constitutes a 'second skin' and on the visual level, Karim-Mowgli is compelled to accept a fake colonial identity in a metaphorical surgery that bisects the Anglicised boy from the stereotypical Indian savage.

Shadwell, another theatre director that Karim meets, provides penetrating definitions that stress the condition of hybridity more than the heritage of postcoloniality: "The immigrant is the Everyman of the twentieth century [and it is] your destiny, which is to be a half-caste in England" (*BS*, 141). The operation that Karim sustains does not stem from the act of writing back to the Empire, but concerns a revisitation of the ethnic issue of identity. Second generation immigrants cannot rely on the mind-constructed India and therefore opt for exploring new ways of being through pop culture, drugs, fashion. It is interesting to note that however even their fathers bear a confused viewpoint, split between their Indian homeland and their new English life. On the one hand, they complain about Indian difficult conditions of life, criticizing what in their eyes now appears as a hellish Third World country, corroded by harsh poverty, religious divisions and climatic adversities. At the same time, the fathers feel they cannot consider themselves fully integrated, though they still do not hint at the emergence of hybridity, and as a result they proudly express their various forms of 'otherness.' The following passage shows how Anwar and Haroon reinvent the ideal map of India, juxtaposed with the grim reality of the Asian country:

> Now, as they aged and seemed settled here, Anwar and Dad appeared to be returning internally to India, or at least to be resisting the English here. It was puzzling: neither of them expressed any desire actually to see their origins again. 'Why would I want to go there again?' Anwar grumbled 'It's filthy and hot and it's a big pain-in-the-arse to get anything done. If I went anywhere it would be Florida and Las Vegas for gambling!' And my father was too involved with things here to consider returning. (*BS*, 64)

It is the adverb 'internally' that witnesses the friction of attitudes of the two Indian characters and designates a nostalgia for a mental image of the subcontinent. India does not constitute a real homeland but the ethnic call for Haroon to deny a western vision of life and mark his line of difference from the son; whereas Karim defines himself as "an Englishman bred and born, almost," Haroon does not become the victim of post-imperial assimilation: "I have lived in the West for most of my life, and I will die here, yet I remain to all intents and purposes an Indian man. I will never be anything but an Indian" (*BS*, 263). It is true that probably such statements incorporate an expression of nationalism and chauvinism (especially if we consider that they are pronounced in front of journalists who are interested in the guru's activity), but they also function as a genuine reflection on the life of the exiles, in which the displacement does not annihilate the geographic and human roots. The Egyptian-born and now America-settled intellectual Ihab Hassan speculates on the magnetic idea of the diaspora, the cathartic connotation of the migrant's re-shaping of countries: "Homes are not places, and they are not where hearts are, since we all carry our hearts where we go. Home is an attitude, a readiness for *death and dispossession*, a kind of self-heedlessness that makes the entire universe a home."[6]

Exile then, though Hassan prefers the term 'displacement,' shows such a powerful determination to face 'death and dispossession' and eventually opens up a new quest. Imagined Indias can be illusory islands of the mind, shelters that protect émigrés from the racist assaults but their scope is even wider and suggests a cosmic seduction for mankind and the ego. The desire to fabricate a fictitious country may represent a temporary escapism, but diasporic authors admonish about such easy dreamland pictures. Farrukh Dhondy, for instance, warns about the misleading safety of a quick *escamotage* in his novel *Bombay Duck* in which the theatre impresario David Stream, who wants to stage a new, ethnic-conscious version of the *Ramayana*, the classic Indian epic, stresses the fragmentary constitution of the subcontinent and suggests that the captivating quintessence of multiculturalism must consider its inner divisions and separatism:

> Ok, I've read you that to be fair. India is not the great peace-loving monolith that we are trying through our internationalised world to construct. India is in the mind. In parts of it Hindus kill Sikhs, in

> other parts Muslims kill Hindus and so it goes on and so does life. As it does in Northern Ireland. I want you all to think it over because our play is not propaganda for peace, like soviet Youth Congress. It is the cat's cradle of pressures itself.[7]

In this quotation we are shown an echo of the sense of 'death' exposed by Hassan: the violence that lacerates dolorously and sadly the country carves the frame of mind of the émigré too. The wandering man now finds himself precariously poised on a razor's edge. Kureishi has in mind mainly the second generation of Asian diasporic subjects, who are rather different from those Commonwealth migrants who arrived over the post-war period, in the 1950s and 1960s.

His unique position tends to cement the principle of ethnicity, and hence the struggle against racism within small communities and the questions of constructed categories of identity (Englishness versus Indianness/Asianness), with the acceptance of hybridity, embroiled in the reproduction of the self. Hybridity thus invests characters like Karim and Shahid through a series of dichotomies: the former is an actor and a student, is straight and gay, metropolitan and marginalized, English and Indian; the latter is secular and religiously fervent, westernised and curious about fundamentalism. Such oppositions contribute to the outcome of the new nation-making process, a cultural momentum that is being possible only in contemporary England. The danger of 'showing off' the intercultural melting pot is connected with the questions on the manipulation of small communities and the ethic regulation of powers. Dhondy, through his Parsee protagonist Xerses, expresses his reluctance to the iconoclastic mechanisms of acceptance: "It was the age of America and Americanness, where ethnicity—Jewishness, blackness, etc.—mattered to anybody. If you didn't have that as a badge to wear in all those competing cultures, well then, you found something else for which 'they' victimised you. It started with wanting to be part of a victim group and moved on to asserting that together you were tough!"[8]

For both Dhondy and Kureishi, ethnicity should not be regarded as a composite system of 'cultural fragments' but rather as the signs that constitute a broader social system and its changes. Unlike what Kureishi and other recent diasporic authors depict, the first generation migrants of the 1950s believed in a sort of internal hierarchy so that people from the Commonwealth somewhat felt privileged, in virtue of their belonging to the Empire. In fact this characteristic provided a tacit inscription into the common denominator of Britishness, perceived as an enhancing factor. In Sam Selvon's *The Lonely Londoners* (1956), the Caribbean protagonist Moses acknowledges the differentiated legal status of his community from the Eastern Europe congregation; while talking about the owner of a restaurant in Ipswich, he vehemently asserts his inner view of national identity in terms of labour and action: "The Pole who have that restaurant, he ain't have no more right in this country than we. In fact, we is British subjects and he is only a foreigner, we have more than any people from the damn continent to live and work in this country, and enjoy what this country have, because is we who bleed to make this country prosperous."[9] In his non-standard, creolised English, Moses develops the subject-based stasis that characterises the initial flow of migrant from overseas colonies. Whereas in such type of narrative, the intrusion of memory and the Tiresias-like role are given strong emphasis, in Kureishi's (and Dhondy's) fiction we are facing the elaboration of the new ethnic element, not the regression into a stereotypical or orientalised 'other.' Kureishi uses the concept of hybridity to modulate a polyphonic discourse: his urban émigrés constitute a catalogue of different typologies, from the feminist Jamila, to the scheming Asif, from the clumsy Changez, to more complex characters like Karim and Shahid.

They all express a plurality of values, which are mitigated by their compulsory exile, and nonetheless they try to react and manifest their own cultural essence. The story of Jamila and Changez, for all its social and intercultural implications, mirrors the paralysed condition of the migrant, abruptly split between a modern, secular context in Britain and a strict imposition and upholding of traditions. Uncle Anwar compels his daughter Jamila to marry a man from India and the cliché of arranged marriages already employed in the plays with the hunger strike device to force the girl's decision, is here reiterated, with a touch of bitter irony as the act of coupling Jamila and Changez identifies with that of imagining, of fancying but it eventually becomes a sign of the deterioration of the masculine element and the patriarchal order.

Before this episode takes place, Anwar's sense of modernity and progressive attitude permits Jamila to have a promiscuous, careless social life and great freedom, but then her father switches into the role of the devout Muslim. According to Karim, such return to religious beliefs and traditionalism is paralleled by Haroon's pose as a neighbourhood guru, and in both instances the reasons for such choices should be detected in their remote roots, nearly implying a feeling of inevitability: "Perhaps it was the immigrant condition living itself out through them" (*BS*, 64). The older generation migrant finds himself trapped in a cultural grid, imprisoned between the memory of a self-constructed India and a half-absorbed England. Anwar rejects his Hindu identity and assumes a Muslim rigidity: paradoxically, the immigrant displays a resistance and perseverance that is matched neither in the East nor in the West. Obviously, the practice of marrying off (or even selling) daughters to endowed selected men, which is still quite common and socially accepted in Indian society, is here comically adapted to a broader cultural horizon. Usually accompanied by the presentation of a dowry, the tradition of arranged marriages is very hard to uproot; Vrinda Nabar observes that in India "the spectre of having one's daughter rejected and unmarried or worse, of having the marriage called off at the eleventh hour if the price paid does not match the expectations seems to deaden the scepticism of the most self-avowedly progressive fathers."[10]

Anwar, who runs a small corner shop in the suburbs, sometimes even eats pork meat, praises Britain for its democracy, asserts his patriarchal position and eventually leads the daughter to marry Changez; but here Kureishi in his mown prose turns the old, industrious migrant into the victim (literally, since the presence of Changez will contribute to his death) of his own plotting. The girl's husband is described in a grotesque manner: his hair is "sparse, dry and vertical," his stomach "rode out before him" and his only belongings are kept in "two rotting suitcases." The caricature of the stereotyped immigrant covered with rags even acquires the deformity of the 'freak,' a sort of *ludus naturae*, and becomes the paradigm of the alien 'other': his rough grotesqueness is presented so as to reveal the émigré's quintessence, as if the corruption of his crippled body should indicate a pejorative diversity. Changez, indeed, shows a handicapped arm,[11] an element of physical powerlessness that destroys Anwar's plans to convince him to decorate and run his shop.

Changez represents the ultimate image of the stereotype of laziness and passivity associated with the colonised/immigrant, and he seems unable to embody the role of the faithful husband, constantly rejected by Jamila, who holds a strong feminist viewpoint and looks for emancipations. As a reaction towards the imposition of the marriage, not only does she draw away from her family, but eventually she starts a friendship with Changez's Japanese courtesan, Shinko, as if to seek an outer social milieu, protected from male predominance. Such type of same-sex relations can work in both the West and the East but, in Vrinda Nabar's interpretation, "its special nature is conditioned by the differences between the individualistic vision of the West and our own perception of community-membership as a basic duty."[12] However Jamila turns this statement of respect for traditions upside down because her bonding functions in the terms of an operation to rescue the decadent migrant and hybrid context she is living in.

As a consequence of her disastrous and sterile marriage with Changez, Jamila revolutionises her life and joins a commune, a sort of social and political laboratory where her feminist vision can prevail. The young girl then decides to explore human relations and gender politics; she mothers a girl called Leila Kollontai, from Simon, another member of the commune, and at the same time begins a relationship with a woman, the filmmaker Joanna.

Jamila's bearing of a child further develops the feminine issue grafted onto the postcolonial scenario: in a traditional culture and society like that of India, the values of motherhood are deemed as fundamental. Several Hindu goddesses celebrate the woman's biological experience of reproduction: the worships to Durga, Annapoorna, the goddess of food, Grama Devata, the village deity, the "numerous river goddesses like Saraswati, Ganga, Yamuna, Godavari, all share a common base of the female being as the *Ma*, the personification of Mother Earth."[13] However, this powerful collocation of the feminine and the praise to fertility are downgraded by a constant seclusion of the woman, whose freedom is controlled by the male authority though the practice of *purdah*. The feminist debate that presently is underway in India here should amplify and be connected with the migrant's consciousness. For Maithreyi Krishnaraj, the purpose of re-reading and revising motherhood concerns "redefining appropriate terms and conditions, recreating the social structure that can make motherhood conceivably a creative experience, merging as it does the boundaries between child and mother, mediating as it can between nature and history, between the universal and the particular."[14] Jamila seems to adopt these predicaments as a credo to sustain her engagement with the anti-racist politics, gender identification and social/ethnic emancipation. In the form of fiction, this is an attempt to come to terms with the meanings of being a woman and an immigrant, within a double sense of otherness that goes beyond the sociological insight. Changez, whose name echoes the verb 'to change,' passively accepts Jamila's triangular romance and lives in an illusory world, morbidly subjugated by his idea of love. He feels incapable of reacting or having prejudices "except against Pakistanis, which is normal" (*BS*, 273). His sense of national identity thus overcomes his troubled love life:

though it confines him into a marginal zone, it allows an integration into the British pop culture that Changez longs for.

Both Changez and Jamila prove to be characters that can progress and change when engaged with the difficulties of living in Britain. New migrant communities are not pictured as strongholds of fundamentalism and cultural parochialism: because of the urban climate, most of Kureishi's exiled protagonists inaugurate the discourse on hybridity, which "allows an opening to the multiplicity of traditions and cultures within the diaspora without succumbing to the temptations of homogenisation and domination."[15] Such clusters of dislocated subjects still display their ambivalent and fragmented mentality, which is somehow anchored to a process of self-discovery of their Indian roots. Karim, who as an actor plays the role of the immigrant, sometimes feels the loss of a cultural background, an ethnic reference that ought to remind him of a never-forgotten place of origins. But in the end Karim realises that the sense of identity and belonging is a fictional and flexible structure, based upon a merely constructed pattern:

> But I did feel, looking at these strange creatures now—the Indians—that in some way these were my people, and that I'd spent my life denying or avoiding that fact. I felt ashamed and incomplete at the same time, as if half of me were missing, and as if I'd been colluding with my enemies, those whites who wanted Indians to be like them. Partly I blamed Dad for this . . . *so if I wanted the additional personality bonus of an Indian past, I would have to create it*. (*BS*, 212-13. My emphasis)

Initially shocked by the juxtaposition with his own people, after a closer scrutiny the young protagonist comprehends that the retrospective journey through the labyrinths of ancestral memory, and the quest for a national identity, is self-governed, and the outcome shapes the hybrid dynamics of being, on the backdrop of the post-colonial heritage. Karim's speculations suggest that the Indian frame of mind should be regarded as constructed category of knowledge rather than a re-discovered distinctiveness. The same search for cultural awareness is employed by Dhondy when he sketches the encounter between Xerses, a Parsee teacher in London, and Sonya, his mixed-race pupil of Asian descent. The girl hopes to be guided by the man, and her curiosity is delivered as a verbal operation to acquire self-confidence:

> 'I want you to tell me lots of stories. My mum doesn't. She's the Indian side and I don't have grandparents and my parents don't much mix with Indians and I feel deprived. So I've latched on to you. OK?'
>
> 'Very OK,' I said.
>
> 'I'm culturally deprived. Some of the girls in the sixth form think you're cute and the boys think you're a wally. I think you're both and lots more and I want to find out.'[16]

Sonia and Xerses unearth two typical positions of the migrant's world: on the one hand, the absence of homeland and the atavistic culture assume the form of exploration through the memories and narratives, namely the "stories" that the girl reclaims; on the other, the mimic tendency of the educated expatriate reveals a multi-layered accretion of cultural notions. Thus, Karim is partially akin to Sonia, and their inquiry regards the protection of the ethnic self.

But what Karim finds out centres on the artificiality of the ego, the anxiety of collocating one's self into a specific category, far away from the Cartesian structure that defines the independent subject ('I think therefore I am'). In Foucault's opinion, the existing order of society shapes the vision but the individual undermines social norms of being and Lacan, too, has spoken of the crucial psychoanalysis of the unstable identity. Not only does the Anglo-Indian protagonist have to retrieve his Indian past, but he is also expected to re-invent the corollary of elements pertaining to the cultural and social dimensions. The principle of 'anthropo-poiesis'[17] illuminates the malleability of codes, of behaviours, of norms of coming into being, which all share a common denominator based on the propensity towards being shaped. Karim has to move past crossroads and foster an hybridising vision: his negotiations of layers of different cultures, absorbing the verve of 1970s Britain, canonical literature and art in general, do not give him the role of a privileged member of the Indian community, but depict a precursor to the practices of the intercultural discourse.

The scattering of identities in Karim is made further evident in his stage experiences, which force him to assume a hyphenated position: a 'real-fake' Indian/Pakistani boy as the Kiplingian Mowgli, a disturbing label that evokes or pretends to evoke what the director Shadwell defines as "authenticity," a goal that can be reached by wearing make-up and carefully posing. In Kureishi's rebus-like attempt to metafictionalise Karim, the creation of Tariq, the newly arrived immigrant modelled on clumsy Changez, is instrumental in the ironic process of de/construction of characters within the novel; Karim/Tariq is provided with a carnivalesque costume, wearing "high white platform boots, wide cherry flares that stuck to my arse like sweet paper and flapped around my ankles, and a spotted shirt with a wide 'Concorde' collar" (*BS*, 220), defining him as an ironic and postcolonial Arlecchino of the now globalised world.

The series of oppositions positioned at the edge of cultures that Kureishi sets in motion dismantles the congealing fixity of Englishness/Indianness. Whilst the young actor has to re-codify his Indian terms, Englishness also appears as a constructed product, which, according to Simon Gikandi, has been a useful tool to reinforce the fabrication of the imperial/metropolitan frame of mind, and to impose a hegemonic gaze onto the colony. Fragments of Englishness (the game of cricket, Shakespeare, canonical literature) define the colonial purpose of forging new totems of significance, which have survived even after the independence of overseas territories. For Gikandi,

> the persistent and enforcement of colonial categories in their moment of disappearance points us in two related directions: in the formerly colonised space itself, we encounter the foremost insignias of colonial culture overdetermining the making of what were supposed to be decolonised identities; in the metropolis itself, we

> see the same categories returning, in their phenomenality and ghostliness, to call into question the axioms of Englishness.[18]

Myths like the Monarchy or William the Conqueror (who is believed by students of all ages across the Commonwealth to be the very first English king and not a Norman invader) cease to be monolithic paradigms of cultural superiority. Gikandi's deconstruction of images also operates through an iconographic analysis of portraits of sovereigns: whereas the glorious Ditchley portrait of Elizabeth I (circa 1592) concerns a towering figure that rises from the cartography of the world, the portrait of Elizabeth II by Pietro Annignoni (1969) carries a compelling sense of unease and witnesses the post-imperial void generated by the discordant re-adaptation of the English power. The emptiness that surrounds the monarch may symbolise the disintegrating sense of identity, a colonial memory and a nostalgia that paved the way to Thatcherism.

This scheme of invented identities also applies to Karim's relationship with Margaret, his mother, because in response to her pungent affirmation ("'Who gave birth to you? You're an Englishman, I'm glad to say'" [*BS*, 232]), the boy's words justify his chameleon-like appearance by heading for new social and cultural interstices: "'I'm an actor. It's my job,'" whereas the artistic performance in its composition of memories and references re-creates the meaning of identity in the postcolonial age. The capitulation of Karim to the spectre of subtle English imperialism embodied by the shadow of Kipling (Jamila bitterly reproaches the boy for the disgusting costume, the phoney accent, and the political implications: "'The play is completely neo-fascist'") is counterbalanced by the parodic perception of the English quintessence. In the penultimate chapter, set in New York, Karim re-joins Charlie, now a famous singer who denies his English origin and proclaims his Americanised aesthetic vision,

> 'Sit down, Karim, for God's sake,' said Charlie. 'Stop farting about. You're not in Beckenham now.'
>
> 'I know that.'

> 'Well then, can't you stop standing there and looking so English?'
>
> 'What d'you mean, English?'
>
> 'So shocked, so self-righteous and moral, so loveless and incapable of dancing. They are narrow, the English. It's a kingdom of Prejudice over there. Don't be like it!' (*BS*, 254)

Charlie, now voluntarily deprived of his British personality, admonishes Karim and prompts him to experiment new modes of being. Along with a dose of criticism, ("I heard an American voice say 'these English are animals. Their whole culture has fallen through the floor!'"), the American context modulates the perception of the young actor as a typical Englishman, now translated into an inhabitant of some decaying wasteland.

Finally it may be possible to draw a parallel between the restless, chaotic and active characters and the sites of generative social ferment, like Karim's suburbs, Jamila's commune and Charlie's central London. Therefore the novel in all its complicated ramifications "provides a marvellous ocular itinerary of the transgressive possibilities of the hitherto unimagined communities."[19] Both characters and locations are pervaded by the force that dictates the subversion of political choices, and the cinematic style that accelerates the plot.

I would like to quote Kureishi's shorter fiction as well in order to illustrate his treatment of the indicators of nationalism and racism; "We're not Jews," from the collection *Love in a Blue Time*, is a salient example. Witnessed though the eyes of a mixed-race child, Azhar, the story juxtaposes the world of verbal intolerance and racial abuse, embodied by two rough characters, Big Billy and Little Billy, and the narrow existence of the boy's family, on the backdrop of a 'secondclassness' of Pakistani émigrés. Riding back home on a double-decker bus, Azhar and his mother are approached by the two Billys, their nuisance neighbours. The woman, being rudely addressed and laughed at, deploys a makeshift to protect her cultural and ethnic background: "We're not Jews" is her reply that should declare the emergence of human dignity and personal identity. From the very title, by starting up with a West-generated stereotype of the much-denigrated Jews, Kureishi orchestrates the defence of the ironic writing towards the levelling and standardisation operated by a globalising vision. Yvonne, the English mother of Azhar, and Big Billy have suffered the years of the war but such experience does not grant the sharing of the same social ground. On the contrary, the English-born woman is bitterly accused to have married a "darkie," and the racial prejudice is explicitly shown.

But Azhar's mother, a character who is not familiar with Urdu, loathes sunburnt places and curry dishes, assumes the role of the spokesperson of the integrated émigrés and, by shifting the emphasis from claims of origin and the notion of home, she is involved in a process that places herself on a safe and comfortable social level. Denouncing her distance from the Jews, she insists on being part of an unspecified but self-declared broad-minded community, created by the global transformations, which however feels entitled to deliver ethnicity-based insults. The paradox here inscribed permits the author to treat with a great density of irony Bhabha's definition of vernacular cosmopolitanism, when he says that ethnic minorities across Britain are "compelled to make a tryst with cultural translation as an act of survival."[20]

Azhar's mother is then counterbalanced by another character, the unnamed husband briefly defined as 'Father': his search for a sense of homeplace, having previously lived between China and India, is not given a primary thematising light, rather it is his thirst for knowledge and narrative propensity that distinguishes him as a typical Kureishian intellectual. The father fails to gain success on the literary scene as his English, with his Bombay variety 'mish and mash,' has a defamiliarising effect and avoids expressing the functions and circumstances that hybridisation should develop. Father, like Granpop and Uncle Asif, belongs to the group of relatives described as those used to "talking loudly in Urdu or Punjabi, using some English words but gesticulating and slapping one another in a way English people never did" (*LBT*, 50), where the frenzy movements clash with the social matrix of upholding traditions. The concluding paragraph hints at the disturbing patterns of verbal and non-verbal languages modulated by an in-between platform of hybridity-making, where lights and shadows are equally and generously cast:

> Azhar was accustomed to being with his family while grasping only fragments of what they said. He endeavoured to decipher the gist of it, laughing, as he always did, when the men laughed, and silently moving his lisp without knowing what the words meant, whirling, all the while, in incomprehension. (*LBT*, 50-51)

The passage suggests an elusive degree of communication and Kureishi's prose has to undermine the rhetoric of integration, so extensively associated with the unifying policy of globalisation, as a principle of cultural hegemony.

Elsewhere in Kureishi's fiction, both in the novels and plays, we are shown contextualised patterns of denunciation pivoting on pejorative lexical items like 'Paki,' 'gypo' or 'brown mug,' in which the annihilating power of such insults is set out to clarify a world torn between the idea of migrancy on the one hand (with the metaphor of the wandering Jew, trespassing physical and mental boundaries, following a diasporic utopia) and the social milieu, on the other hand, struck by violence and cultural changes. In *The Black Album* an appropriation of the racist stereotype of the Jew is included even within the Pakistani community, when Chili, the protagonist's brother, dramatizes the disparity of social status and citizenship, affirming:

> You see them, our people, the Pakis, in their dirty shops, surly, humourless, their fat sons and ugly daughters watching you, taking the money. [. . .] The new Jews, everyone hates them. In a few years, the kids will kick their parents in the teeth. Sitting in some crummy shop, it won't be enough for them. (*BA*, 201)

The social and generational aspirations are here posited to further the clash between the émigrés and their homeland, by mounting the argument of incomprehension and incommunicability and eroding the father and son relationship, when the scope of integration appears to dislodge the younger generation from society. Furthermore, Chili, through his recalcitrant illegal activities, reinvigorates the racist equation which identifies the immigrants and confines them in the roles of delinquents and outcasts, unfit to practice an ethnic harmony inside the new society's ranks.

In a parallel manner there is an affiliation of the text towards the genre of the 'university novel,' whose corpus (let us think about David Lodge) sanctions the "presumed social inclusiveness of English studies—and the model of national belonging which the discipline symbolises—by non-white immigrants in post-war Britain."[21] This aspect of Kureishi's fiction should be read as an operation of updating and corroding the myth of 'Britishness,' which actually seems to dawn at the turn of the century. In the novel, Deedee's unconventional lectures offer an attempt to change the traditional college syllabus, with a special emphasis on colonial and postcolonial literatures, to reach, with a touch of irony, the edge of postmodernism: "She and the other post-modern types encouraged their students to study anything that took their interest, from Madonna's hair to a history of the leather jacket" (*BA*, 26). The closeness to reality, with distant metafictional tones, is reinforced by the fact that the novel opens with a sort of Islamic/pagan rite of burning books, with clear references to the dramatic episodes of violence that characterised the publication of Rushdie's *The Satanic Verses*. 'High' canonical literature is thus linked to the question of ethnicity.

In the end, Kureishi's representation of Asian Britain has shown a pluralistic and manifold viewpoint that rescues his Indo-Pakistani heritage and projects a new insight into the future sense of national belonging and personal/collective identity. Kureishi's hybrid use of hybridity, a pun frequently suggested by critics themselves, is motivated by the writer's purpose to depict the contradictions of the modern world: storytelling through drama, fiction and cinema brings to light a variety of issues that accompany the anxieties of postcolonialism, postmodernism and globalisation.

NOTES

1. Kenneth C. Kaleta, cited: 220.
2. Cf. "In Pakistan people were keen to know not only about Asia and the Middle East, but about Europe and the United States. They sought out information about the whole world. They needed it. They ordered books from Europe, listened to international radio and chewed up visiting academics like pieces of orange. In Britain today, among the middle class, thinking and argument are almost entirely taboo" (*MBL*, 33).
3. Traditionally *Everyman*, which has become a canonical example of morality plays, is believed to be a translation from the Dutch. Probably written anonymously in 1485, it was published after 1528 or 1529.
4. Seema Jena, "From Victims to Survivors," *Wasafiri*, No. 17, Spring 1993: 4. See also David Galloway, *The Absurd Hero* (Austin and London: University of Texas Press, 1966), where we read "With the absurd hero, achievement ceases to be a question of victory or defeat but is rather a success in sustaining an elemental disproportion": 12.
5. Here I borrow an expression coined by Kureishi himself, used in his Introduction to *Collected Screenplays* (London: Faber and Faber, 2002).
6. Ihab Hassan, "Beyond Exile: A Postcolonial Intellectual Abroad," *The Southern Review*, 29: 3, Summer 1993: 460. (My emphasis).
7. Farrukh Dhondy, cited: 108.
8. *Ibid.*, 147.
9. Sam Selvon, *The Lonely Londoners* (1956) (London: Longman, 1999): 40.
10. Vrinda Nabar, *Caste as Woman* (New Delhi: Penguin India, 1995): 160.
11. "Changez's left arm was withered in some way, and stuck on the end of the attenuated lump of hard flesh the size of a golf ball, a small fist, with only a tiny thumb projecting from the solid mass where there should have been nimble, shop-painting, box-carrying fingers. It looked as if Changez had stuck his hand into a fire had had flesh, bone and sinew melted together" (*BS*, 81).
12. Vrinda Nabar, cited: 37.
13. Alladi Uma, cited: 6.

14. Maithreyi Krishnaraj, "Motherhood. Power and Powerlessness," in Jasodhara Bagchi, ed., *Indian Women. Myth and Reality* (Hyderabad: Sangam Books, 1995): 35.
15. Monika Fludernik, "The Constitution of Hybridity: Postcolonial Interventions" in Monika Fludernik, ed., *Hybridity and Postcolonialism* (Tübingen: Stauffenburg-Verlag, 1998): 21.
16. Farrukh Dhondy, cited: 185.
17. Anthropo-poiesis, in Francesco Remotti's interpretation, takes into account the non-biological aspects of the human being and concentrates on the persistent cultural components. Processes of formation of the self, then, even in its unconscious forms, concern formative influence; such phenomena regard every society every any life phase of the individual. In particular, the young people are to experience anthopo-poietic practices: from infancy and childhood they evolve into early adulthood by developing their own vision of the world, but unlike what happened in ancient communities, where the whole metamorphosis was 'contained' within one single rite of passage, in modern societies the generational transformation covers an undefined time and includes different manifestations. See Francesco Remotti "Esigenze Antropo-poietiche giovanili e comunicazione interculturale" in the Proceedings of the Conference "Giovani e Intercultura," Turin, 20th September 2001, ed. Davide Rigallo and Anna Ferrero: 32-35.
18. Simon Gikandi, *Maps of Englishness. Writing the Identity in the Culture of Colonialism* (New York: Columbia University Press, 1996): 9.
19. Sangeeta Ray, "The Nation in Performance: Bhabha, Mukherjee and Kureishi," in Monika Fludernik, ed., cited: 232.
20. Homi Bhabha, "The Vernacular Cosmopolitans," cited: 139.
21. Bart Moore-Gilbert, cited: 112.

Little Indias in Britain: Meera Syal's Novels of Innocence and Experience

> And why, today, on the day that my life is to be wrung dry of all memory, why do such images steer strong in my consciousness, the child sits with her chin in her chest, submitting slowly to her strange fate, once you were wrenched from my womb, with less violence she thinks, against my will, my muscles tightened within me, and you were forced to flood your lungs with painful air, and hours from now you will descend into the sulphurous brine that is the air of my polluted home, perhaps like her mother, she will have to sit late into the dark with her, soothing her tired chest muscles with hot mustard oil, for as a child she had suffered form a weak chest.
>
> Sunetra Gupta, *Memories of Rain* (p. 163)

Meera Syal is a versatile artist who started her career by joining a theatre society when she was a young student, and continued by writing novels and scripts and acting in films and shows. Born in 1962, she was raised in Essington, a mining village in the West Midlands, after her parents from Bombay decided to settle in post-industrial Northern England. Before going to Manchester University, where she read English and Drama, she attended Queen Mary's High School in Walsall. During her higher education years, she came into contact with reciting and writing: she commenced then her prolific creative production. Indeed, she belongs to that circle of diasporic artists who move incessantly among different genres, from literature to cinema, from media to theatre. Such category is wide and includes Hanif Kureishi, Ayub Khan-Din, Farrukh Dhondy, Ruth Prawer Jhabvala, Firdaus Kanga amongst the others. Her two novels, *Anita and Me* (1996), set in Northern England and imbued

46). The author insists on the strident characterisation of Anita to the detriment of naïve Tracey and, in this way, significantly builds up a pole of attraction for displaced Meena, seduced by the girl that she conceives as a strong herald of Britishness.

The focal point in Syal's novel resides in the treatment of hybridity: whereas Bhabha views it as a privileged site of negotiation, a zone of in-betweenness that regulates the experience of the diaspora, Syal argues a different interpretation of such notion and warns about its confusing powers. Hybridity in its procedure of digesting cultural entities and neutralising peculiar differences erodes the inner space of the self-making and, in the case of a young girl like Meena, darkens the perceptive skills. The framework that results from this clash is partial and unstable and does not allow a full development of the character. Meena feels she cannot be neither a proper English nor an authentic Indian girl, and this climate of personal uncertainty, unlike Karim's manipulation of Britishness, expresses a psychological anxiety mixed with ethnic dislocation. Syal's style highlights a sympathetic gaze upon the derelict white community of northern shires and, in so doing, it differs from Rushdie's fiction, structured around a utopian or dystopian act of confrontation of cultures. Drawing on her own treasure of memories, the author creates a character that is a pure synecdoche of an entire community, sketched in the historical processes of mutation, namely the diasporic act of re-drawing the contours of British society.

To corroborate Meena's sense of displacement, the author moulds a colloquial, vernacular vocabulary: the young protagonist in her impetuous and sometimes clumsy attempt to imitate the British youth discards her little knowledge of Indian languages and practises a vivacious slang. Her mother, born in a small village close to Chandigarh in Punjab, uses her capacity of a teacher to berate her daughter and convince her to abandon impolite words and adopt correct English: "A 'piece' being a peculiar Tollington for sandwich which my mother had banned me from saying in the house. 'Just because the English can't speak English themselves, does not mean you have to talk like an urchin. You take the best from their culture, not the worst. You'll be swearing and urinating in telephone boxes next, like that Lowbridge boy'" (*AM*, 53). Positioned in the new social environment, Meena relies on the linguistic competence as a tactic to conceal her solitude in a web of gossips, small talks and chatting. As a matter of fact she strives to claim her entitlement to the multitude and anonymity of 'ordinary' English speakers and delete her detested label of Indian girl. In her stubbornness, she does not want to sound like her father, whose fluency of English is still blurred by Indian interferences: "He spoke in his characteristic blend of Punjabi and English, but enough for me to understand" (*AM*, 74).

Conversely, Meena prefers a Brummie accent to affirm her reimagined value of belonging. Furthermore her young age and unclear worldview affect and galvanise the linguistic frenzy that accompanies the first-person narration. David Lodge explains this device with the Russian term *skaz*, which describes the apparently inarticulate (but actually intelligently constructed by the author) teenage jargon of many novels of formation.[4] Meena defines her identity with reference to 'street credibility' inscribed into social hierarchies of gangs and groups: by imitating Anita, the 'other,' she designates the self. A sharp dialogic relationship thus links the two girls and dictates a system of attraction and repulsion. The writer eschews tones of morbidity and delicately paints a portrait of rough characters endowed with freshness and honesty. Compared with *The Buddha of Suburbia*, we can observe that this narrative strategy operates in a different manner: whereas the intense bond established between Karim and Charlie is ambiguous, sometimes even violent, and grounded on the notion of switching identities through devices like music and drugs, in Syal's case, the two girls project their feelings and aspirations on the semi-rural backdrop of a village and seek relief in the glossy pages of magazines and comics, and in the gossips about invented or real romances.

However, this fragile balance breaks when the Punjabi girl examines her tie with the English friend, who has also a racist behaviour, and finds her own doubts painted on the face of the other: "In fact, sometimes, when I looked into her eyes, all I could see and cling to was my own questioning reflection" (*AM*, 150). The lack of faith in the girl betrays a revisitation of Meena's plans to conquer Englishness and when she is excoriated by the different forms of racist intolerance, the protagonist, endowed with her limited tools of comprehension, has to face up to the operation of reciting roles and working out identities. The abrupt reaction towards migrants involves the sharp verbal abuse and physical assault. Two examples in particular show the deplorable semantic transformation, that modern sociolinguistics has defined as an ideological weapon to suffocate or marginalise the voices of Otherness, through the establishment of ethnic or social categories. For instance, Meena is appalled to learn that the name of the dog kept by the Rutters is "Nigger," a pejorative lexeme that evokes racist connotations. Another insult ("Bloody stupid wog. Stupid woggy wog. Stupid." [*AM*, 97]) comes unexpectedly from a quiet old English lady, almost a stereotype of kind manners, made aggressive by parochial bigotry. This scene occurs when Meena's mother is clumsily driving and provokes a long queue on a countryside road; the puzzled girl succumbs to the bitter offence, and the scene reminds one of the humiliating experiences that Salman Rushdie sketches in his "The Courter."[5] The brutal vulgarity of some suburban delinquents is close to the impoliteness shown by the old lady, and in both cases the devastating effect strikes adolescent innocence. In Syal's novel, the dramatic experience is further intensified when news about the aggression of an Asian person appears in the local paper and Meena has to reconsider her relationship with the white community because the accident "was too close to home, and for the first time, I wondered if Tollington would ever truly be home again" (*AM*, 275).

The writer's textual strategy alternates the genre of comedy with the dark mood of tragedy, for the novel is not immune from death, violence and betrayal and as a whole it sketches the difficult passage from innocence to experience. In its effort to argue the evolution of British society in the 1960s, it even hints at sad domestic episodes of actual missing of children in the Manchester area in that period. Such bittersweet technique of representation forges the double relation which joins and divides Anita and Meena, and mirrors the protagonist's crisis and quest for identity, in a perpetual nervous oscillation between Englishness and Indianness. In this manner, the narrative structure witnesses a dual act of bulimic assumption, or devouring, of English customs and slang expressions (Meena defines Anita as "my passport to acceptance" [*AM*, 148]) and anorexic refusal to conformity and compromises. Here Syal elaborates on a metaphorical and physiological imagery discriminating the individual body and the intercultural surroundings. As a matter of fact, the novel covers two years of Meena's puberty and highlights the maelstrom of physical and psychological fervour; it also depicts a mutable scenario, in which the notions of collective society and ethnic belonging are dismantled and re-constructed.

While Mr. Kumar points out a typical western misinterpretation of ethnic diversity ("You ask any men on the street to tell the difference between us and a Jamaican fellow, he will still see us as the same colour" [*AM*, 150]), the critical discourse upon the meaning of skin and body reveals plenty of applications. Postmodernism and (post)feminism have drawn attention to the centrality of the body and its representations through visual and verbal arts, and stressed the intimate connection with the construction of identity. The colour of the skin that preoccupies postcolonial literatures and their rewriting of canonical texts (let us think about the story of *Othello* reimagined by Caryl Phillips in *The Nature of Blood*, 1997) becomes a fundamental issue: it bears a pregnant element of personal identity and records an atavistic ascendance. Meera Syal's witty prose tackles the subject with cunning methods and abundant irony in the words of Meena so that when at school her teacher "Mr. Williams had asked where the moors came from [. . .] I had put up my hand

and answered confidently, 'Yorkshire, sir!'" (*AM*, 213). The confounding geography of otherness is here mocked by the author, who insists on the schematic constructedness of cultural identities and topographic clichés.

Within the discursive analysis of the body, skin works as an interface between the outsideness and the insideness, between the self and the other; thus it may be seen as a 'barrier' and a 'wrapping,' or a 'container.' Through skin, the body communicates with the surrounding atmosphere and at the same time it protects the individual from external infections. It also has the function of an inner thermometre, signalling health problems with dots or sheltering the body with specific secretions. Not only does it display the physical condition of the person, but it also exhibits feelings, emotions and thoughts for the individual can blush, become pale or knit the brows. Whether Meena feels the humiliation of the insult 'nigger,' a very offensive word that comes from the Latin root *niger*, she also finds it difficult to come to terms with her own body, given the meaningful interrelation between the physical aspect and the ethnic origin: "I always got told off, but I was beginning not to care. I knew I was a freak of some kind, too mouthy, clumsy and scabby to be a real Indian girl, too Indian to be a real Tollington wench, but living in the grey area between all categories felt by increasingly like home" (*AM*, 149-50). By constructing her idiosyncratic zone of in-betweenness, the opaque condition of difference that characterises the migrant's displacement, the girl's social management of the body affects the private and public spheres of perception. As the sociologists Sue Scott and David Morgan sustain, "there is, indeed, something fluid and indeterminate in the interplay between individual and societal representations and concerns with bodies."[6] Thus the question of the body which is central to the practice of everyday life should be addressed in terms of both individual bodies and collective identities, in a metonymic frame of picturing a more embodied society in its wholeness and fragmentariness as well.

Meena percolates into a state of halfway ethnic awareness and does not seem to fit in her body, which is perceived as an immutable hindrance that annihilates the cultural translation and communication between East and West. Here lies the seminal difference with Kureishi's *The Buddha of Suburbia*, a text in which the writing of the body is articulated by virtue of a metaphorical dismemberment, a splitting-up of images and costumes. For Karim, the glittering world of theatre unfolds a circus-like atmosphere, one in which the training of actors coincides with a transformation of the artistic and fictional body; through exercises, performances and miming, they can also alter their inner selves. In the case of Karim, we further observe a veiled trace of gender switching due to echoes of sexual promiscuity, flashy clothes and ambiguous gestures. The same could be applied, to a certain extent, to his brother Allie, whose fashion artistry turns him into an extravagant, modern dandy; as a matter of fact, his body transformation is rendered through the creation of clothes.[7] For Kureishi, the only exception in this cathartic treatment of bodies and identities regards the Bengali immigrant Changez: imprisoned in a deformed body and considered as a *ludus naturae* from the East, he cannot dismantle the worn but still solid stereotype of the needy migrant covered with rags[8] though, as the name symbolically suggests, he will eventually change in his effort to understand English lifestyle. The displacement of mundane and rough Changez, catapulted from the rural and 'underdeveloped' Indian context into the frenetic, metropolitan chaos of London, motivates the clash between nature and culture that sociologists tend to refer to as the representations of the grotesque and classical bodies. The novelist here introduces the radical potentiality of physical otherness and re-interprets the theory of powerful bodies in a sarcastic light because "the grotesque body represents the symbolic power of the natural, a capacity for violence and sheer physical dominance, highlighting the potential fragility of respectable society [and] in reversal of the conventional equation, it is a man's apparent unmediated links with nature, in all its earthiness and unpredictability, that provides the power of the grotesque body."[9] Therefore in his awkwardness, Changez undermines the site of construction of social bodies and corrodes rational constructs of respectability and order.

Meena's sense of inadequacy epitomises the corporeal aspect and originates from her broken identity, divided between the English social setting and the Indian family milieu. The body then, Syal seems to suggest, operates as a mirror that exposes personal experiences and psychological tensions. Meena denounces the nullifying prerogative of threatening hybridity not just in a visual performance, but also in the concreteness of the body of the migrant. For the juvenile protagonist, the act of watching her body changing physically and the awareness of undergoing a generational crisis bring her to a paradigmatic crossroads, which is a significant turning point in her life. Whereas Freud links the importance of the self with the material entity of the body, modern psychoanalysis, Jacques Lacan for instance, has sustained the primacy of the visual in the perception of the self and the making of identity through the act of vision.

However, tactility and the feeling of the body too manifest a conspicuous part of one's personal identity and biological evolution, or ageing, because of the somatic features, scars, wrinkles, tattoos or piercing. The investigation into the mysteries of the body also allows a reflection on the moral or linguistic ban pertaining to the erogenous areas. When Anita boldly inserts sexual references in her gross conversations, she pretends to be a mature young woman and, in this respect, becomes a model for malleable Meena. The Punjabi girl's crisis of identity coincides with a fastidious rejection of her body, a typical childish act which also displays a sense of unbelonging of the body, perceived as a rigid line of demarcation between genuine Indianness and captivating Englishness, which she fears she cannot cope with. Had she been a character of the 1990s, Meena might perhaps have turned to piercing and tattooing by using her skin as a site to construct or modify her alternative identity like a postmodern heroine. It would work as a kind of *tabula rasa*, the blank slate upon which the making of the ego gradually writes itself by virtue of epidermic variations and inscriptions. Nowadays psychoanalysts explore the dynamic status of the self and the constant endeavour of the individual to evolve into a different state, and such practice may also include earrings, cuts, piercing, lifting, tattoos, or other means of corporeal transformation. These indelible signs eventually influence the structure of identity and determine the return to the intimacy of the self.[10]

The question of the body is also tackled in Kureishi's *Intimacy*, albeit the perspective here is quite different: as the title suggests, it is a text that evokes confidential complicity and physical closeness. The novella was made into a film, also based on other stories like "Nightlight" and "Strangers when we meet," both collected in *Love in a Blue Time*. In the film, a persistent and morbid scrutiny of the body, exposed in a complete and shocking nakedness, works as a leitmotif and a catalysis. Hanif Kureishi and Patrice Chéreau, the French director, argued about the frayed storyline and its cinematic transformation. The film furthermore stresses the tactile image instead of the oral performance because the verbal communication is almost neglected and the two protagonists rely on touching and effusions rather than words and phrases. This leads to the metaphorical depreciation of the body on the one hand (in a certain time, during a war for instance, we may assume the body is slighted) and to the alternative function of sex as a partial system of communication:

> After the twentieth century it is, it seems, a culture of disgust and of shock that we inhabit, in which humans are reduced to zero, the achievements of culture rendered meaningless—a stance often called the human condition. Yet this kind of fastidious despair can become an aesthetic pose, creating its own cultural privileges and becoming a kind of vanity. [. . .] Patrice seemed interested in the power of impersonal sexuality, in passion without relationship, in the way people can be narcissistically fascinated by one another's bodies and their own sexual pleasure, while keeping away strong feeling and emotional complexity. (*DS*, 229)

This is the key for comprehending the film, Kureishi seems to suggest, whose scope and purpose are not to scandalise the prudish British audience but to detect the intricate web of human relations as well as the notion of the body and sex in contemporary society. Kureishi's pessimistic challenge, modulated through a voyeuristic intermission, concerns the obscure self-perception as the individual undergoes the inevitable process of ageing. Indeed, this is the central motif of his very recent novella "The Body" (2002), which from the very title ambivalently alternates the dark tones of a postmodern search for identity with the disturbing atmosphere of gothic literature. Grounded upon a highly suggestive intertextuality that pays an oblique homage to works as diverse as Wilde's *The Picture of Dorian Gray* and Mary Shelley's *Frankenstein*, or Dostoevsky's *The Double*, this novella however is shaped by modern and postmodern anxieties of the contemporary age and coldly depicts a conflict between concreteness and thought, between the idea of being and appearing. The protagonist, an elder writer and playwright symbolically bearing the name Adam, is given the chance to have his brain and mind transplanted into a new, young and handsome body. The absurd proposal, which seems to have been borrowed from a science fiction romance, turns the protagonist into a wandering Dorian Gray. However, it is not just the wish for eternal youth that motivates Adam to opt for this miraculous operation, but rather the possibility of experimenting an alternative existence and scanning the meaningful interstices of life.

In the aseptic atmosphere of the mysterious hospital, where a sort of Orwell's Newspeak provides a classification of "Newbodies" and "Oldbodies," Adam faces up to the doctor, a futurist wizard who deals with both organic material and mental essence. Their encounter, confronting the positions of the intellectual and the scientist, is worth citing at full length:

> 'Words are your living' he said. 'Bodies are mine. But I would imagine so.'

> 'The existence of Newbodies, as you call them, will create considerable confusion, won't it? How will we know who is new and who old?'
>
> 'The thinking in this area is yet to be done,' he said. 'Just as there has been argument over abortion, genetic engineering, cloning and organ transplants, or any other medical advances, so there will be over this.'
>
> 'Surely this is of a different order,' I said. 'Parents the same age as their children, or even younger, for instance. What will that mean?'
>
> 'That is for the philosophers, priests, poets and television pundits to say. My work is only to extend life.' (*BSS*, 22)

The surgeon's explanation dilates the narrative scope and conveys a philosophical enquiry, one in which postmodernity highlights the centrality of the body, imagined through discursive practices and visual or textual performances. As the new Millennium age brings the double technique of staging the body, in a bulimic assimilation, 'devouring' images and simulacra on the one hand, and anorexic refusal to conformity, as generational conflicts and crumbling traditions show, on the other, the body affirms anew its pivotal role in current thinking and perception.

By becoming a metaphor imbued with Faustus-like echoes, the body is coldly reformulated by the author as a commodity that may be sold or bought, an object or simulacrum that testifies to the disruption of the individual, lost in an existential void. By way of parallelism, we consider the monster of Frankenstein, who is also a chimera, a fictional 'object' and, to misquote the French philosopher Jean-Jacques Lecercle,[11] the body of the monster gives voice to the others and illuminates their discursive contradictions. The body in Kureishi's story and the monster in Shelley's text bind together the different frayed narrative levels; and they serve as a site of cathartic transformations. It is an organic metaphor which requires a new taxonomy in order to describe both the components of the body and the textual structures.

Under the guise of a fantastic tale, Kureishi seems to hold that the complementarities between body and mind are overwhelmed by the postmodern disintegration. Representing or manifesting the body becomes an ambivalent act that oscillates between the social situations that require and legitimate the body or neglect the bodily exploitation. This is due to several causes and in a sociological interpretation, "the ambiguities in this area reflect the complexities of a modern society, the multiplicities of overlapping reference groups or fields of meaning and the struggles and negotiations around the legitimacy or otherwise of different forms of embodied activities."[12]

To return to Syal's writing, Meena's intolerance with her own Indian body has to undergo a cultural mediation when she is pungently confronted with her own people, the other Punjabi immigrants. While arguing with Sam Lowbridge, the local, handsome braggart,[13] who also embodies a skinhead turbulence matched with a confused, juvenile point of view, Meena strives to erase the concept of difference by admitting the ethnic awareness behind the migrant condition, and her inclusion in such category. After watching him causing a riot at the circus, she understands he is guilty of the assault on the miserable Indian victim previously reported in the paper and her anger explodes:

> For all his bluster, I had the feeling that Sam was truly nothing more than a puppet and the knowledge that he would never have the character to cut the wires made me furious, for the waste, for his cowardice, for both of us.
>
> 'Those things you said at the spring fete, what were you trying to do?' I tasted grit, maybe I had ground my molars into dust.
>
> Sam shrugged and dragged his heel along a muddy edge. 'I wanted to make people listen.' He said finally.
>
> 'You wanted to hurt people, you mean!' I yelled at him. 'How could you say it, in front of me? My dad? To anyone? How can you believe that shit?'
>
> Sam grabbed me by the wrists and I sucked in the air and held it. 'When I said them,' he rasped, 'I never meant you, Meena! It was all the others, not yow!' I put my face right up to his; I could smell the smoke on his breath. 'You mean the others like the Bank

> Manager?' Sam looked confused. 'The man from the building site. The Indian man. I know you did it. I am the *others*, Sam. You did mean me.' (*AM*, 313-14. Author's emphasis)

In the novel, the dramatic encounter between the two is problematic for a number of reasons: on the one hand, it fractures the monolithic conception of white racism by presenting the uncertain character of Sam, who indolently proves to be a violent extremist and cannot probably motivate his deplorable actions; on the other, it endorses Meena's recognition of her own community. The protagonist's limited idea of hybridity tends to bisect the world into the distinguished realms of Englishness and Indianness and therefore the girl experiences the collision with an alienating context: "The song made me realise that there was a corner of me that would be forever not England" (*AM*, 112).

Two thematic elements restore Meena's desire to see India and to become integrated within the Punjabi community: the traditional court of aunties and uncles that enlarge Indian families and the arrival of Nanima, the maternal grandmother who performs a portrait of Mother India. Under the influences of these devices, Syal awards Meena a gradual process of formation and maturity, a feeling of awareness while it is possible to view an autobiographical frame that illustrates the prejudices of Britain and its rejection of immigrants from former colonies. The writer, in an interview given to the BBC, admitted that the novel incorporates some echoes of her childhood: this combination of narrative fiction and memories works because "the emotional landscape is very much how I felt growing up, being the only Asian family in such a tiny miming environment."[14] In the end Meena achieves a stronger self-confidence and overthrows her own fears and clichés.[15]

It is worth noticing the controversial role assumed by 'aunties' in Indian culture; in their profound marginality, they tumultuously extend the domestic space of the Hindu family and constitute a symphonic texture of intertwined traditions and family ramifications. Syal treats the figure of the auntie with a generous injection of irony and demolishes the grave image to paint a caricature, a light-hearted personage. To justify her choice, she even states that the "pleasure of writing as an Asian woman is the pleasure of exploding stereotypes."[16] As a matter of fact, being linked to time-honoured social and religious conventions, aunties "are distanced voices of exile, women who are 'partioned' within the crowded *oikumene* constituted by the traditional household of the Hindus [and] their inferior position reflects a hierarchical division or separation of the domestic space."[17] Many diasporic or Indian novels in English are devoted to the feminine issue of aunties, often associated with a shadowed state of widowhood (which in Hindu culture represents a polluting and burdensome condition), but here the case is different. Contravening the custom of encircling aunties within the restricted space of the *zenana*, a sort of gynaecium in the Hindu home, place exclusively dedicated to women, the author frees them from such segregating claustrophobia to revive the hybrid scenario and to assemble a crowded family reunion:

> The Aunties all had their individual names and distinct personalities, but fell into the role of Greek chorus to mama's epic solo role in my life. Although none of them, nor their husbands, the uncles, were actually related to me by blood, Auntie and Uncle were the natural respectful terms given to them, to any Asian person old enough to boss me around. This was an endless source of confusion to our English neighbours, who would watch tight-lipped as mama and papa's friends would phut-phut into the communal dirt yard and heave themselves and their several kids out of their hatchbacks, unfurling shimmering saris and clicking with jewellery, holding up their embroidered hemlines from the dirt floor. As I dutifully kissed every powdered or stubbly cheek with a 'Namaste Auntie, Namaste Uncle' and led them towards our back door, I could see our neighbours shift uncomfortably, contemplating the apparent size of my family and the fact we had somehow managed to bring every one of them over here. I once tried to explain to our next door neighbour, Mrs. Worrall, why my parents seemed to have so many siblings. 'It's just being polite, you see.' I said. 'Like saying sir or madam, to call them Auntie or Uncle. 'Cos we have different words for

> proper relatives, like my dad's younger brother is called a *Chacha*, his elder brother is called a *Taya*. But me mom's sister is called a *Masee*, and my dad's sister a *Buaji*. . . . So you know the difference between pretended ones and real ones." (*AM*, 29-30)

In their anarchic exorbitance, aunties and partially uncles remind Meena of her indissoluble cultural background and stimulate her apparently mild interest in India. The above-quoted humorous presentation also deals with introductory intercultural education and interferes with the rigidity of social conventions of the English white population. As the young protagonist explains, the epithets of 'auntie' or 'uncle' function as polite forms of address, for they may also indicate people or acquaintances who are not "blood relatives but connected by something deeper, India."[18] Illustrated like characters taken from popular comics, aunties actually prove to be holders of traditions and memories and this aspect fascinates Meena and influences her progress.

The strategic roles of aunties as intermediaries within family disputes and community conflicts is reiterated in Syal's second novel *Life Isn't All Ha Ha Hee Hee*, which is grounded on a fragmented and more complex structure. Here we encounter the same sarcastic representation of aunties as spry and messy women of modern times. Sunita, for instance, describes the legion of her aunties and uncles in an affectionate manner:

> There are too many aunties and uncles to remember their names, so I gave them my own titles, based on their most memorable characteristics. There were the obvious ones like Ginger Auntie (over fond of the henna bottle), Car Keys Uncle (hands for ever in his pockets jingling things, at least I hoped they were his keys), Halitosis Uncle (no explanation needed), My Bobby Auntie (never stopped boasting about her fat son who, incidentally, ended up serving time for fraud) and my personal favourite, Existential Uncle, a tall thin man who never spoke when spoken to, but would occasionally interrupt other's conversation without warning, with loud comments such as 'Why it is, huh?' or 'They spoil everything, bastards!' I finally settled on Modern Auntie as my confidante. It almost felt wrong to bestow the auntie label on her as she was

> nothing like the overweight fussy women who seemed to live at my house at weekends. Modern Auntie was beautiful, really beautiful, with sharp aquiline features and sleek black hair like a Mughal miniature, except her hair was cut short in a fashionable bob. And she wore make-up. But not the usual auntie warpaint of bright orange lipstick (much of it on the front teeth) and alarming smears of eyeshadow. She used it to give her face shadows and contours. (*LAH*, 79-80)

Both Meena and Sunita, albeit the blatant difference of age (Sunita is a depressed woman in her thirties) recognise the need to cling to tradition and family union, which in the case of Indian culture translates an extended family tree. The vivacious style that they employ to picture aunties and uncles mirrors a humorous modernity that replaces the strict notion of *purdah*, the segregating division of women from men, with urban cheerfulness: in the social architecture of diasporic writing, Syal testifies to the partial secularisation of Indian membership and revisitation of religious zeal.

Sunita's amusing account of her relatives obliquely subverts social manners and family customs and is further reinforced by the actual nickname that Modern Auntie is given by her own community: Divorced Auntie, a title which clearly has a shocking effect. Sunita herself views the label as a menace, a shameful stain that may corrupt the purity of tradition: "Divorce was one of the English diseases my mum was afraid we would catch if we hung around Willis' Fish Bar too much, along with short skirts, bad skin and bland food. I had only seen Asian divorces in the Hindi films we would watch around Gadget Uncle's house, the one person we knew who owned a video recorder" (*LAH*, 81). Her naïve perception of reality has to refer to kitsch Bollywood productions to figure the loathsome practice of divorce, interpreted by the Indians as another polluting threat of the West.

In Syal's fiction, the rehearsal of the female body does not solely replicate a discursive analysis *à la* Simone de Beauvoir, one in which the biological condition and the constructed image of womanhood coincide. Rather the Indian author foregrounds the narrative bodily elaboration, with all its implications concerning skin colour as a divide that cannot be violated. Paradoxically the body of the Indian woman is shown by the segregating norm of the *purdah* because "in Indian society, the normative thrust has increasingly been towards the concealment of the female body,"[19] and this marks the migrant's process of self-perception in the new location. While the novelist clearly condemns and parodically challenges the female marginalisation of the East, a textual parallelism complies the bodily representation of both Asian and English female protagonists inasmuch as Meena and Anita pursue a bespangled appearance. The ironic and subversive interpretation of the body is also present in those films that tackle ethnic issues, like *East is East*, and invests the physicality of English girls too. Defined by their harsh manners, strong make-up and provocative clothes, they join Indian girls in a fierce competition for identities.

Meena, after brooding over her tormented life, feels a strong desire to re-appropriate the so far avoided cultural heritage she has always questioned; she now even plans to fly to the subcontinent as if she would be entitled to obtain a moral refund for the unjust abuses caused by the English. The destiny of the girl is evocative of second generation immigrants who have to cope with their displacement. Unconsciously she rejects and at the same time is mesmerised by Punjabi and such linguistic tension incorporates the wandering of the postcolonial and diasporic individual, endowed with a diaglossic tool of communication:

> It felt so strange to hear Punjabi under the stars. It was an indoor language to me, an almost guilty secret which the Elders would only share away from prying English eyes and ears. On the street, in shops, on buses, in parks, I noticed how the volume would go up, when they spoke English, telling us kids to not wander off, asking the price of something; and yet when they wanted to say something intimate, personal, about feelings opposed acquisitions, they switched to Punjabi and the volume became a conspiratorial whisper. [. . .] I stood uncertainly on the front porch and watched helplessly as the Aunties and Uncles began reclaiming the

> Tollington night in big Indian portions, guffawing Punjabi over fences and hedges, wafting curried vegetable smells through tight-mouthed letterboxes, sprinkling notes from old Hindi film songs over jagged rooftops, challenging the single street light on the crossroads with their twinkling jewels and brazen silks. (*AM*, 203-4)

The disturbing presence of more languages at work, which is a typical characteristic of postcolonial literatures,[20] also challenges Meena's assumption of the language: in her pendulum-like movement, the young protagonist understands she has to head for a new perception of the self, beyond ethnicity and stereotypes. The optimistic end of the novel reminds one of the epilogue of *The Buddha of Suburbia* because both Meena and Karim have dismantled the clichés of alluring Englishness and indelible Indianness and inaugurated a new way of interpreting and living the diasporic difference and contemporary hybridity.

Apart from such linguistic outburst, also food is a significant sign of culture and it is dramatised within the textual interstices, following a similar technique exploited by Rushdie, to evoke memory and construct a treasure of references that bridges individuals across time and space. In their fragrance, boiling curries and crispy samosas become narrative ingredients that Syal uses not only to reveal the mundane aspect of a migrant family, but also to allude to the cultural heritage of the immigrants, who uphold traditions and in thus doing construe a collective identity:

> My mother would right now be standing in a haze of spicy steam, crowded by huge babbling saucepans where onions and tomatoes simmered and spat, molehills of chopped vegetables and fresh herbs jostling for space with bitter, bright heaps of turmeric, masala, cumin and coarse black pepper whilst a softly breathing mound of dough would be waiting in a china bowl, ready to be divided and flattened into round, grainy chapatti. And she, sweaty and absorbed, would move from one chaotic work surface to another, preparing the fresh home-made meal that my father expected, needed like air, after a day at the office about which he never talked. [. . .] This food was not just something to fill a hole, it

> was soul food, it was the food their far-away mothers made and came seasoned with memory and longing, this was the nearest they would get for many years, to home. (*AM*, 61)

The dense expression "soul food" is particularly meaningful and may even refer to the sphere of Hinduism and the religious lore in its prescriptive norms of dealing with food in the contexts of both common life and specific rites. Before Meena's eyes, the role of the female cook is given a magical aura and a connection with a remote past. Similar to the archetype of Great Goddesses, the Indian woman churns delicacies that have the power to call into mind an entire world pictured in its social stratifications. The passage should not be read solely as a 'textual gastronomic bazaar,' a miscellany of exotic recipes and ingredients, because in a Rushdinian style Syal underscores the 'mnemonic function' of food as a strategy to revitalise the remembrance of homeland through the earthly rite of cooking and serving food. It is a discriminating procedure that separates the Indian world from the English context: we should not forget that Sunita's mother, as I have previously quoted from *Life Isn't All Ha Ha Hee Hee*, considers "bland food," a label which idiosyncratically indicates tasteless western dishes, as blameworthy as "divorce, short skirts and bad skins," namely what she terms as "English diseases."

The dietary practices of Meena's parents sustain a pragmatic effort to maintain their identity and in this fashion they permute the miniature village of Tollington with distant rural Punjab. However food is also viewed as a generational hindrance because Meena in her 'anglicising' campaign avoids traditional dal soup, pakoras and paneer: "'I don't want that . . . that stuff! I want fishfingers! Fried! And chips! Why can't I eat what I want to eat?'" (*AM*, 60). We can observe this aspect of her rebellious character as an act of digesting cultural components of English lifestyle, rather than childish tantrum. Again, we have an instance of the girl's twofold tactic of bulimic resistance, which is the refusal of Indian food, and anorexic assimilation, exemplified in the typical English dishes, to escape from the domestic prison-shelter, made up by magazines, toys, books and fantasy.

Whether food and the other cultural procedures such as those viewed previously are dividing structures that in the narrative construct a polarised dichotomy representing India and England, Syal calls into question such strict social norms and codes of behaviour: in fact, her fiction is grounded "on a mixture of debunking myths and poking fun at Indian traditions."[21] With her novels, Syal's style shifts from the world of innocence textualised by the complex character of Meena to that of experience, pictured by adults and their entangled lives. Obviously this is a general consideration because in the two texts the narrative confines are often blurred. *Life Isn't All Ha Ha Hee Hee* maintains a subversive re-interpretation of the Asian community in London and breaks the plot into a series of episodic events, in a modernist fashion. The text alternates an omniscient narrator with a first-person account of the intersecting stories revolving around three Indian women: Sunita, Tania and Chila. Their close friendship constitutes an atypical sisterhood characterised by the ethnic sense of belonging. Indeed the female viewpoint dominates the novel and Meera Syal employs it as a tool to dismantle fixed clichés or collective stereotypes regarding both the Indian and English communities whereas the male characters play a minor role or are put in a subaltern position.

Set in contemporary London, in the East End's shelter for migrants, the three protagonists contribute to a manifold representation of Punjabi womanhood collocated in a diasporic context. Each of them shows individual features and has to survive through peculiar circumstances: Sunita embodies the sad and bored housewife, Tania tries to achieve a high rank in the world of media and Chila performs the timid and naïve bride, predicated by the notion of having a proper Indian marriage. The author cannot completely be identified in any of them, but it is evident that, subtly, autobiography is again amalgamated with fiction.

In spite of its quality of weightlessness, a term judged positively by Rushdie himself, the texture is rooted into the diasporic consciousness that meticulously discriminates and simultaneously, by virtue of hybridity, blends together two opposite cultural modes. Tania, Chila and Sunita have to compromise their Indian background with modern English lifestyle. It is a curious, multifaceted and sometimes even amusing process as Tania holds that "behaving like a Brit is so dependant on the weather" (*LAH*, 53), a quotation that seems to have been borrowed from a known passage by Homi Bhabha. Meera Syal is familiar with diverse genres, from literature to cinema but her narrative manoeuvre may be justified by the fact that "the migrant novel itself draws attention to the regenerative experience of straddling worlds [and being] grown fat on their different cultural riches, it brings into prominence the translations and migrations of which it is itself a product."[22] The three women testify to the inner conflicts that disturb the Asian community and their perception of the female condition with its dense bonds.

Tania is a dynamic character who works as a video maker and fights for her career in the world of media. Supported by those "magazines or papers that claim I am now officially the voice of Brit-Asian Yoof" (*LAH*, 316), she is a modern, nonconformist and emancipated witness of the migrant community. We should, however, analyse her behaviour vis-à-vis her English boyfriend, Martin. The two make up an unusual couple, symbolised by two antithetical poles. The girl seems to deny her ethnic belonging and neglects her connection with the tradition, whereas the boy profoundly longs for a sense of the East:

> It was true, there was a part of Tania he would always find fascinatingly alien, and he did not know if that was a racial or a female thing. It was not, as people often asked, anything to do with her family, she rarely saw them and talked about them even less. It was not ostensibly a cultural barrier: she understood basic Punjabi but didn't speak it; Martin had been to India and she hadn't; it was Martin who brought home the latest fusions CDs and had to prise her away form Frank Sinatra to listen to them; it was him who

> brought home fireworks for Diwali or booked tickets for a Dussehra festival, and her had always refused to join in. 'Ghetto groupie' she had called him, only half joking. Although nowadays, fashion victim would have been a more accurate term, as brown was indeed the new black, in couture, in music, in design, on the high street, judging by the number of plump white girls prancing around wearing bindis on their heads and henna on their hands. (*LAH*, 108-9)

They both overthrow their identities in a reversal of roles substantiated by a postcolonial contamination. The citation depicts a contradictory social scenario, one in which the cross-cultural pollination bears a re-visitation of values and symbols. Whether the personage of Martin is built as a type of Tania's alter ego, their relationship synthesises the hybrid urban context of the metropolis re-forged by the migrant contact. The constant reference to music, for instance, framed by ethnic vibrancy, elevates another form of culture extensively practised by diasporic individuals. This is linked to the artistic and literary phenomenon called Black Performance poetry, one in which music serves as an instrument to give prominence to identity and difference.

Such acts of cutting cultural gestures and recomposing a mixed intra-ethnic collage, which the novel hints at, should be deconstructed as a strategy of resistance against globalising hegemony. Syal's migrant characters are fond of music because the author conceives it as a linking device between East and West: Chila and her husband Deepak, for example, appreciate a particular kind of music called 'Asian fusion' for "it resembled a collision between an Indian film from the early Seventies and Salvador Dali on his day off" (*LAH*, 58). The peculiar intermix metaphorically sustains again the migrant's metamorphosis in the new urban milieu.

Syal's heroines display an energised reaction towards gender discrimination that stems from traditional Indian lore. However it is worth noting that her operation goes beyond a feminist prototype, or a postmodern updating: while the Indian 'mother' culture is well rooted in space and time and bans the intercultural agency of crossover, the condition of the urbanised exile becomes impermeable and paradoxically problematic. Given this premise, the social and novelistic picturing of women acquires in the East a very different value from the one sustained in the West. Therefore the role of the woman has to conform to prescriptive norms and in this respect the author moulds her fiction in a feminine perspective so as to dispute social constraints. The Indian critic Vrinda Nabar states: "the secretive manner in which all aspects relating to female sexuality are glossed over in India should make it apparent why some of the obsessions of western feminist would not apply to our situation."[23] Within the diasporic context, the novelist has to balance English modernity, adopted by her protagonists, and the Indian concept of belonging.

Chila, who is described by her relatives in terms of naivety and marginality, occupies the weakest position in Syal's trinity and is subjugated by parochial customs; the practice of arranged marriages as a mechanism to protect the Asian community and keep the purity of families forces her into an opaque, silent life, loaded with drudgery and surrogated amenities provided by the opulent West. In her idiosyncratic stream of consciousness, Tania comments on the destiny of her friend and illustrates a typical pattern of postcolonial literature by female writers:

> Chila didn't have much choice. Coming from the most traditional family and obviously not college material, they were lining up boys for her before she left school. Ironic, really, that the girl who most wanted to Do the Right Thing was considered defective material. Her parents assaulted the marriage markets on all fronts: the matrimonial bureaux where they find a perfect match by matching up your heights and income brackets, the notice boards in the temples and community centres where your personal details are displayed along with the times for yoga classes and the winner of the under sevens trampolining competition, and, of course, the gossip grapevine. [. . .] I don't know how Chila kept her dignity, I hated her fucking family for what they were offering her, hated the other bastards for what they thought she was worth. And the amazing thing was, under all that pressure, Chila always said no. She would

> wait, she said. I don't know for what, we all thought. (*LAH*, 148-49)

By organising her marriage and arranging all the details of her own life, Chila's parents uphold a prescriptive oral law and contrast the frenetic instability of second generation migrants and their propensity to iron out the ethnic difference: they draw a divide that fractions the mirage of multiculturalism. Tania assesses the gesture in a bitter way and denounces the truncated identity of the girl, sacrificed to the perpetuations of an antiquated law. Chila in the end marries Deepak, albeit the parents of the man do not agree with this decision, and by doing thus she performs the 'ideal' role of the Punjabi girl, guided and protected within the patriarchal family system. The narration encircled with single episodes does not follow a linear order but rather amalgamates memories, gossips and events by offering a tripartite viewpoint. Chila's uneasy pregnancy further accomplishes the status of imposed 'tamed domesticity' and calibrates the paradoxical condition of Indian womanhood, one in which maternity is regarded as a feature of prestige and yet does not allow to achieve a higher social position. In this respect, Tania embodies the opposite alter ego of Chila for she does not want to have children and affirms obstinately her resourcefulness, being a "media wallah on the make."[24]

Nonetheless, her refusal of rules and labels renders her an indecipherable character, oscillating in a borderline definition: she is neither Indian nor English. This is mirrored in the linguistic dimension too, which works as a barrier, a Babel-generated discrimination that amplifies the ambiguous relation of East and West, of Tania and Martin:

> Of course, he could identify spoken Punjabi, but he somewhat never associated it with Tania. [. . .] Martin was struck by the intimacy that a shared language could evoke, and how his writer's ear heard different tunes in each one. French always sounded dirty and indolent, provocative pillow chat, even if a couple happened to be arguing over who last unloaded the dishwasher. Spanish was pas-

> sionate and slightly amused, as if the speaker knew it was obligatory to lose their temper about something inappropriate before the end of the sentence, and then forget about it two sentences later. Russian depressed him, in the way a good vodka hangover did, and Mandarin was noble and slightly condescending. He had heard Malayalam once, in a south Indian vegetarian restaurant, he chose it as his favourite so far, as the babbles and rolling tongue plosives sounded like a large man farting in the bath. But Punjabi, he decided, he hated. It was crude, soil-bound, back-slapping macho sounding, no spaces to listen as Tania and the Bloke seemed to constantly talk over each other. (*LAH*, 126-27)

In this cacophonic representation, Syal stresses the unconventionality of the girl and jeeringly portrays a character who may stand as a muse for a modern artist (a student of history of art once defined her body as a 'Picasso,' during her sleep, and a 'Modigliani,' when she was awake) in search for originality. Her verve, however, is bound to affect and later break the balance of the sisterhood, when she shares a licentious adventure with Deepak, and sanctions the fading of the female bond.

The author does not bring forth a univocal accusation against her because she ambitiously tries to picture the human and psychological diversity by widening the scope of her prose. Thus the ethnic element is not overvalued: "The book is not just about one community, to me it is about relationships and they just so happen to be Asian."[25] The miscellany of characters finds a metaphor about the difficulties of mundane life in the title of the novel, which is actually a phrase said firstly by Mr. Kumar in *Anita and Me* and in thus doing, the reiterated formula seals a link between childhood and adulthood. With the personage of Sunita, Meera Syal proposes another type of Indian woman and speculates afresh on the idea of marriage. To scan her convulse existence, we have to turn to Tania's words when, in one of her dramatic monologues, she presents her friend:

> For Sunita, it was different. Her parents were considered the coolest around. Yeah, her brothers got away with murder, but her mum

> and dad always insisted she should get her education and then think about marriage if she wanted. They offered to do some introductions, and even said if she found someone herself, they wouldn't mind (unless he was a black Muslim with no job, in which case they would kill her). The subtext was, choose anyone you like, preferably a Hindu Punjabi with prospects. . . . I would love to have interview her folk for the doc. Her dad insisted they call it 'Assisted marriage, no arranging in this house. We help, we advise and we leave it to her. Just like your upper classes, although I would never have put Diana and Charles together. Whoever matched them needs a good slap.' (*LAH*, 149)

This may sound like the description of a modern, progressive Asian family with an open-minded perspective, but in spite of the ironic colour and provocative note of banning Muslims, it actually alludes to a compromise between the ancient law and the secularised environment. Further sarcasm emerges from the unusual label, "assisted marriage," which may probably be read as a hypocritical tag for concealing the real intention of the family to preserve the daughter's decency. The text is adorned by puns and the author's jesting attitude cuts the otherwise claustrophobic domestic setting, regulated by severe codes and hierarchies.

Sunita cannot perhaps be compared with vivacious Tania and yet displays a mild degree of emancipation, though she is obviously not allowed to revolutionise her life, constantly safeguarded by her close community. She then becomes a mother and her children, Sunil and Nikita, reflect the controversial interpolation of prestige and liminality that is usually grafted onto the notion of maternity in Indian culture[26]: on the one hand, the woman is praised as a giver of life and thus connected with ancestral rites and mythical figures, on the other, her duties are doubled and now include looking after their children. The woman is compelled to perform her twin role egregiously and in the end she succumbs to the prospective of a numb position within family life. Yet in Syal's writing, such topics are mocked, so that Sunita's husband, the therapist Akash, turns out to be a captivating caricature of manhood, and due to his passion for alternative medicine and eastern religions, he partially acquires some of the typical traits of Haroon, Karim's father, a debonair exploiter of the absurd western construction of the Orient: "And there he was. The best of East and West in one perfectly formed package and I knew how lucky I was to have found him before anyone else" (*LAH*, 89).

The story of Sunita transmitted as an intricate gaze into the past betrays a silent tension which infringes a fixed formality. It derives from her own family context because her mother as well had to endure the burdensome, subaltern condition of the *zenana* that regulated her life and limited her identity:

> My mum has always had this weird habit, she has never called my father by his real name (in fact, for years I thought his full name was Darling Sharma), preferring endearments such as jaan and ji and sometimes, when she was feeling fruity, husband-sahib. During my rebellious phase, when I was monitoring how many times my dad and brothers left my mother alone in the kitchen while they stared at the TV, I challenged her about this. (*LAH*, 234)

Sarcastically this passage revisits the numerous polite forms of address of the eastern tradition and suggests, in a bittersweet overtone, the harsh condition experienced by women within immigrant family life. The way Sunita delineates her background does not constitute solely a reaction against the inviolability of traditions: her significance has to be confronted with the personal experience of both Tania and Chila. Again Syal tends to deepen her psychological analysis of characters by taking an autobiographical turn. Bearing in mind her progressive family, she ponders the social factor too: "I think most of the families I knew were like mine. [. . .] it has a lot to do with the sort of life they led in India. It is not really a race issue, it is a class issue. I found it strange to hear about these families who treat their women in such a dogmatic way, and it is always the bad cases that get the most publicity."[27] Thus her criticism of patriarchal rules and woman discrimination, dramatised by updated urban images of *purdah* in liberal London, oscillates between actual examples, hidden behind the respectability of Asian families, and the equally disturbing diffusion of British stereotypes, often emphasised by the media. In the end, the three protagonists cast doubts on the integral and sound image of Punjabi women in modern West: they disrupt clichés and draw a self-parody that is close to the style Syal adapts in other works like the TV comedy show *Goodness Gracious Me*, produced for the BBC.

The two novels show how this fiction is deeply rooted in contemporary reality and provides a testimonial of the life of immigrants in Britain through time and space, from 1960s Tollington to the chaotic London of the 1990s. Many of the themes dealt with in literature are also observed and examined in the social and educational sectors. Nadya Kassam, for instance, a Kutchi/Gujarati woman born and raised in Tanzania, accepted to coordinate a project involving manuscripts by young Asian women in the UK. The collection was later published by The Women's Press under the title *Telling It Like It Is.*[28] Being active in a Black women's newspaper and in an Asian women's support group, she collaborated with and stimulated schools, refuges, writing workshops, youth groups and community centres. The issues that emerge from the various contributions cover a wide thematic area and the correlation between this piece of non-fiction and Syal's narrative unearths the paradigmatic space of diaspora, one that creates meanings in the global redrawing of confines and cultures. Both Syal's characters and the contributors of Kassam's project subvert the imposition of a ghetto order and empower the marginal areas of society. As Bhabha holds, "it is in the emergence of the interstices—the overlap and displacement of domains of difference—that the intersubjective and collective experiences of *nationness*, community interest or cultural value are negotiated."[29] Indeed such crevices of memory may be seen as momentous epiphanies of the radical displacement experienced by the exile.

The papers collected by Kassam[30] in their unsophisticated freshness are aimed at a salutary exercise of recording reality and unburdening social anxieties. They constitute the creative literary workshop of a community in its intricate process of overflowing cultural borders. Let us compare, for example, how the festival of Diwali[31] is dealt with in non-fiction and fiction. In Kassam's book, the theme is exploited by a Hindu girl named Harsha, whose parents and brothers were born in Tanzania and Kenya. The connection with Asia or Africa does not seem to disturb the girl's consciousness because she relies, a bit optimistically maybe, on London as an intercultural setting ("I was born here, in London and have grown up in this country, surrounded by all religions and cultures"[32]). Harsha and her literary counterpart Meena have to find a corresponding event of western culture to explain the importance of Diwali. Harsha's report, almost similar to a naïve documentary, reads:

> Everyone has time off work or school to celebrate Christmas, but for Diwali, which is our New Year, we have to book our leave in advance and sometimes, when this gets difficult, you don't enjoy yourself as much. In India, people have time off for Diwali and can celebrate it properly. They get holiday time for it, just like Christmas holidays in Britain. [. . .] Diwali is enjoyable here, but in India, people can dance in the street because the climate is better. In London this can happen in certain areas, but you have to get up really early in order to miss the traffic! Diwali is a time to dress up, get together with your family, make special foods and generally party, but you still have to worry about waking up early the next day so you can go to work or school.[33]

Syal's heroine too laments the scarce visibility of Diwali, languished by hostility and ignorance and made into an alien rite that has to be compared to or maybe even assimilated by the main Christian holiday, namely Christmas:

> Mama had been cooking and cleaning for weeks it seemed because today was Diwali—'Our Christmas, Mrs. Worrall,' mama had told her, not wanting to go into huge detail about the Hindu Festival of Light and why the date changed each year, being a lunar festival, and how we did not give presents but put on all the lights in the house and gambled instead to welcome the goddess Lakshmi into

> our lives, hoping she would bring luck and wealth with her. Christmas was not the best comparison to use in front of me because I naturally expected a carload of presents and the generally festive communal atmosphere that overtook the village somewhere around late November and continued into January. But no one else in the world seemed to care that today was our Christmas. There was no holiday, except it happened to be a weekend. (*AM*, 91-92)

The two passages convey an identical interpretation of the ancient festival, one that is a notable component of the lore of Indian Hindu migrants, and its adaptation in England. The meaning of keeping the community's habits and religious functions implies setting the focus on the contours of ethnic identity. Yet we should regard it as the hybrid reconstruction of pregnant sites of postcolonial modernity, a definition that only apparently may sound like a sort of curious oxymoron. Celebrating Diwali in the West is a means to maintain the relation with India and at the same time serves as an agency of transformation: it is how 'newness' enters Britain, to paraphrase Rushdie and Bhabha. Meera Syal's technique consists of elaborating on personal memories and drawing events from the media: by textualising some traits of actuality she sanctions her light-hearted, self-ironic and sincere commitment to the migrant question.

NOTES

1. The author substitutes her own name, which indicates the ocean or the sea, with a name that was once popular in Scotland, as the familiar form of Wilhelmina. Compare Maneka Gandhi, cited: 246, and Iseabail Macloed and Terry Freedman, *Dictionary of First Names* (Ware: Wordsworth Editions, 1995): 159.
2. *Anita and Me* (GB, 2003), Portman Film, The Film Council and BBC Films. Screenplay by Meera Syal, director of photography Cinders Forshaw. The film's cast includes Meera Syal herself and other famous British-Indian actors, well-known to the British audience like Sanjeev Bhaskar, who was the presenter of *The Kumars at No. 42*, a BBC entertainment show. Here the family name is an

indicator of Indianness and comes from the TV series *Goodness Gracious Me*; Syal plays the role of a cunning grandmother.

3. Anita Roy, "Tollington Lassies," *The Guardian*, 5 April 1996: 26.
4. See Lodge, cited: 18-20.
5. Compare the racist aggression depicted by Rushdie, which is reinforced by overwhelming rudeness: "The second Beatle had taken out something from an inside pocket. A blade caught the light. 'Fucking wogs,' he said. 'You fucking come over here, you don't fucking know to fucking behave. Why don't' you fucking fuck off to fucking Wogistan? Fuck your fucking wog arses" (*EW*, 204).
6. D.H.J. Morgan and Sue Scott, "Bodies in a Social Landscape," in Sue Scott and David Morgan, eds., *Body Matters* (London: The Falmer Press, 1993): 15.
7. "I could see he had become pretty zooty, little Allie. His clothes were Italian and immaculate, daring and colourful, without being vulgar, and all-expensive and just right: the zips fitted, the seams were straight, and the socks were perfect—you can always tell a quality dresser by the socks. He didn't even look out of place sitting there on Mum's fake leather sofa, and the flowery pouf in front of him, his shoes resting on Mum's Oxfam rag like jewels on toilet paper. Some people know how to do things, and I was glad to see that my brother was one of them. Allie had money, too: he was working for a clothes designer. He and I talked like grown-ups; we had to. But we were shy and slightly embarrassed" (*BS*, 267). Here the ritual of changing and inventing garments is a metaphor that partially corresponds to the growth of Karim, Charlie and Allie who pursue their own maturity through theatre, music or fashion. See Chapter Two.
8. This is exactly the image that emerges from the BBC version of the novel; Kureishi himself acknowledged the difficulties in finding a suitable actor to play Changez, and director Roger Michell flew to India to continue the casting. In the end they opted for Harish Patel: "The dialogue I'd written for him was in strange Anglo-Indian grammar; the sentences ran like mazes. Roger found Harish Patel in Bombay. He was the last actor they saw on that casting trip. I met Harish a couple of times after he'd set foot for the first time in London. He'd been thinking hard about how Changez talked, walked and used his crippled hand, determined to include

his own amazement and confusion at this country in the part" (*DS*, 210).

9. David Morgan, "You Too Can Have a Body Like Mine: Reflections on the Male Body and Masculinities," in Sue Scott and David Morgan, cited: 83.
10. Concerning the mutability of the body and skin in particular, with reference to self-formation, see Betti Marenko, *Segni indelebili* (Milan: Feltrinelli, 2002). For a psychoanalytic interpretation, see Umberto Galimberti, *Il corpo* (Milan: Feltrinelli, 2000). The exploration of the sexual meaning of the body is also treated in Jean Baudrillard, *L'échange symbolique et la mort* (Paris: Editions Gallimard, 1976), especially chapter four. On the notion of piercing and tattoos as stratagems to transform the body-mind relation, see Francesca Alfano Miglietti, *Nessun tempo, nessun corpo* (Milan: Skira, 2001). The subject of the body in the intercultural mediation is dealt with in Anna Ferrero, ed., *Corpi individuali e contesti interculturali* (Turin: L'Harmattan Italia, 2003).
11. See Jean-Jacques Lecercle, *Frankenstein: mythe et philosophie* (Paris: Presses Universitaires de France, 1988).
12. David Morgan, cited: 79.
13. "Sam Lowbridge was generally considered the Yard's Bad Boy. He'd managed to acquire a criminal record by the age of sixteen and supplemented it with wearing black leather and an obligatory sneer" (*AM*, 55). The appearance of the body is worked out anew by a specific costume, with typical details of a modern villain. However we ought to detect a notable rural maladjustment and generational indeterminacy as core reasons for such attitude.
14. See the interview by Jason Best, available on the Internet at the following address: www.bbc.co/uk/films/2002/10/23meera_syal_anita_and_me_interview.shtml.
15. Also the relationship between Meena and Anita's mother is representative of the British behaviour toward the immigrants who, from the 1950s onward, started moving into the UK by benefitting from the open door policy of the post-war time. "Mama and I both picked up Deirdre's tone, which was not one of hostility but disbelief, she was waiting for an answer to the question that obviously puzzled her and upset her, how could we possibly think ourselves better than her? I had always been a little afraid of Deirdre, with her scarlet gash of a mouth and her backhanded conversation, but I

now could see something else, something unexpected in her face—she was frightened of us. Of course it made sense; we were not one of those faceless hordes depicted in the television news, arriving at airports with baggage and children, lost and already defeated, begging for sanctuary. We were not the barely literate, perpetually grinning idiots I occasionally saw in TV comedies or the confused, helpless innocents I spotted in bus and supermarket queues whilst they tried to make sense of their small change or the gesticulating wanderers who would sometimes stop my papa for directions, holding up pieces of paper with 'Mr. Singh, Wolverhampton, England' written on them" (*AM*, 215-16).

16. Interview by Caroline Marshall available at http://carolinescomedybase.tripod.com/meera/html
17. Alessandro Monti, "Mad 'Aunties' and 'Madi' Women: Patterns of Resistance and Intimations of Marginality in the Representation of Hindu Widows," in A. Monti and R.K. Dhawan, eds., *Discussing Indian Women Writers* (New Delhi: Prestige, 2002): 21.
18. See Interview by Caroline Marshall, cited.
19. Vrinda Nabar, cited: 41. The critic explains that the reference to the condition of female body "may be analysed as a literal and metaphorical extension of purdah: since literal purdah ('curtain') denotes various modes of physical constraints on the public display of the female body, metaphorical purdah marks a shift in emphasis to what is socially considered proper behaviour for a woman. This emphasis has withstood the media revolution, and holds sway over the popular consciousness in spite of the determined if dubious onslaught of the advertising industry": 41.
20. See Bill Ashcroft, Gareth Griffiths, Helen Tiffin, *The Empire Writes Back* (London: Routledge, 1989). In particular, chapter two.
21. Akim Ojumu, "All About Meera," *The Observer*, Sunday 16 June 2002: 28.
22. Elleke Boehmer, cited: 241.
23. Vrinda Nabar, cited: 40.
24. Sudeep Chakravarti, "London Calling," *India Today*, 20 September 1999: 24.
25. Alex O'Connel, "Meera Cracked," *The Times—Metro*, 16 June 1999: 16.
26. See Ashapurna Devi, "Indian Women. Myth and Reality" in Jasodhara Bagchi, cited: 19-23.

27. Alex O'Connel, cited: 17.
28. Nadya Kassam, ed., *Telling It like It Is* (London: The Women's Press, 1997).
29. Homi Bhabha, cited: 2. Author's emphasis.
30. These are some of the titles: "Facing up to Bullying," "Making My Own Culture," "I don't Look like One," "A Ugandan Indian in Britain," "In a Bengali Family."
31. We first have to refer to the term *deepa* to find the meaning of Diwali: "One who becomes illuminated and illuminates others is Deepa or lamp. In the evening the Deepa is lit and verses are recited in its honour. The Deepa is offered to God and this offering is known as Aarati. In the honour of river, Deepas are floated on her waters in the evening. [. . .] In India lamps of different sizes and shapes are made. Lamp-stand in the form of tree is lit in the temples." M.L. Varadpande, cited: 35. Concerning Diwali, often spelt as Dipavali, its most common definition reads: "A grand Indian festival of lights, Dipavali, falls in the month of Kartika (October-November) when every house is illuminated with the row of well lit oil lamps and days and night reverberate with the sound and fury of crackers and spectacular fireworks. Lakshmi Pujan or worship of goddess of wealth, Lakshmi, is the main feature of Dipavali festival," Varadpande, cited: 37. Lakshimi is also the goddess of good fortune, and the wife of Vishnu. See also http://www.hindunet.org/god/Goddesses/lakshimi
32. Nadya Kassam, cited: 37.
33. *Ibid.*: 38.

The Pen and the Screen: An Overview of Nomadic Subjects from Diasporic Literature to Cinema

> Inside the hall, popular songs were played one after the other: Lata Mangeshkar, Rafi, Noor Jehan, all. When the lights went off, the world changed. On the screen were our actors and actresses, our jokes, romantic stories, the scenery of our land. The stories were mostly of the injustices suffered by the poor, the weak and the lovers at the hands of the rich and the heartless. [. . .] And although such things never happened in real life, the clever mixture of these plots with beautiful girls and their songs and dances was a culture of our dreams which at once entertained and wrenched our souls in this foreign land. Often I forgot where I was until a few seconds after the lights came back on. When the film had in it terrible things done to people and their families, many of us started to weep. One thing I have seen here, when we leave our country and come to another, our hearts grow soft.
>
> Abdullah Hussein, *Émigré Journeys* (p. 45)

The stylistic features that shape Syal's texts are clearly indebted to other cultural media like music, cinema and theatre and their influence witnesses the author's involvement in several intellectual experiences. The abundant list of her television credits and filmography includes the well-known comedy show *Goodness Gracious Me* and films like the eponymous *Anita and Me*, *Beautiful Thing* (1996), *Sammie and Rosie Get Laid* (1987), and more. Her narrative vein also brought her to work for the radio and quality papers with sporadic articles in *The Guardian*, but also for the theatre, with the play

My Sister Wife, initially conceived as a three-part BBC television series.[1] She even participated in the production of an impressive musical entitled *Bombay Dreams*, by Andrew Lloyd Webber, inspired by Bollywood productions, which premiered in 2002 and is currently running at Apollo Victoria Theatre in London.

Syal's storytelling is dramatised in several kinds of format and points out an intense impulse to narrate, to deal with the word and operate in a creative manner. In an interview, she extends the scope of writing, also perceived as a therapeutic act of self-analysis that may shift one into a fictional context:

> I do believe that you have a writing muscle like any other muscle. I think it's really good to try to write every day, even if it's crap, even if it's a letter to somebody that you have to compose and use your emotions in, it's all really good because it helps develop your voice and that is in the end what makes you want to read a book. It's not necessary that it's the most fantastic story ever told. I mean what stories are original? We tell the same ones over and over again. It is the tone of a voice, a writing voice that makes you want to read something and that I think you only find through writing a lot.[2]

Writing is part of the process of growing up and developing intellectual skills then, or is even an attempt to achieve maturity. In her informal vivacity, she endorses the narrative practice as a discursive instrument to decipher actuality, from ordinary, everyday episodes to the aftermath of grand paths of history.

The recent boom of films like *Bend it like Beckham* directed by Gurinder Chadha or the hypnotic music by groups like Panjabi MC has further accelerated the cultural phenomenon of mongrelisation: as a consequence, ethnic or 'efnic,' to quote a pungent and provocative miswriting coined by Syal herself, artists are now in the limelight. Tackling the field of arts that are rearranged or influenced by the British Asian community, it is inevitable to turn to Hanif Kureishi, who was probably the first to exploit diverse genres like literature, theatre and cinema. Notwithstanding, clouded by his characteristic cynicism, he provokingly demolishes the sacredness of the artist as creator of beautiful things in favour of the commercial purpose. His cold vision of the relationship between writing and cinema may also be applied to the diasporic context, if we consider not only his films (either written or directed) but also the other texts, in their various forms, produced by the Asian community:

> These days writers are more likely to work in other areas of the media. As literature and academia have moved farther apart, the profession of writing seems closer to the rest of the media: print, television and film. Most writers, these days, fancy writing and directing their own films, or at least having their work made into films, which is a good way of extending one's income and reaching a larger audience. [. . .] With a film there are usually two significant creators, the writer and the director. Occasionally, as with Bergman, this can be the same person. Usually it is not, as writing and directing are different types of talent. The writer does his work first, after which it is used in various ways by the director. The writer almost always receives less recognition than the director and often less than the actors. (*DS*, 263)

Kureishi's kinship to cinema may date back to his dramaturgic experience: having been appointed Writer in Residence at the Royal Court Theatre, he cunningly shifted to protest 'fringe' theatre, one in which social and political matters could be scrutinised in depth, and then he converted himself to the big screen. With the only exception of *London Kills Me* (1991), which he also personally directed, all the other films are written by him or based on his stories: *My Beautiful Laundrette*, *Sammie and Rosie Get Laid*, *The Buddha of Suburbia* (a four-part TV film for the BBC from the eponymous novel), *My Son the Fanatic*, *Intimacy*, *The Mother*. They make up a rather variegated stock of motifs and styles and they mirror Kureishi's adoption of diverse techniques of storytelling in various phases of his career.

His early cinematic productions (*My Beautiful Laundrette* and *Sammie and Rosie Get Laid*) were directed by Stephen Frears and produced by Tim Bevan. They should be observed in opposition to mainstream tendency of British cinema, then dominated by two main categories: 'Raj Revival' and 'Heritage' cinema. Such labels include respectively films like *Gandhi* (1982) by Richard Attenborough (Rushdie condemned it because it "presents false portraits of most of the leaders of the independence struggle," *IM*, 104[3]) and *A Room with a View* (1986) by James Ivory. The first type, 'Raj Revival,' masks historical sequences of British domination as a sort of nostalgic museum piece: Kureishi on the contrary adverts about the threatening ideology that from the past is recuperated and instilled in modern England. His narrative revenge therefore subverts the paradigm of colonial hierarchy so that in opposition to the film version of *A Passage to India*, he elaborates on an ironic redrawing of ranks: consequently in the suburban London depicted in *My Beautiful Laundrette* the Indian employer (Omar) has a subaltern white employee (John).

Let us consider the different treatment that Kureishi in his films applies to the issues of topographic collocation, gender discourse and political implication. Also 'Heritage' cinema directs its gaze into an idealised past of imperial glory and in so doing it praises the constructed myths of British superiority. Conversely Kureishi's films erode this degree of steady stability and revisited historiography: they are centred on the actual socio-cultural transformations that propagate throughout Britain. Whether 'Heritage' cinema prefers a pastoral, Eden-like English countryside and considers large metropolitan centres as virulent places of decay, slums corrupted by the otherness of immigration, Kureishi's films lay great emphasis on London and main British cities as functional sites of hybridity at work. *Sammy and Rosie Get Laid*, for instance, is a significant study case as it unfolds a dynamic representation of London, with echoes *à la* Dickens. As a matter of fact, Sammy, one of the protagonists, affirms the bursting vitality of the city, in which identities are processed and polished according to a transnational metamorphosis: "We love our city and we belong to it. Neither of us are English, we are Londoners you see."[4] Such statement functions as a manifesto of revised Englishness and describes the osmotic relationship that binds together the individual self and the geographic site through the alchemic mutation operated as it is by diaspora.

The subject pertaining to sexuality is exploited by 'Heritage' cinema so as to furnish a moral and even puritan order, which is completely transfigured in Kureishi. The salient examples are Omar, John, Karim, Jamila, Rosie, amongst others, and they have the function to investigate into gender-related questions: they redraw the borders of the perception of sex and introduce alternatives to androcentric models. The influence of feminism indeed challenges the canonical act of filing female characters in marginal discursive areas.

Kureishi's political satire that arises from his unconventional filmography excoriates the Tory's policy of privatisation and capitalism introduced during the 1980s. *Sammy and Rosie Get Laid* ends with a rhetorical and pompous announcement by Margaret Thatcher, whose voice-over celebrates the progress of the British nation in a populist fashion. Of course the message belongs to the author's bantering attitude but we ought to discern his complex political reaction as a counterattack to the hegemony of the New Right: his support of the Left is problematic and demanding. In his films Kureishi adopts a double technique to undermine the imposed conception of social, moral and political order: he introduces the members of what may defined as the "rainbow coalition," namely the individuals discriminated from the point of view of race, culture, gender, sexuality or class, and then he equips his characters with alternative lifestyles, or unorthodox behavioural patterns. These rebellious gestures are often connected with music, fashion, squatting in abandoned flats, or even sexual activity and the use of drugs; symbolically they revert the imposition of duties and discipline endorsed by the New Right and Thatcherism.

Kureishi envisages a utopian dream of assembling multicultural, or rather intercultural, forces that from the periphery remould the centre. This does not mean exclusively a rise of minor social categories, a refusal of their fastidious rung: Kureishi's contingent of drop-outs (like Johnny in *My Beautiful Laundrette*), immigrants (Ali and Parvez in *My Son the Fanatic*), drug addicts (Clint in *London Kills Me*) or disillusioned pessimists (Jay in *Intimacy*) "point out the possibility of a new sense of national community built on the idea of pluralism and of non-hierarchical conceptions of difference."[5] The enticing outcome concerns the building of revisited contemporary Englishness, which replaces anachronistic clichés of the imperial heritage with a chaotic and productive miscellany of present human experiences. In this instance, the fragmentariness of the films is justified and enhanced by a pluralistic or polyphonic viewpoint; as a matter of fact, in *Sammy and Rosie Get Laid* "contradictory shards are incorporated into the story through Kureishi's mode of storytelling to convey his themes of contemporary political and cultural paradox."[6]

The textual archaeology of the films, however, is marked by technical and structural imperfections: although Kureishi had in mind classic, canonical films—let us think about Italian realism with *Bicycle Thieves* (1948) by De Sica or *La Dolce Vita* (1948) by Federico Fellini—his cinematic works lack the solidity of a specific genre. The author motivates his stylistic rearrangements but irreparably his films (at least the ones released in the Eighties) were penalised by a continuous shortage of funds and limited time plans (*My Beautiful Laundrette* was shot in three weeks between February and March 1985, while the filming of *Sammy and Rosie Get Laid* occurred in 1987 and again took a short time).

In their inclusive act that absorbs and extrapolates citations and keynotes, these films weakly function as a kind of collage dominated by a capricious or frayed unity. Let us contemplate *Sammy and Rosie Get Laid* for example, whose plot is dilated into a grotesque act of staging "London, a psychological investigation of the mind of a torturer, an analysis of contemporary gender relations, and a series of thinly-sketched love stories" (*MBL*, 43). Thus the visual narration proposes a swinging montage that, however, fails to embody coherently the eclectic social composition of the city and, albeit the dispersive panoramic sequences are partially contrasted by meaningful close-ups, the characters do not seem to be able to fulfil completely the premises. Kureishi, who wrote the screenplay of *My Beautiful Laundrette* while visiting relatives in Karachi, largely based his work on the effect of irony because, in his mind, it "is the modern mode, a way of commenting on the bleakness and cruelty without falling into darkness and didacticism."[7]

The same climate of uncertain co-ordination may be found in *London Kills Me*, a cinematic odyssey across the miserable areas and derelict castes of the city. Whether we interpret the film as a parodic homage to *The Wizard of Oz*, directed by Victor Fleming in 1939 (Clint's surreal endeavour to find a suitable pair of shoes, in order to obtain a much agonised job, is a parallel of Dorothy's quest for the magical ruby slippers in the land of Oz),[8] we have to record that the whole project suffers from a messy directing and editing. The enervating ambiguity that seems to characterise the film's outlandish trio (Cliff, Muffdiver and Sylvie) overrides dialogues and scenes too and places the film in a divergent position from the original script.

This broad introduction to Kureishi's films has shown the limits of his cinematic production which is not often matched with his mastery of storytelling. Harsh criticism arose from both the audience and the experts. Amusingly, the writer recalls how a distant aunt bitterly protested about the release of *My Beautiful Laundrette*, which, in her opinion, depicted a pejorative portrait of the Indian community. The relative sent a ferocious letter to Kureishi's father accusing the author of sustaining and widening British stereotypes of the immigrants.[9] Also the recent films are not immune from the lack of a sound frame constructed around a central topic. Although the entire project of *London Kills Me*, in which Kureishi is both screenplay writer and director, is motivated by the intention to experiment film-making as an alternative way to narrate ("The editing, like writing, I realized, would also be a form of exploration and testing of the material. It was all, even this, an attempt to tell a story

Genre-breaking is another feature of Dattani's style and it emerges in *Seven Steps across the Fire*, a play which only apparently uses the frame of crime fiction. The investigation that Uma Rao, wife of the Chief Superintendent of Bangalore and a post-graduate student of sociology, carries into the case of murder of the *hijra* Kamila becomes a metaphor for the confront between the moral barrier that bisects tradition and modernity. The unconventional heroine has to deal with the hostility of a whole community, willingly eager to eradicate an embarrassing episode. Mahesh Dattani seems to admonish about how dolorous events may be manipulated and falsely reconstructed in order to silence scandalous diversity. Given the strict code of reference, this is a courageous challenge to the conscience and the Indian heritage.

Besides the radio dramas written for the BBC, his oeuvre may also include or hint at diasporic subjects like the sense of displacement, the peregrination of the migrant and the tough adaptation to a new country. *Tara*, firstly performed as *Twinkle Tara* in 1990 in Bangalore, narrates about two conjoined twins, Chandan and Tara, raised and separated by a traditional Indian family. The 'malecentric' principle indeed elevates the boy and excludes the girl. Chandan, also known as Dan, is an aspiring novelist who migrates to Britain so as to come to terms with the haunting remorse that blurs his identity. Technically the play requires a multi-level set as a stratagem to highlight the discrepancies of the temporal phases and here the theatrical machinery helps the author to visualise the various acting of the personages. The incipit presents a long soliloquy of Chandan, who after settling in London tries to record his experience of life and transforms his own pain into words. The metanarrative quality of the text unveils a bitter reflection on the idea of writing as a practice to exorcise inner fears. The tone is similar to diasporic literature and overlaps the voice of the migrant with that of the writer by recording their communal solitude:

> Yes. I have my memories. Locking myself in a bedsitter in a seedy suburb of London, thousands of miles from home hasn't put

> enough distance between us. [. . .] My battery charger helps on some occasions. But now I want them to come back. To masticate my memories in my mind and spit out the result to the world of anger. (*Picks up the sheet he has been typing.*) My progress, so far, I must admit has been zero. [. . .] But that's all done with. Tonight I drop everything I've desperately wanted to be in my years in England. (*Mimes removing a mask and throwing it away.*) The desperate immigrant (*Mimes removing yet another.*) The mysterious brown with the phoney accent. The last being in the hardest to drop having spent two whole years in acquiring it. And what remains is what I intend making capital of. My freakishness. I am a freak. (Pause) Now, a freak doesn't have to look very far for inspiration. (*Moves to his table.*) But what is hard is to let go. Allow memories to flood in. (*Winds another sheet on the typewriter and then stops.*) To tell you the truth, I had even forgotten I had a twin sister. (*Music fades in slowly.*) Until I thought of her as subject matter for my next literary attempt. Or maybe I didn't forget her. She was lying deep inside, out of reach.[11]

Dattani's analysis stresses the intimate link between Chandan and Tara and their painful separation. The chirurgical operation that separates the two is paradigmatic of the Indian frame of mind that marginalises women. The twins represent more than a brother and a sister because in the paradoxical vision of the playwright they constitute the one and the self and join together the terms of gender. By deconstructing personal histories and identities, the author explores human relations and gender hierarchies, which are still perceived as monolithic and unchangeable assumptions in congealed India. Clearly, Dattani's theatrical creations are dissimilar from Kureishi's urbanised rebels, Syal's emancipated career girls or Rushdie's grotesque and mystical migrants. They belong to different national or transnational literatures. Nonetheless there is a certain affinity that pushes these authors to operate in the same thematic and discursive area. Symbolically the native Indian authors remind the diasporic writers of the paradox of the postcoloniality, which is the condition of double identity, fragmented and united by the registers of English.

Let us journey back to the UK. When in 2000 Meera Syal was appointed 'Media Personality of the Year' by the Commission for Racial Equality as part of the 'Race in Media Awards,' they recognised her involvement in a multitude of creative projects. In her fertile career, a significant point that introduced her to the large British audience probably resides in *Goodness Gracious Me*,[12] originally conceived as a radio show and then adjusted for BBC2 in 1998. It was an instant hit and immediately appealed to a very mixed crowd of viewers. Structured through short colourful sketches, the series dismantles British preconceptions of Asian communities and mocks expectations of both Indian migrants, who desperately try to discharge their burdensome heritage and acquire an Anglicised identity, and the British neighbourhood, blindly unable to understand different cultures. Interestingly it is the style of comedy that permits a critical gaze on the stereotypes created by both factions. Undoubtedly drama represents a very popular form of television entertainment in the UK and according to Raymond Williams, "as an experience is now an intrinsic part of everyday life, at a quantitative level which is so very much greater than any precedent as to seem a fundamental qualitative change"[13]; Syal and the producers however pinpoint the highly subversive role of parodic and comic fiction, which can be manipulated through widespread television. By transforming the not always peaceful cohabitation of Indians and the English into kitsch and pungent vignettes, Syal gives prominence to peripheral figures: the immigrants, with their fantasies of belonging and identity. The core topics of diaspora are here displayed through the modes of parody and pungently exploited in a project of appropriation and abrogation of Englishness and Indianness.

Fixed images of British life like the traditional Sunday barbecue or the regular visit to the pub are assimilated by the immigrant and re-imagined as a new socialising rite. However the process is double because whether the Indians conquer Englishness, simultaneously they have to negotiate their own Indianness. What stems from this act of contamination and disruption regards postcolonial hybridity.

Syal, who is both a screenwriter and an actor of *Goodness Gracious Me*, seems to reflect on the notion of mimicry as the key term for deciphering behavioural patterns and linguistic instances. In post-colonial criticism, it is a technical device that regulates the mixed relationship between coloniser and colonised and it artfully inter-plays with similarities and dissimilarities. The Indians pictured in the series perform a shift of identity and this inner slippage may be comprehended inasmuch as they reject the burden of otherness, thrown onto them by the authoritative centre, and strive to penetrate the English circle of social acceptability. As a consequence, names have to be changed, from Kapur to Cooper, Indian tonic water is polemically refused, given its 'dangerous' provenience, and looking for one's roots in the subcontinent is considered absolutely unacceptable.

Instead of solo performances, the series relies on choral representations and while it recognises its connection with variety-theatres, it clearly absorbs several elements from the world of television such as "the exploring 'eye of the camera,' the feel for everyday ordinary life, the newly respected rhythms of the speech of work and the streets and of authentic privacy."[14] The humoristic sketches, constructed with the technique of collage, actually may embody racial and social issues of contemporary England. As a matter of fact, the 'comicasation' of the harsh lives of migrants does not coincide with a watering down of serious themes. On the contrary, the skilful operation leads to a dialogic confrontation between two cultural traditions. In other words, Syal by exposing the Asian community in a ludicrous, exaggerated manner, stimulates the discussion on the collective identity and cultural memory, and her purpose is to go beyond the ethnic conflict.

Let us observe a couple of examples to understand how comedy operates a subtle inversion of roles. In the episode "East Meets Pest," the very title instils the tactic of parody: a woman whose house is infested by pests asks for qualified help to solve her problem. However she is rather shocked by the expert who visits her place: it is indeed a Buddhist monk, dressed in the traditional orange gown and his methods consist in chants and prayers that should convince the mice to flee away. The ridicule scene unmasks mesmerising mysticism, perceived as an absurd way to deal with the mundane world. It also denotes the clash of cultures because the woman, who is Indian, expects a modern, technological system to get rid of the vermin and rejects the archaic return of the native. In the sequence titled "Go for Authentic," it is the British viewpoint to be mocked. A British artefacts buyer in India seeks traditional objects and ethnographic items but her silly orientalism, being stubbornly determined to find the roots of Indian civilisation like an explorer of long-gone colonial times, makes her the ideal victim of astute local swindlers. They highly charge her for a heap of useless stuff and in thus doing the comic revenge towards the former imperial centre is achieved. 'Authentic' Indianness and Englishness collide in a yeasty performance of mimicry—the coloniser who wishes to expropriate the 'exotic' heritage with false philanthropy—which is a pure caricature of the relations between East and West.

It is rather interesting to scrutinise the linguistic variation that we find in *Goodness Gracious Me*, ranging from RP (the standard language of the centre and the authority) to Punjabi-influenced English or even Indian English. In spite of their 'rhotic' pronunciation, the Indian characters employ English to flaunt a much-agonised inscription into the canonical collective identity of Britain. The innovative strength that characterises the show lies in the recourse to the techniques of comedy and not drama or tragedy, which in variable measure affect diasporic novels and films. Indeed a laughable matter, in the intention of the producers, seems to overthrow rigid schemes and open a new discursive space. The weightlessness of the sketches is not concerned with ethnic clownery but rather illuminates a controversial cross-cultural scenario; its *modus operandi* is ambivalent as "it casts doubts as to expectations of 'subaltern' behaviour and it confers a blurred sense of national and cultural identity."[15] Meera Syal wittily lampoons the fake myth of the purity of races and hierarchies and her textual strategy, which should not be confused with a fashionable pretension of teaching intercultural education, is endowed on the television medium, a popular tool to argue in a global community.

The author has continued to operate in the terrains of literature and cinema. In 2002 she wrote the script of the film based on her novel *Anita and Me*. Obviously the story line had to be adapted—the time of the action is for instance moved a bit forward into the 1970s—but the magnetic bevy of the novel is maintained so as to delineate a bittersweet polyphonic tone. Anita Rutter, for instance, is aptly seen as a complex character, more than an adolescent 'seductress' whereas Meena, brilliantly played by Chandeep Uppal, charts the viewpoint of the whole film during her pathway of formation. From a technical point of view, unlike the other 'ethnic' films I take into account here, *Anita and Me* mainly relies upon the use of voice-over and clearly this device gives the Punjabi protagonist a salient position, although in cinema, the textual narration adopts a large set of techniques and strategies of representation. Moreover, "the different components of cinematic narration [. . .] usually work in consort, but sometimes the implied author creates an ironic tension"[16] and this degree of internal discrepancy is mirrored in the unstable relationship between Meena and Anita, who in spite of her irruptive vitality cannot emerge from her shadowed role. Meera Syal herself is part of the cast and acts as a chubby, gossipy Auntie: in this role, she is not akin to the protagonists of *Goodness Gracious Me* but embodies an inflexible upholder of traditions, always bemoaning about Meena's scarce competence of Punjabi.

The linguistic factor, which indicates the tension between the English community and the Indian family, is a paradigmatic structure of cultural identity along with social acts. Whether in the film the British speak varieties of northern accents, from 'Brummie' to 'Mancunian,' the Kumar family sway within a creolised continuum, with English and Punjabi as its extreme borders. Irony is again on alert in the film and celebrates idiomatic puns: when Meena's father at a wedding party is called onstage to sing a "traditional Punjabi" song, he mouths in his tone-deaf voice the Italian lyrics of *Volare* by Domenico Modugno. No wonder all the guests are devastatingly puzzled and taken aback by such unexpected climax! The festive confusion of the diaspora, which blinks at all generations of immigrants, replaces the stiff rigidity of English costumes. The semi-detached house of the Kumar, smelling of curries and upholstered with saris, interrupts the privacy of English homes which dot the pastoral rural milieu of Tollington. To conclude the crescendo of paradoxes, the screenplay smoothes over the typical prestigious figures of an English village: the local Anglican priest, for example, shares his time between ecumenical duties and his passion for rock music. And when he decides to leave, the new minister shocks the whole community just for the black colour of his skin. Once again the speculation on the ethnic body is given prominence and the terms of sarcasm destabilise expectations and preconceptions.

A similar level of humour characterises *Bend it like Beckham*, a typical British comedy, 'currified' rather than 'chutnified' through the Sikh protagonist. This time the racial issues are re-invented in a populist manner and made available to the general public: the device used by director Gurinder Chadha consists of a 'mythicised' element of western popular culture, namely football. More than a national game, it is considered as a social activity, a kind of entertainment that may bind together individuals with different backgrounds. The issue of football has frequently inspired cinema and in this case a possible model of reference may be *Fever Pitch* (1997) directed by David Evans and based on the eponymous novel by Nick Hornby, which represents the crisis of the protagonist Paul, torn between teaching English at school and his enthusiastic supporting of Arsenal. Again soccer becomes, perhaps in an oversimplified way, a metaphor for harmonising social groups. This is the wish that both Jasminda Singh, commonly called Jess, and Jules, her blonde English friend, share. However Jess's family judge playing in a female soccer team an immoral and disrespectful abolition of traditions. Therefore the girl has to cheat her parents in order to play and at the same time cannot negate her heritage. Whether football functions as a linking mechanism, the intercultural discrimination is acted out by the ceremony of the Punjabi wedding and the ritual preparation of food. As postcolonial and diasporic novelists have extensively expressed, food is a valuable symbol that evokes the notion of belonging and in the film learning to cook a "full Indian dinner" means to adopt a specific identity and reject instances of polluting hybridity. Jess's mother wants her daughter to be able to prepare a tasty *aloo gobi* and in so doing proclaims a sharp divide between the suitable and proper Indian behaviour and the indecent alienating English life. On the intertextual level she is close to Sunita's mother in *Life isn't All Ha Ha Hee Hee*.

Although in the film women, from Mrs. Sing to Jess's sister, Pinky, and all the sundry aunties, are depicted emphatically, the young protagonist is segregated by patriarchal rules and reminds one of the female characters that we have encountered so far: Meena, Chila, Jamila and all the others who strive for their emancipation. As a whole, the film, whose title refers to Beckham's technique for curving kicks around a series of defenders, is structured as a comedy of intrigues and it "interweaves the underdog theme of *Billy Elliot* with Indian coming-of-age films like *East is East* and *Monsoon Wedding*, adding a healthy dose of MTV flavour in the appropriate spots."[17] Gurinder Chadha, who co-wrote the script along with Paul Mayera Berges, matches the generational conflicts with the inter-racial dilemma of second generation immigrants, being torn betwixt two cultures. This is the second movie of the director who, after a prolific collaboration with the BBC and Channel 4, launched her debut film *Bhaji on the Beach* (1993), written by Meera Syal.

Chadha's strategy operates in a twin way so that the cinematic structure is grounded on the image of soccer as a metaphorical intercultural and social glue, and is further defined by the temporal set, which is contemporary suburban London. The latter element is crucial for, unlike what happens in films like *Anita and Me* or *East is East*, the identification with present times indicates a milder degree of generational conflict, one in which strict parents grant their children some concessions. Jess's quarrelling with her relatives avoids verbal abuse or physical violence that haunt other British Asian movies. Moreover hybridity is observed in its process of affecting social and cultural structures inasmuch as Pinky leads a rather westernised life and yet wants her, curiously enough, non-arranged marriage in the classic Punjabi tradition.

The energetic direction reaches its climactic peak through the use of alternate montage: Pinky's exuberant wedding ceremony—whose gaudy and eclectic taste derive from Bollywood's follies—is juxtaposed to Jess's victorious performance on the pit, a real arena of emotions for the English. The two orgasmic episodes intermittently promote a procedure of globalisation, in a dual and contradictory act of staging the East and the West, whose contradictory practices are 'metabolised' by virtue of the cinematic medium. The exorbitant Indian ethnicity is ritualised into a carnival that is an attempt to undermine orientalism but Chadha's aesthetics renders the films an enjoyable and reassuring folk-tale, whose happy ending claims a visionary and feeble demarginalisation of the migrant. Gaining social respectability as a token for sportive activities comes into collision with the Sikh repertoire of signs of belonging. The itinerant focus of the film illuminates the notion of keeping cultural roots and preserving the idea of home, the migrant's treasure of *oikumene*, by peeping into the semi-detached house of the Singh family, dominated by religious icons and richly decorated on the wedding occasion. The filmic structure approaches the inter-pollination of the diaspora but tends to expound a kitsch scenario of giddy dances in sari and mouth-watering piles of spicy food. This atmosphere of ambiguity concerns the threat of 'unhomeliness' of which Homi Bhabha speaks:

> That is the condition of extra-territorial and cross-cultural initiations. To be unhomed is not to be homeless, nor can the 'un-

> homely' be easily accommodated in that familiar division of social life into public and private spheres. [. . .] The recesses of the domestic space become sites for history's most intricate invasions. In that displacement the borders between home and world become confused; and, uncannily, the private and the public become part of each other, forcing upon us a vision that is as divided as it is disorienting.[18]

To come full circle with British films devoted to the exploration of Asian communities, we must draw our attention to the frequently cited *East is East*, directed by Damien O'Donnel. The script by Ayub Khan Din, who played the role of Sammie in *Sammie and Rosie Get Laid*, was originally designed to be staged at the Royal Court Theatre in London and subsequently made into a movie in 1998. The plot which is quite known pivots around a Pakistani family in Salford, in the Manchester area and the time is the beginning of 1970s, during the political campaigns of racist Enoch Powel, before the rise of Margaret Thatcher. The contrast between the Khan family and the surrounding English milieu is depicted through symbols and images, so that a thriving fish and chips shop run by migrants goes beyond a shocking inversion of stereotypes and becomes a connector with the town. The cheerful dimension is activated from the very opening by the Khan sons who join a Catholic procession down the streets. In their eyes, the act functions as a kind of game or a means to (mis)represent their camouflaged identity in a theatrical manner that, however, ignores the religious implications behind the alien parade. George Khan strongly believes in a proper Pakistani and Muslim education for his whole family: the generational friction that stems from this family web is further complicated by his English wife, Ella, who simultaneously contrasts and sustains the patriarchal authority.

The director's *mise en abime* interpolates comic and dramatic overtones as it unfolds the questioning of double belonging and self-perception. Like Karim, the Khan sons pursue the mundane traits of Englishness like entertainment activities (connected with typical places like the pub or the disco) or alternative lifestyles (colourful and fashionable clothes of the 1970s instead of the traditional *salwar kameez*). In spite of their father's assiduous insistence, they reject Urdu and assume a northern variety of English: by so doing they ratify their idiosyncratic process of self-determination and emerge anew as hybridised characters. The screenplay is based on a type of representation which foregrounds both the verbal and the visual axes: the former is monitored by the inter-language experience (George's exploding wrath, for instance) while the latter is exemplified in the images of Powell delivering a racist speech concerning the "policy of assisted repatriation and resettlement," transmitted on TV. However the blatant extremism of this political vignette is subtly mocked by the Khan juniors who sit around the TV set and enjoy crispy bacon and sausages. The scene portrays a dual inversion of canonical inscriptions into specific categories: by violating Muslim dietary norms and jokingly pretending to support the xenophobic enemy *par excellence*, they mould a new space of identity, one in which hybridity may translate the mongrel essence of the migrant.

O'Donel and Din seem to suggest that dealing with the diaspora implies an impact of worlds and words. In this respect, cultural topographies are stressed and alert the audience of what lies behind the façade of Asian otherness. Significant is the visit the Khan family pay to relatives and friends in Bradford, an emblematic town in North England which houses a massive ethnic yearly festival called Mela, a Hindi word for 'celebration.' Bradford, to which Kureishi dedicates an essay now collected in *Dreaming and Scheming*, constitutes a sort of privileged shelter for peoples from Pakistan, India and Bangladesh and makes use of its racial pandemonium as an instrument to discern the single nationalities within a diasporic spectrum, which is wrongly perceived as a stereotyped wholeness according to the western viewpoint. The sign on the road leading to the city, "Welcome to Bradford," has been astutely re-written and now reads "Welcome to Bradistan." The pun that arises from the semantic shift expresses the Pakistani consciousness that seems to govern the whole place. It stands as the exact opposite of what Rushdie terms as the example of British intolerance: "Wogistan." Yet we should interpret such dichotomy as a linguistic experiment in cross-cultural cartography, one which substitutes Bradford for Pakistan, in the migrant's vision, and London for distypic Orient, in the mind of the racist hooligan. The Khan's journey actually conceals the plot of an arranged marriage, planned by George and his friend, the Mullah, between Abdul and Tariq and the daughters of Mr. Shah.

The picaresque development of the story brings to light the sweet and sour taste of the void that separates the Pakistani father from the Anglicised family. Ella, however, manages to balance her hard condition of English womanhood and motherhood conjugated to Muslim faith and codes. Interestingly the decision-making aspect of the linguistic communication is performed by George Khan and other Pakistani members of the community and excludes the real social actors of this peculiar act of transaction.[19] The breaking of the linguistic relationship is further accompanied by divergent behavioural patterns: the young Khans abrogate severe prescriptions pertaining to their ethnic heritage and switch into a different zone of ego-making. Therefore, as sociolinguistics has demonstrated, the feeling of belonging and creating an organic community is orchestrated by virtue of linguistic performances and social acts as well. By emulating rebellious gestures of Britishness, like clubbing, drinking at the pub or dressing up, the Khan sons celebrate their allegiance to hybridised modes of being through a pragmatic process of assimilation. It is not a weak capitulation to globalising practices but rather an endorsement of a circumstantial metamorphosis. Whether Bradford may apparently serve as a synecdoche of Pakistan, second generation migrants react by drawing a hybrid identity, whose imprecise contours fluctuate in the experience of the diaspora and double belonging.

To come to a conclusion, I would argue how both the rhetorical style of contemporary writing in English and the analytic quality of cinema have exploited the condition of migrants as subjects of our uncertain, post-Millennium age. In Britain, given the large presence of migrants, mostly from former colonies, it is plausible to register the need and demand of cultural productions related to ethnic issues. Decorated by off-camera anecdotes, the movies of this category have gradually obtained visibility and an independent space in socio-cultural discourses. In a diachronic perspective, Hanif Kureishi may be considered a sort of initiator, who bravely dared to turn the spotlight towards the marginalised subjects, those individuals neutralised through ideological and political procedures of segregation that liberal Britain supported under the auspices of Enoch Powell and Margaret Thatcher. Afterwards, this unusual genre, quite akin to off-Broadway productions of 'fringe' theatre, manifested its disturbing presence by challenging monochromatic, canonical British cinema. However we should recall that it never strived to penetrate the niche of *cinéma d'essay*, but rather its purpose was to stimulate or provoke the audience. By now it has probably achieved a respected status, given the present preoccupations of society that it seeks to deconstruct.

The migrant question has indeed entered all forms of cultural representation and intellectual argument. Broadly speaking, we have to add that the reproducibility of diasporic issues, shifted from the terrain of fiction onto the big and small screens is also conceived as a commercial operation to sell a 'new' product. It is somehow a revitalised form of orientalism by which racial and cultural differences are reduced to instances of entertainment: here the focus is on the vibrant, garish otherness of the migrancy filed in a reassuring stereotype to the benefit of the avid eye of the western viewer; e.g. let us consider the fabricated blissful ending of Jess's story. Combined with the renaissance of British cinema, from the late 1980s onwards with directors like Ken Loach, Kenneth Branagh or Mike Lee, the introduction of diasporic themes found its way in spite of an initial hostile reaction. This fashion created blockbuster movies so that the transition from marginality to visibility was definitely sanctioned, although sometimes to the detriment of quality.

Obviously these films cannot be compared with Bollywood works because of the profound and incompatible differences of their own cultural modes and structures. However some recurring motifs of Indian films, such as arranged marriages, impossible romances or traditional patriarchal families, are echoed or adapted so as to be incorporated in diasporic cinema. It is worth remembering that the Indian cinematic industry functions as a technological instrument that stages narratives, that is to say a popular way to modernise the very Indian practice of storytelling through the eye of the camera. Veiled references from the *Arabian Nights* to the *Mahabharata* are indeed disguised behind mundane tribulations, in a sort of 'quasi-mythical,' endless soap-opera. However, the messy cluster of Bollywood films clearly appears tasteless to the western audience and even the ethnographic element is often observed as an alienating barrier.

Salman Rushdie comments upon the scarce quality of Hindi films, but reminds one of the pleasures of weightlessness they offer. As a matter of fact, the numerous references to forms of popular Hindi culture abound in his novels and add a carnivalesque, polyphonic euphoria that is also endowed with disruptive energy. As Nandini Bhattacharya reminds, "in Bombay cinema's absolute defiance of cinematic norms (as established by the West), its amazing capacity to incorporate disjointed and incongruous items such as songs, dance, violence, sex, all within one elastic and grotesque form, its complete disregard of Aristotelian dictums of unity and structure, its almost child-like irreverence of all logic and rationality, makes it for Rushdie a potent symbol of subversion and dissent."[20] Whether these Indian forms of entertainment may be interpreted as hegemonic instruments to control masses and impose a constructed order, Rushdie rejects such schemes and emphasises the liberating eruption of cinema, seen as a site to undermine political or social impositions. Not only does he use Bollywood texts and stories to decorate his deft prose, but he also turns to western cin-

the delusion he gathered from that experience is soothed by the fact that now his screenplays of *Midnight's Children* are used in the theatre by the Royal Shakespeare Company, under the direction of Tim Supple, who has also performed an adapted version of *Haroun and the Sea of Stories*.

Both Salman Rushdie and Hanif Kureishi have experienced the stressful re-adjusting of their own literary works into scripts instead of handling them onto professional writers. This witnesses the intricate link between the artist-creator and the moulded word, between the page and the stage, between the 'inky' character and the 'ocular' movement. In adapting, apart from the much-debated question of fidelity, we should perhaps move to the notion of analogy, which tries to parallel the stylistic features of the original text through the use of editorial cutting, accelerated motion and other devices.[21] Diasporic or postcolonial authors writing or adapting for cinema or television express a throbbing anxiety by exposing the novelty of intercultural forces at work in British society to the western showbiz. The assessment of their results may vary or alert the audience of the peril of ambiguous hybridity that distorts the empty concept of assimilation by cementing the 'us versus them' dichotomy. The migrant's *modus operandi* is structured via either resistance or mimicry, and in Britain this new kind of cinema should be viewed as an effort to stage the contradictions and turmoil of ethnic minorities, loaded with the burden of mixed belonging. This constitutes a fragment, to wit, of a nation to come, with the expanded meaning or rather questioning of Englishness.

NOTES

1. The play was later included in a collection titled *Six Plays by Black and Asian Women Writers* (London: Aurora Metro Publications, 1995).
2. Interview with Caroline Marshall, cited.
3. See also in the same collection, "Outside the Whale": 87-101.

4. Hanif Kureishi, *Sammie and Rosie Get Laid* (London: Faber and Faber, 1988): 33. The depiction of the city reminds one of T.S. Eliot's lines that describe London as an "unreal city / under the brown fog of a winter moon." See T.S. Eliot, *The Waste Land.* On the motif of London in modernist literature, see Valerio Fissore, "La storia è la città," in Valeria Gianolio, ed., *Le tradizioni del moderno* (Turin: Tirannia Stampatori, 2002): 31-40.
5. Bart Moore-Gilbert, cited: 92.
6. Kenneth C. Kaleta, cited: 53.
7. Hanif Kureishi, *My Beautiful Laundrette and The Rainbow Sign* (London: Faber and Faber, 1986): 43.
8. By extension, the film hints at the nomadic condition of the migrant, downloaded by an impetus to wander before settling down. The diasporic displacement is suffered by the English themselves, made into miserable exiles in their country. As a matter of fact, "modern-day migrants undertake trips down a yellow brick road that lead beyond Dorothy and Toto's Oz to some psychological destinations on an internalised map," Kenneth Kaleta, cited: 15. The reference to *The Wizard of Oz* corroborates as well the indication of the "rainbow coalition" that the author seems to deploy in delineating characters in his fiction.
9. The episode is narrated in "Some Time with Stephen: a Diary," which accompanies the script of *Sammie and Rosie Get Laid.* It is now collected in *Dreaming and Scheming.*
10. Sally Avens, "A Note on the Play": 115 in Mahesh Dattani, *Collected Plays* (New Delhi: Penguin, 2000). She then goes on and adds: "Mahesh also made music work for him within the story—the playing of M.S. Subbalakshmi's Meera bhajans and the popular tunes of Bollywood sung by the liftman in Mumbai underline the north and south union of the two families."
11. Mahesh Dattani, cited: 323-24. On the relevancy of intra-gender explorations in Dattani's drama, see Corrado Micheli, "The Male Other. New Gendered Spaces of India: A Critical Overview" in Alessandro Monti, ed., *Hindu Masculinities across the Ages: Updating the Past* (Turin: L'Harmattan Italia, 2002): 157-70.
12. References are made to the episodes contained in the BBC videotape *Goodness Gracious Me*, (The Very Best of Series 1 plus Unseen Out-takes). Screenplay by Meera Syal, Sanjeev Bhaskar, Anil Gupta, Nina Wadia, Sanjeev Kholi, Sharat Sardana and Richard

Pinto. The show is produced by Anil Gupta and directed by Nick Wood. The episodes were originally screened between 12 January and 16 February 1998 on BBC2. For a punctual analysis of the series, see Sandra Campagna, "Can the 'Subaltern' Laugh? A Weightless Migrant Metaphor" in Alessandro Monti and John Douthwaite, eds., *Migrating the Texts: Hybridity as a Postcolonial Literary Construct* (Turin: L'Harmattan Italia, 2003): 77-112.

13. Raymond Williams, *Television. Technology and Culture* (New York: Schocken Books, 1975): 59.
14. *Ibid.*: 57.
15. Sandra Campagna, "Can the 'Subaltern' Laugh? A Weightless Migrant Metaphor," cited: 109.
16. Seymour Chatman, *Coming to Terms* (Ithaca and London: Cornell University Press, 1990): 135.
17. Review by Darrin Keene, available at http://www.filmthreat.com
18. Homi Bhabha, cited: 9.
19. See Sandra Campagna, "Voices from Bradistan: the Sense of Belonging in Multiracial Societies," *Textus: English Studies in Italy*, Vol. XIV, No. 2, 2002, Special Issue: "'Languaging' in and across Human Groups. Perspectives on Difference and Symmetry," ed. Giuseppina Cortese and Dell Hymes: 263-86.
20. Nandini Bhattacharya, "Hegemony or Subversion? Ideology of Popular Culture and the Novels of Salman Rushdie," in *The Atlantic Critical Review*, cited: 167.
21. Concerning the aspects of adaptation, see Seymour Chatman, cited, in particular chapter ten, "A New Kind of Adaptation: *The French Lieutenant's Woman*": 161-83.

Select Bibliography

1.1 Primary Sources

Kureishi, Hanif, *Plays One* (London: Faber and Faber, 1999).

_____, *The Buddha of Suburbia* (London: Faber and Faber, 1990).

_____, *The Black Album* (London: Faber and Faber, 1995).

_____, *Love in a Blue Time* (London: Faber and Faber, 1998).

_____, *Intimacy* (London: Faber and Faber, 1998).

_____, *Midnight All Day* (London: Faber and Faber, 2000).

_____, *Sleep with Me* (London: Faber and Faber, 1999).

_____, *The Body and Seven Stories* (London: Faber and Faber, 2002).

_____, *My Ear at His Heart* (London, Faber and Faber, 2004).

Rushdie, Salman, *Midnight's Children* (London: Vintage, 1995).

_____, *Shame* (London: Picador, 1984).

_____, *The Satanic Verses* (London: Vintage, 1998).

_____. *East, West* (London: Vintage, 1995).

_____, *The Ground beneath Her Feet* (London: Jonathan Cape, 1999).

_____, *Imaginary Homelands* (London: Granta, 1992).

_____, *Step across This Line* (London: Jonathan Cape, 2002).

Syal, Meera, *Anita and Me* (London: Flamingo, 1997).

_____, *Life Isn't All Ha Ha Hee Hee* (London: Anchor, 2000).

1.2 Other Authors/Other Texts of Reference

Chaudhuri, Amit, *Afternoon Rag* (London: Vintage, 1998).

Dattani, Mahesh, *Collected Plays* (New Delhi: Penguin India, 2000).

Dhondy, Farrukh, *Bombay Duck* (New Delhi: Penguin India, 1999).

Gupta, Sunetra, *Memories of Rain* (London: Phoenix, 1995).

Hussein, Abdullah, *Émigré Journeys* (London: Serpent's Tail, 2000).

Rushdie, Salman and Elizabeth West, *The Vintage Book of Indian Writing 1947-1997* (London: Vintage, 1997).

Smith, Zadie, *White Teeth* (London: Penguin, 2001).

2.0 Secondary Sources

2.1 Critical Works

Albertazzi, Silvia, *Abbecedario postcoloniale* (Macerata: Quodlibet, 2001).

Ahmad, Aijaz, *In Theory* (London: Verso, 1992).

Ashcroft, Bill, Gareth Griffith and Helen Tiffin, *The Empire Writes Back* (London: Routledge, 1989).

Bhabha, Homi, *The Location of Culture* (London and New York: Routledge, 1994).

Brennan, Timothy, *Salman Rushdie and the Third World. Myths of the Nation* (London: Macmillan, 1989).

Boehmer, Elleke, *Colonial and Postcolonial Literature* (Oxford: Oxford University Press, 1995).

Dennis, Ferdinand and Khasan, Naseem, eds., *Voices of the Crossing* (London: Serpent's Tail, 2000).

Deleuze, Gilles and Felix Guattari, *A Thousand Plateaus: Capitalism and Schizophrenia* (London: The Athlone Press, 1988).

_____, *Nomadologia. Pensieri per il mondo che verrà* (Italian translation) (Rome: Castelvecchi, 1995).

_____, *Rizoma* (Italian translation, edited by Franco Berardi) (Rome: Castelvecchi, 1997).

Dhawan, R.K., ed., *Writers of the Indian Diaspora* (New Delhi: Prestige Books, 2001).

Fletcher, D.M., ed., *Reading Rushdie. Perspectives on the Fiction of Salman Rushdie* (Amsterdam: Rodopi, 1994).

Fludernik, Monika, ed., *Hybridity and Postcolonialism* (Tübingen: Stauffenburg-Verlag: 1998).

Gandhi, Leela, *Postcolonial Theory* (Edinburgh: Edinburgh University Press, 1998).

Gikandi, Simon, *Maps of Englishness. Writing the Identity in the Culture of Colonialism* (New York: Columbia University Press, 1996).

Gilroy, Paul, *There Ain't No Black in the Union Jack* (London: Routledge, 2002).

Goonetilleke, D.C.R.A., *Salman Rushdie* (London: Macmillan, 1998).

Grant, Damian, *Salman Rushdie* (Plymouth: Northcote House, 1999).

Hennard Dutheil de la Rochère, Martine. *Origin and Originality* (Bern: Peter Lang, 1999).

Kaleta, Kenneth C., *Hanif Kureishi—Postcolonial Storyteller* (Austin: University of Texas, 1998).

Kuortti, Joel, *Fictions to Live in. Narration as an Argument for Fiction in Salman Rushdie's Novels* (Frankfurt am Main: Peterlang, 1998).

Kureishi, Hanif, *Dreaming and Scheming* (London: Faber and Faber, 2002).

Lee, A. Robert, ed., *Other Britain, Other British* (London: Pluto Press, 1995).

Manferlotti, Stefano, *Dopo l'Impero. Romanzo ed etnia in Gran Bretagna* (Naples: Liguori, 1995).

Mongia, Padmini, ed., *Contemporary Postcolonial Theory* (New Delhi: Oxford University Press, 1996).

Monti, Alessandro, *Durga Marga: la via difficile* (Rome: Bulzoni, 1995).

_____ and John Douthwaite, eds., *Migrating the Texts: Hybridity as a Postcolonial Literary Construct* (Turin: L'Harmattan Italia, 2003).

Moore-Gilbert, Bart, *Hanif Kureishi* (Manchester and New York: Manchester University Press, 2001).

Pandit, M.L., *New Commonwealth Writing: a Critical Response* (New Delhi: Prestige, 1996).

Parameswaran, Uma, *The Perforated Sheet. Essays on Salman Rushdie's Art* (New Delhi: Affiliated East-West Press, 1988).

Phillips, Mike and Trevor Phillips, *Windrush. The Irresistible Rise of Multiracial Britain* (London: Harper Collins, 1999).

Punter, David, *Postcolonial Imaginings* (Edinburgh: Edinburgh University Press, 2000).

Rao, Madhusudhana M., *Salman Rushdie's Fiction* (New Delhi: Sterling, 1992).

Said, Edward, *Orientalism* (1978) (Harmondsworth: Penguin, 1995).

_____, *Culture and Imperialism* (London: Vintage, 1994).

Taneja, G.R. and R.K. Dhawan, eds., *The Novels of Salman Rushdie* (New Delhi: Indian Society for Commonwealth Studies, 1992).

Venkata Reddy, K., *Critical Studies in Commonwealth Literature* (New Delhi: Prestige, 1994).

2.2 Articles and Reviews

Adami, Esterino, "The Reinvention of Tradition: English/Banglish Dishes and Diasporic Texts," in Alessandro Monti, Marina Goglio and Esterino Adami, eds., *Feeding the Self, Feeling the Way in Ancient and Contemporary South Asian Cultures* (Turin: L'Harmattan Italia, 2005).

_____, "Hanif Kureishi's Storytelling as a Kind of Artistry: *The Body and Seven Stories*," *Indian Journal of World Literature and Culture*. Forthcoming.

Allen; Richard, "Men Need History. V.S. Naipaul, Barry Unsworth and Hanif Kureishi," in Nilufer E. Bharucha and Vrinda Nabar, eds., *Postcolonial Indian Literature in English* (New Delhi: Vision Books, 1998): 213-23.

Alliot, Bénédicte, "Misplacement in Hanif Kureishi's *The Buddha of Suburbia*," *Commonwealth Essays and Studies*. Special Issue, Nos. 1-4 (1989-97): 95-100.

Akliyar, Vidyut, "*Haroun and the Sea of Stories*: Metamorphosis of an Old Metaphor," *Commonwealth Novel in English*. Volume 6, Number 1-2 (Spring-Fall 1993): 1-12.

Bassi, Shaul, "Salman Rushdie's Special Effects," in Linguanti, Elsa and Carmen Concilio, eds., *Coterminous Worlds. Magical Realism and Contemporary Post-Colonial Literature in English* (Amsterdam: Rodopi, 1999): 47-60.

Bhaduri, Seema, "Interplay of Dualities; A Look at the Structural Motifs in *Midnight's Children* and *Shame*," *The Atlantic Critical Review—Quarterly*. Volume 1, Number 2 (July-September): 44-53.

Bhattacharya, Nandini, "Hegemony or Subversion: Ideology of Popular Culture and the Novels of Salman Rushdie," *The Atlantic Critical Review—Quarterly*. Volume 1, Number 2 (July-September): 161-69.

Beck, Rudolf, "Close Encounters of the Third Type: Salman Rushdie's Short Story Cycle *East, West*," *Anglia*. 116.3 (1998): 355-80.

Begum, Jameela, "Multiculturalism and Canadian Literary Diaspora," *College English Review*. Vol. 3, No. 4 (October-December 1999): 4-8.

Booker, M. Keith, "*Finnegans Wake* and *The Satanic Verses*: Two Modern Myths of the Fall," *Critique—Studies in Contemporary Fiction*. Volume XXXII, No. 3 (Spring 1991): 190-207.

Campagna, Sandra, "Voices from Brandistan: the Sense of Belonging in Multiracial Societies," in Giuseppina Cortese and Dell Hymes, eds., *Textus*, Vol. XIV, Number 2, Special Issue "'Languaging' in and across Human Groups. Perspectives on Difference and Asymmetry" (2001): 236-86.

Carey, Cynthia, "Hanif Kureishi's *The Buddha of Suburbia* as a Post-Colonial Novel," *Commonwealth Essays and Studies*. Special Issue, Nos. 1-4 (1997): 119-25.

Chakravarti, Sudeep, "London Calling," *India Today*. 20 September 1999: 24.

Chaturvedi, Nagesh, "Indian Myths in Salman Rushdie's *Midnight's Children*," *Language Forum*. Volume 19, Number 1-2 (January-December 1993): 173-81.

Concilio, Carmen, "Città postcoloniali o città postmoderne? Toronto, Bombay (Mumbai), Johannesburg fra oblio e memoria," in Gianolio, Valeria, ed., *Le tradizioni del moderno* (Turin: Tirrenia Stampatori, 2002): 95-134.

_____, "'Worthy of the World': the Narrator/Photographer in Salman Rushdie's *The Ground beneath Her Feet*," *The Atlantic Critical Review—Quarterly*. Volume 1, Number 2 (July-September): 141-50.

Conner, Marc C., "*Midnight's Children* and the Apocalypse of the Form," *Critique: Studies in Contemporary Fiction*. Number 38, Volume 4 (Summer 1997): 288-99.

Crane, Ralph J., "Like a Distant Drum Beating Loudly: the Exiled Pen of Salman Rushdie," *The CRNLE Review Journal*. Number 2 (1993): 11-18.

Dell'Aversano, Carmen, "Mitopoiesi o mistificazione? L'epos postmoderno di *Midnight's Children*," *Strumenti Critici*. a. x, Number 3 (September 1995): 341-66.

_____, "Worlds, Things, Words. Rushdie's Style from *Grimus* to *Midnight's Children*," in Elsa Linguanti and Carmen Concilio, eds.,

Coterminous Worlds. Magical Realism and Contemporary Post-Colonial Literature in English (Amsterdam: Rodopi, 1999): 61-69.

Dhillon, Amit, "Life in Exile," *India Today*. 15 March 1999: 126.

Dissanayake, Wimal, "Towards a Decolonised English: South Asian Creativity in Fiction," *World Englishes*. Vol. 4, No. 2 (1985): 233-42.

Ganguly, Debjani, "Of Unremarkable, Un-Rushdie-like Lives: the Diasporic 'Local' in the Latest Fiction of Amit Chaudhuri," *CRNLE Journal*. Special Issue: *Sri Lanka and Indian Diasporic Writing*. (2000): 84-95.

Doyle, Waddick, "The Space between Identity and Otherness in Hanif Kureishi's *The Buddha of Suburbia*," *Commonwealth Essays and Studies*. Special Issue, Nos. 1-4 (1997): 110-18.

D'Souza, Florence, "Salman Rushdie's *Midnight's Children*: A Remythologisation of India's Contemporary History," *The Atlantic Critical Review—Quarterly*. Volume 1, Number 2 (July-September): 19-32.

Ganapathy-Doré, Geetha, "Mapping Continents: the Journey Home in Salman Rushdie, Michael Ondaatje and Bharati Mukherjee," *Commonwealth Essays and Studies*. Volume 17, No. 1 (Autumn 1994): 3-9.

Haffenden, John, "Salman Rushdie," *Novelists in Interview* (London: Methuen, 1985): 231-61.

Hand, Felicity, "How British Are the Asians?," *Wasafiri*. Issue Number 21 (1995): 9-13.

Hassan, Ihab, "Beyond Exile: a Postcolonial Intellectual Abroad," *The Southern Review*. Volume 3, Number 29 (Summer 1993): 453-64.

Hashmi, Alamgir. "Hanif Kureishi and the Tradition of the Novel," *Commonwealth Novel in English*. Volume 6, Number 1 (Spring-Fall 1993): 50-60.

Hashmi, Asif, "The Buddha of Suburbia," *Artrage*. (Dec.-Jan. 1994): 18-19.

Hensen, Michael, "'Our Stable Ego of the Character': Identity in the Novels of Rushdie," *The Atlantic Literary Review*. Volume 2, Number 3 (July-September 2001): 123-33.

Hopkin, James, "The Horror of Being Hanif," *The Guardian.* 30 October 1999: 10.

Jena, Seema, "From Victors to Survivors," *Wasafiri.* Issue Number 17 (Spring 1993): 3-6.

Jussawalla, Feroza, "Rushdie's *Daastan-e-Dilruba*: *The Satanic Verses* as Rushdie's Love Letter to Islam," *Diacritics.* Volume 26, Number 1 (Spring 1996): 50-73.

Kirpal, Viney, "Postmodern Strategies in the Indian English Novel," *LITTCRIT.* No. 43, Volume 22, Number 22 (December 1996): 21-33.

Knippling, Alpana Sharma. "Hanif Kureishi," in Emmanuel S. Nelson, ed., *Writers of the Indian Diaspora* (West Port, Connecticut: Greenwood Press, 1993): 159-69.

Kortenaar, Neil Ten, "*Midnight's Children* and the Allegory of History," *Ariel.* Volume 26, Number 2 (April 1995): 41-61.

_____, "Postcolonial Ekphrasis: Salman Rushdie Gives the Finger Back to the Empire," *Contemporary Literature.* Volume 30, Number 2 (Summer 1997): 232-59.

Kuortti, Joel, "Enslaving Readings: Salman Rushdie's *The Satanic Verses* and Textuality," *The Commonwealth Review.* Volume X, Number 2 (1998-1999): 44-56.

_____. "Intercultural Identification and Salman Rushdie's *The Satanic Verses*," *The Commonwealth Review.* Volume X, Number 2 (1998-1999): 57-70.

Linguanti, Elsa, "Origin, Origins, Originality: *East, West, Antipodes* and *The Womb of Space*," *Africa, America, Asia, Australia*, Number 22 (1999): 7-18.

Lakshmi, Vijay, "Rushdie's Fiction: the World Beyond the Looking Glass," in Emmanuel S. Nelson, *Reworlding. The Literature of the Indian Diaspora* (New York-West Port, Connecticut: Greenwood Press, 1992): 149-55.

Leith, William, "Sex, Drugs and a Mid-life Crisis," *The Observer/Life.* 23rd March 1997: 6-8.

Linguanti, Elsa, "Rushdie's *The Ground beneath Her Feet*: Different Whatnesses," *The Atlantic Critical Review—Quarterly.* Volume 1, Number 2 (July-September): 118-32.

Macdonald, Marianne, "Acts of Betrayal," *Night & Day*. April 1999: 16-21.

Mahjoub, Jamal, "Love in a Blue Time," *Wasafiri*. Issue No. 27, Spring 1998: 51.

Mahoney, Blair, "Rushdie and his World: the Carnivalesque, Masquerade, and Grotesque Realism in his Fiction," *The Atlantic Literary Review*. Volume 2, Number 1 (January-March, 2001): 84-104.

Manferlotti, Stefano, "La città degli immigrati. Spazio e memoria in Salman Rushdie e Hanif Kureishi," in Carlo Pagetti, ed., *La città senza confini* (Rome: Bulzoni, 1995): 301-11.

_____. "East or West? Le due culture nella narrativa breve di Salman Rushdie," in Mirella Billi, ed., *Voci sull'India e dall'India 1947-1957* (Viterbo: Settecittà, 2001): 87-103.

Mathur, O.P., "A Metaphor of Reality: a Study of the Protagonist in Rushdie's *Midnight's Children*," in Ayyappa K. Paniker, ed., *Indian English Literature since Independence* (New Delhi: The Indian Association for English Studies, 1991): 69-78.

Massé, Sophie, "Language versus Languages in *The Satanic Verses*," *Commonwealth Essays and Studies*. Volume 1, No. 1 (Autumn 1997): 72-76.

Merivale, Patricia, "Saleem Fathered by Oskar: Intertextual Strategies in *Midnight's Children* and *The Tin Drum*," *Ariel*. Volume 21, Number 3 (July 1990): 5-21.

Mishra, Vijay, "Postcolonial Differed: Diasporic Narratives of Salman Rushdie," *Ariel*. Volume 26, Number 3 (July 1995): 7-45.

Misrahi-Barak, "Yoga and the *Bildungsroman* in Hanif Kureishi's *The Buddha of Suburbia*," *Commonwealth Essays and Studies*. Special Issue, Nos. 1-4 (1989-97): 88-94.

Monti, Alessandro, "Chutnifying the Text: A View on the Split of Synchronicity and Literary Globalisation," *The Atlantic Literary Review*, Volume 2, Number 2 (October-December 2001): 190-201.

_____, "Mad 'Aunties' and 'Madi' Women: Patterns of Resistance and Intimations of Marginality in the Representation of Hindu Widows," in A. Monti and R.K. Dhawan, eds., *Discussing Indian Women Writers* (New Delhi: Prestige, 2002): 21-38.

Mookerja, Sourayan, "Irradiations of History: the Author, Cosmopolitanism and *The Satanic Verses*," *World Literature Written in English*. Volume 32-33, Nos. 2-1 (1992-93): 107-21.

Moore-Gilbert, Bart, "London in Hanif Kureishi's Films: Hanif Kureishi in Interview with Bart Moore-Gilbert," *Kunapipi*. Volume XXI, Number 2 (1991): 5-14.

Mujeebuddin, Syed, "Centres and Margins: *Shame*'s 'Other' Nation," in M.K. Bhatnagar and M. Rajeshwar, eds., *Post-Modernism and English Literature* (New Delhi: Atlantic, 1999): 103-19.

O'Connel, Alex. "Meera Syal," *The Times*. 16-22 October 1999: 16-17.

Oubechan, Jamel, "The Barbarians and Philistines in *The Buddha of Suburbia*: Dis/locating Culture," *Commonwealth Essays and Studies*. Special Issue, Nos. 1-4 (1989-97): 101-9.

Owen, Kate, "Love and Loathing," *The Guardian-Metro*. 30 October/ 5 November 1999: 21.

Paranjape, Makarand, "Indo-Anglian as Anglo-Indian: Ideology, Politics and Cross-Cultural Representation," *New Quest*. Number 110 (March-April 1995): 133-42.

Patra, Pradip Kumar. "Race, Colonialism and Nation: a Study of *Midnight's Children* and *Shame*," *The Quest*. Volume 14, Number 2 (December 2000): 39-44.

Purushotham, K., "Rushdie's Images of *Bharateeya Nari* in *Midnight's Children*," *Kakatiya Journal of English Studies*. Volume XIII (1993): 90-103.

Ramachandran, C.N., "Critical Response to Rushdie," *The Commonwealth Review*. Volume X, Number 2 (1998-1999): 27-35.

Richards, Cameron, "Postmodernism or Postcolonialism Tomorrow? The Relevance of a Dialogic Framework for Postcolonial Criticism," *SPAN*. Special Issue, Volume 1 (October 1993): 65-74.

Roy, Anita, "Tollington Lassies," *The Guardian*. 5 April 1996: 26.

Rushdie, Salman, "Minority Literatures in a Multicultural Society," in Kirsten Holst Petersen and Anna Rutherford, *Displaced Persons* (Sydney: Dangaroo Press, 1988): 33-42.

Sangheera, Sathnam, "Asian Giveaway," *Financial Times*. 23/24 October 1999: 4.

Sarma, M. Madan, "Fantasy as Method in *Midnight's Children*," *The Atlantic Critical Review—Quarterly*. Volume 1, Number 2 (July-September): 39-43.

Schoene-Harwood, Berthold, "Beyond (T)race: Building and Proprioception in Meera Syal's *Anita and Me*," *The Journal of Commonwealth Literature*. Volume 34, Number 1 (1999): 159-69.

Scott Langeland, Agnes, "Rushdie's Language," *English Today*. Vol. 12, No. 1 (January 1996): 16-22.

Singh, Sushila. "Salman Rushdie's Novels: from Fantasy to Reality." *The Commonwealth Review*. Volume 1, Number 1 (1989): 111-24.

Srinivas, V., "Tradition and Experiment in the Novels of G.V. Desani and Salman Rushdie." Dissertation, Department of English, Kakatiya University (1998).

Vivan, Itala, "The Impact of Postcolonial Hybridisation on the Britishness of British Literature," in S. Bassi, S. Bertacco and Bonicelli, eds., *In That Village of Open Doors* (Venice: Cafoscarina, 2002): 27-43.

3.0 Reference Books and Other Materials

3.1 Essays, Books and Dictionaries

Acharya, K.T., *A Historical Dictionary of Indian Food* (New Delhi: Oxford University Press, 2002).

Amselle, Jean-Loup, *Logiche meticce* (Turin, Bollati Boringhieri, 1999).

Anderson, Benedict, *Imagined Communities* (London: Verso, 1991).

Bagchi, Jasodhara, ed., *Indian Women. Myth and Reality* (Hyderabad: Sangam Books, 1995).

Chatman, Seymour, *Coming to Terms* (Ithaca and London: Cornell University Press, 1990).

Elam, Keir, *The Semiotics of Theatre and Drama* (London and New York: Routledge, 2nd Edition 2002).

Fox, Kate, *Watching the English* (London: Hodder, 2004).

Galloway, David, *The Absurd Hero* (Austin and London: University of Texas Press, 1966).

Gandhi, Maneka, *The Penguin Book of Hindu Names* (New Delhi: Viking Penguin India, 1989).

Hall, Stuart, *Critical Dialogues in Cultural Studies* (London: Routledge, 1996).

Hutcheon, Linda, *The Canadian Postmodern* (Toronto: Oxford University Press, 1988).

Kassam, Nadya, ed., *Telling it like it is. Young Asian Women Talk* (London: The Women's Press, 1997).

Shukla, Sandhya, *India Abroad* (Princeton: Princeton University Press, 2003).

Smaro, Kamboureli, *Scandalous Bodies. Diasporic Literature in English Canada* (Toronto: Oxford University Press Canada, 2000).

Spargo, Tasmin, *Foucault and Queer Theory* (Cambridge: Icon Books, 1999).

Sue, Scott and David Morgan, eds., *Body Matters* (London: The Falmer Press, 1993).

Thieme, John, *Postcolonial Con-texts* (London and New York: Continuum, 2001).

Uma, Alladi, *Woman and Her Family. Indian and Afro-American: A Literary Perspective* (New Delhi: Sterling, 1989).

Varadpande, M.L., *A Dictionary of Indian Culture* (New Delhi: Arnold, 1994).

Vrinda Nabar, *Caste as Woman* (New Delhi: Penguin India, 1995).

Williams, Raymond, *Television. Technology and Cultural Form* (New York: Schocken, 1975).

Yule, Henry and A.C. Burnell, *Hobson-Jobson. The Anglo-Dictionary* (Ware: Wordsworth Editions, 1996).

3.2 Feature Films and TV Materials

My Beautiful Laundrette (Directed by Stephen Frears; screenplay by Hanif Kureishi, starring Danny Day-Lewis, Richard Graham, Derrick Branche, Roshan Seth; 1985).

Sammy and Rosie Get Laid (Directed by Steven Frears; screenplay by Hanif Kureishi; starring Shashi Kapoor, Ayub Khan Din, Meera Syal, Roland Gift; 1987).